Connie Mack's
First Dynasty

ALSO BY LEW FREEDMAN
AND FROM MCFARLAND

*Baseball's Funnymen: Twenty-Four Jokers,
Screwballs, Pranksters and Storytellers* (2017)

The Boyer Brothers of Baseball (2015)

Joe Louis: The Life of a Heavyweight (2013)

*DiMaggio's Yankees:
A History of the 1936–1944 Dynasty* (2011)

*The Day All the Stars Came Out: Major League
Baseball's First All-Star Game, 1933* (2010)

*Hard-Luck Harvey Haddix
and the Greatest Game Ever Lost* (2009)

*Early Wynn, the Go-Go White Sox
and the 1959 World Series* (2009)

Connie Mack's First Dynasty

The Philadelphia Athletics, 1910–1914

LEW FREEDMAN

McFarland & Company, Inc., Publishers
Jefferson, North Carolina

LIBRARY OF CONGRESS CATALOGUING-IN-PUBLICATION DATA

Names: Freedman, Lew, author.
Title: Connie Mack's first dynasty : the Philadelphia Athletics, 1910–1914 / Lew Freedman.
Description: Jefferson, North Carolina : McFarland & Company, Inc., Publishers, 2017. | Includes bibliographical references and index.
Identifiers: LCCN 2017034404 | ISBN 9780786496273 (softcover : acid free paper) ∞
Subjects: LCSH: Philadelphia Athletics (Baseball team)—History. | Mack, Connie, 1862–1956.
Classification: LCC GV875.P44 F74 2017 | DDC 796.357/640974811—dc23
LC record available at https://lccn.loc.gov/2017034404

BRITISH LIBRARY CATALOGUING DATA ARE AVAILABLE

ISBN (print) 978-0-7864-9627-3
ISBN (ebook) 978-1-4766-2909-4

© 2017 Lew Freedman. All rights reserved

No part of this book may be reproduced or transmitted in any form or by any means, electronic or mechanical, including photocopying or recording, or by any information storage and retrieval system, without permission in writing from the publisher.

The front cover image is a collage of head shots of the 1913 World Series champion Philadelphia Athletics from the *Philadelphia Evening Tribune* (National Baseball Hall of Fame Library, Cooperstown, New York)

Printed in the United States of America

McFarland & Company, Inc., Publishers
 Box 611, Jefferson, North Carolina 28640
  www.mcfarlandpub.com

Table of Contents

Introduction   1

1. Connie Mack Becomes an Athletic   5
2. Rube Waddell and the Foundation   14
3. The Year 1910—The Beginning   22
4. Jack Coombs   31
5. Charles Albert Bender   36
6. The 1910 World Series   42
7. Infielders   52
8. Eddie Collins   59
9. The Year 1911   64
10. The 1911 World Series Foes   71
11. The 1911 World Series Showdown   79
12. Home Run Baker   90
13. The Year 1912   96
14. Eddie Plank   106
15. The Year 1913   112
16. The 1913 World Series   124
17. The Federal League Forms   137
18. The Year 1914   144
19. The 1914 World Series   157
20. The Breakup   170
21. Where They Went   181
22. Connie Mack   196

Chapter Notes   201
Bibliography   207
Index   209

Introduction

Between 1910 and 1914 the Philadelphia Athletics won the World Series three times, in 1910, 1911, and 1913, and lost a fourth Series in 1914. Except for the New York Yankees, only a few teams have matched that accomplishment since the modern era began in 1901 with the founding of the American League.

The A's and the AL were born the same year. The National League was founded in 1876. After fending off some other contenders, the NL held a major league monopoly at the dawn of the 20th century. Ban Johnson, president of the Western League, however, thought big, and using the American League name declared the creation of a second major league for the 1901 season.

Johnson specifically wanted a league presence in Philadelphia to go head-to-head with the established Phillies. That was the justification for the A's existence at first. This was a team pieced together by manager/owner Connie Mack and among the key players in that initial group, and the subsequent dynastic one, were Eddie Collins, Frank "Home Run" Baker, "Chief" Bender, "Rube" Waddell and Eddie Plank, all future Hall of Famers. Although not a significant contributor, Mack's son Earle played on these teams. These A's also featured the so-called "$100,000 infield," which, given inflation and the salaries paid to ball players now, would be called by some other comparatively astronomical figure—a $20 million infield or one even more valuable. The Athletics' "$100,000 infield" included "Stuffy" McInnis, Eddie Collins, Jack Barry and Frank Baker.

Although once a legendary symbol of the team, the white elephant that adorned team uniforms is practically forgotten now. There was no greater opponent of the American League's creation than manager John McGraw. McGraw and Ban Johnson had a falling out that resulted in McGraw leaving the American League Baltimore Orioles behind and jumping to the NL's New York Giants.

No diplomat, McGraw continued verbal sparring with Johnson, but also continuously insulted other American League franchises and individuals. "The American League is a loser and has been from the start," McGraw said. He zeroed in on Philadelphia's principal owner, Ben Shibe (Mack owned a piece of the club), saying his investment was a "white elephant," sure to become a financial drain.[1]

Rallying behind the team, the players and owners reveled in McGraw's pout and began to promote the white elephant. The Athletics out-drew the Phillies by a margin of 4–1 and won their first pennant in 1902. When the team celebrated with a parade along Broad Street, Philadelphia's main downtown drag, floats decorated with white elephants were common. Over the decades, elephants appeared on the cover of many team publications. What McGraw intended as a nasty comment was rebuffed, turned around and used for motivation. The A's made the white elephant cool.

When anyone talks about the Philadelphia A's, most roots grow from Connie Mack, the man who managed, won and lost more games than any other while staying at the helm in his street clothes for more than a half-century. When it came to job security, you couldn't beat Mack's status, since he also owned a chunk of (and eventually all of) the team.

Those Athletics of 1910–1914 represented an extraordinary group of ball players. Their achievements still resonate, as well as their names, especially to baseball historians. They also had the gift of competing in the first so-called "modern" ballpark, Shibe Park. Shared with the National League Phillies when it opened in 1909, Shibe accrued much attention because it was made out of concrete and steel. That was the replacement model for smaller parks constructed of wood that had the unnerving propensity to burn down. Although it changed names (eventually being called Connie Mack Stadium), Shibe remained in the baseball-hosting business until 1970.

The 1910 A's finished with a record of 102–48 and defeated the Chicago Cubs, 4–1, in the World Series. Those were the Cubs of Tinker, Evers and Chance, the poetical double play combination, plus pitcher Mordecai "Three Finger" Brown, a team that won 104 games and was definitely no pushover. Jack Coombs won 31 games for the A's that year, his greatest year.

The 1911 A's finished with a record of 101–50 and defeated John McGraw's New York Giants, 4–2, in the Series. Those were the Giants of pitchers Christy Mathewson and Rube Marquard, and hitters Larry Doyle (who said, "It's great to be young and a Giant") and Chief Meyers. During the regular season, the Athletics outscored teams, 861 to 602.

Introduction

The 1912 Athletics won 90 games, but only finished third in the league. Led by 22-year-old pitcher "Smoky" Joe Wood, this was the Boston Red Sox's year.

The 1913 Athletics finished 96–57 and again won the pennant and the World Series, this time beating the Giants, 4–1. The same core infield was involved, and pitchers Chief Bender and Eddie Plank ruled, with the addition of a young Bob Shawkey and an even younger Herb Pennock, both of whom had bright futures.

The last go-around of glory for this group of A's was 1914, when the Athletics finished 98–53 and outscored foes by 220 runs. They allowed just 529 runs all season, with seven pitchers winning at least ten games. Chief Bender went 17–3.

This being the Deadball Era, the Athletics were built to win with pitching, defense, and situational hitting, not the long ball. The lively ball and Babe Ruth would soon enough revolutionize the game, but that lay several years in the future.

These five seasons represented a fantastic stretch for the Athletics, and it is fair to wonder how long their superlative play might have continued if not for an unforeseen development that interfered. Might they have superseded the Roaring Twenties Yankees in fame and accomplishments? If they had kept it up a few years longer, the Athletics might have been in the conversation with the "Murderers Row" Yankees for the greatest of all teams.

However, by 1914 the competing Federal League was in business, seeking to earn recognition as a third major league. The Federal League made raids on the established American and National Leagues. High-priced offers were made to many players, and the financially conservative Connie Mack refused to match the cost of keeping his players. The A's were dismantled by internal and external forces. Ironically, the landscape of major league ball in 1901, when the Athletics rode the circumstances permitted nurturing a new league into existence, had changed anew less than 15 years later with the advent of an ambitious, hopeful third league, causing the Athletics' temporary demise.

So the American League brought the A's into this world and the Federal League nearly exiled the A's into bankruptcy. As a result, the Athletics dropped from first place in 1914 to last in 1915 and won only 43 games as players deserted the team, one of the most precipitous declines imaginable. It was an artificial ending to the dynasty, but helps to illustrate why it is so difficult to keep teams together and repeat championships.

Mack managed the Athletics through the 1950 season, when he

turned 88. He lived to be 93, passing away in 1956, but was still alive when his team played its final season in Philadelphia in 1954 and began play in Kansas City the next season.

The Athletics live on today, as the Oakland Athletics, if Mack does only in legend.

1

Connie Mack Becomes an Athletic

It all starts with Connie Mack, but Connie Mack did not start with the Athletics. He did not even begin life as Connie Mack.

Born Cornelius McGillicuddy in East Brookfield, Massachusetts, on December 22, 1862, while the Civil War still raged, he was the son of Irish immigrants. His first name was naturally shortened to Connie, thankfully enough for his baseball brethren, and McGillicuddy became the diminutive of Mack just as naturally. The condensed name stuck.

"My family name is McGillicuddy and I was christened Cornelius because there must always be a Cornelius in the male line of the McGillicuddy clan that sprang in County Kildare, Ireland, and sent so many of its sons and daughters across the Atlantic to the land of opportunity," Mack said.[1]

Even his father, of the same name officially, used the identical mini-version of the name, except when handling official business. Mack said his last name, with many fewer letters, definitely came in handy in the baseball world. "The name Mack fitted in a box score of a ball game much snugger than the other, so I did not enlighten players or writers once I got a footing in the major leagues," he said.[2]

However, one time when Mack was catching and managing the Pittsburgh Pirates, he showed up in Pittsburgh only to see his real name, McGillicuddy, in a headline in a local newspaper. He asked the paper's editor how he determined that Mack was not his given name, and the man said he had a friend who was Mack's cousin and who had informed him. Mack took some teasing from his teammates and ragging from the Pirates, perhaps in sing-song fashion as they shouted "McGillicuddy" at him to disturb his concentration on the field. It took a little bit of time for the Pittsburgh razzing to fizzle out.

Mack, who grew to stand 6-foot-2, was tall for his age and tall for his era. He was also skinny at 150 pounds or so, and when he played he was often called "Slats." Photographs taken from his major league days frequently show a man with slightly sunken cheeks. Put a beard on Mack and he might well have resembled Abraham Lincoln, though with a straw boater on his head rather than a black stovepipe hat.

Later, as a manager, Mack earned the nickname "The Tall Tactician." His players, no longer his teammates, called him Mr. Mack. Sportswriters called the ball players on the teams he managed "The Mackmen."

Mack dropped out of school at 14 to help support his family, which was not uncommon at the time, but his diamond education never stopped. By 17 he was playing for his hometown team. He learned he was good at the game. This was a time period when just about every community wanted to field a team. Such devotion to the game, soon to be called "The National Pastime," lasted for decades, supplemental to the professional ranks. There was definitely an "our boys" mentality. You could be a star in your hometown while still working for a living the rest of the week. This was emblematic of the early days of baseball. The first professional team, the touring Cincinnati Red Stockings, was formed in 1869. By 1876, the National League was in business. The American Association was considered a major league from 1882–1891.

The amazing Connie Mack, manager of the Athletics for 50 years, won more games, lost more games and managed more games than any field leader in history while capturing nine American League pennants (National Baseball Hall of Fame Library, Cooperstown, New York).

After several seasons catching for East Brookfield, in 1884 Mack set out to become a professional baseball player. His first minor league job was with a Meriden, Connecticut, team in the Connecticut State League.

1. Connie Mack Becomes an Athletic

Mack showed up, asking for a tryout, and was kept on at $80 a month. At the end of the season he was so popular with the fans that they gave him a gold watch and chain.

Mack moved on to Hartford and then to the Newark Domestics in the Eastern League. By 1886, Mack was in the majors, playing ten games for a horrible Washington Nationals team that finished 28–92 despite Mack's unusual success at bat. A better fielder and field leader than hitter, Mack batted .361 during his debut mini-season. Whether this was foreshadowing of dismal on-field play or not, Washington's home park was named Swampoodle Grounds. The structure held 6,000 fans and was also more officially called Capitol Park, but it did sound as if it belonged in a newspaper comic strip.

The Nationals, who were sometimes called the Statesmen, represented the adage in D.C. that good statesmen are always hard to come by and were swampoodled out of existence after four seasons. Mack latched onto the Pirates after a season in Buffalo, topping 100 games played in a year only once. That Washington .361 was the high-water mark of Mack's big league hitting career. Lifetime, over 11 seasons, he batted .244.

However, for three seasons in his 30s, between 1894 and 1896, Mack was a player-manager. That kicked off his more-than-half-century-long major league managing career, a tenure far exceeding that of any other man's, for him mostly with the Athletics. Mack spent 50-plus years in charge on the A's bench, and one thing that could be counted on was that if he was there for the first pitch, he would be there for the last pitch. Not once during his extraordinarily lengthy time in the job in Philadelphia did Mack get thrown out of a game by an umpire.

Yet, perhaps demonstrating that he was not perfect, Mack was tossed from a ball game—one game out of the 7,792 he managed—while still running the Pirates. On September 6, 1895, when the Pirates were playing the New York Giants in the Polo Grounds, the unthinkable occurred. In the fifth inning of a tie game, a close play at second base infuriated Mack. His old teammate, Hank O'Day, was the umpire, and he called the Giants' runner safe. Mack insisted he was out. A long and loud argument ensued, and O'Day threw Mack out of the game. Even then Mack did not go gently. "They had to call the cops to put me out," Mack said.[3]

After Mack was fired in Pittsburgh (something that would never happen in Philadelphia due to his unique owner-manager position), he surfaced as manager of the then-minor league Milwaukee Brewers. In the minors, then as now, responsibility tends to expand beyond the apparent meaning of a simple title. Mack may have been the field manager, but he was also the general manager and basically the entire front office. It took until 1901 for Mack to gain another major league position, but more mature at nearly 40 and more experienced, he was probably better qualified to run a big league ball club. "I went to the minors of my own volition," Mack said later. "I wanted to learn how to handle men."[4]

He also had $2,500 invested in the new Philadelphia Athletics as the man awarded the franchise by the American League. However, Mack could not afford to be a sole money man and needed backers. Mack, who was privy to all of the inner workings and dealings in the establishment of the league, brought Ben Shibe into the arrangement.

"A century and three-quarters after Benjamin Franklin came to Philadelphia, I arrived here, too," Mack wrote in his autobiography. "I decided that if Ben could become famous here with his 'Poor Richard's Almanack,' I might stand a chance with Connie's Athletics."[5] It was no mystery how the Athletics nickname was chosen for the club. The Philadelphia Athletic Club was long entrenched in the city, and many teams had come and gone over the years that were called Athletics. Management of the new team believed perpetuating the name was a good way to ingratiate itself with fans.

That was the least of the A's start-up problems. It was quite a rush job to get the Athletics into form to start the 1901 season. The team did not have a place to play, and Mack, seemingly joking, indicated that operators might have to use a local playground. Instead, the owners put money down for a ten-year lease on a piece of vacant property that became Columbia Park. The hurriedly manufactured ball park at 29th and Oxford Streets was built for $35,000 and had a surprising capacity of 9,500. It was small, but functional, at least for a little while.

Now that the team had a name and a place to play, Mack needed players to fill out a roster. He always prided himself on his personnel acumen and showed it in a number of ways. Mack's first big amateur signing was plucking southpaw Eddie Plank out of Gettysburg, Pennsylvania, just 140 miles to the west. Plank was born in Gettysburg on a farm and also attended Gettysburg College.

Not only did Plank move right into the A's lineup in 1901, he was still a staff mainstay during the upcoming great years and became a Hall of Famer. That was evidence that Mack did have an eye for talent—in theory anyway, since he was the king of tinkerers, playing 31 different guys during the first year. However, another astute move was talking first-baseman Harry Davis out of retirement. Davis, a local man, was working for the Pennsylvania Railroad when Mack approached him. "I finally succeeded in convincing him that I needed him and had a good opening for him," Mack said. "It was one of my best moves and made possible my first three pennants."[6] Davis had bounced around the game with several teams between 1895 and 1899 and did not play in 1900. He came back, hit .306 in 1901 and .307 in 1902, and led the league in doubles and home runs a couple of times.

Since the National League was doing its best to ignore the upstart American League rather than form any kind of cooperative agreement, Ban Johnson, as president of the new league, felt NL players were up for grabs. Mack went after several members of the Phillies, trying to woo them away. Larry Lajoie was one of the great stars of the early days of the game, as big a name as Ty Cobb would become. Lajoie won five batting titles in a 21-year career and slapped 3,243 hits. When Lajoie, whose nickname was "Nap," played for Cleveland, the franchise called itself The Naps in his honor instead of the Bronchos, all before they became the Indians for keeps.

During that inaugural 1901 season, Lajoie, who was paid $5,000 at a time when the National League tried to impose a salary cap of $2,450 on player salaries, suited up for the Athletics and set an all-time American League batting mark of .426. He led the league in runs, hits, doubles, home runs, RBI, average and on-base percentage. If the Phillies pretended indifference when the A's came into business, they did not respond with docility when Lajoie was hijacked from their roster. They went to court. It took an entire year, until long after Lajoie recorded his stupendous season for the Athletics, but only two days into the 1902 season, the Pennsylvania Supreme Court ruled that no ex-Phillies players (there were others) the A's took from them could remain with the Athletics. Lajoie got into exactly one game in 1902 before the A's had to let him go.

"You have heard the phrase, 'as smart as a Philadelphia lawyer,'" Mack said. "The lawyers for the Phillies lived up to the name."[7] The vindictive Phillies wanted Lajoie to pay a big fine for the privilege of rejoining them, and he refused. So Mack and the A's traded him to Cleveland, since the court order did not apply in Ohio. After taking that bold raiding step on behalf of the American League, in a gesture of solidarity, other teams' owners contributed some players to the Athletics' roster when they were stripped of the former Phillies.

Even without Lajoie, the Athletics were good enough to win the 1902 AL pennant with an 83–53 record. It was Mack's first managerial triumph. There was no World Series yet—that came the next year. The Athletics had six .300 hitters in the starting lineup. Plank wasn't as good as he was about to become, but he still won 20 games as a sophomore.

Building a great team is not an overnight process, and even though Mack was willing to look at the skills of an uncounted number of prospects, he knew who could help the Athletics win and who just represented roster filler. Slowly, gradually, Mack, combing the minors, listening to friends as scouts, found enough very good players to make an impact. In 1902, Rube Waddell joined up. In 1903, Mack's new addition was pitcher Chief Bender. Along with Plank, that meant the A's had three future Hall of Fame pitchers in their rotation at once during the first few years of the 20th century.

In 1905, the Athletics finished 92–56 and claimed their and Mack's second pennant. The first World Series (a sign of a thaw between the American League and the National League) took place in 1903 between Boston and Pittsburgh, with Boston winning. In 1904, the cantankerous Giants manager, John J. McGraw, refused to pit his New York club against the AL-winning Boston Americans (aka Red Sox), so no Series took place.

McGraw finally came around and in 1905, when his team won the NL pennant again, the Giants were the Mackmen's foe in the World Series. The Giants won that Series, 4–1. In the coming years there would be several other confrontations between McGraw's Giants and Mack's Athletics, and contrasts would be drawn between the type of men Mack and McGraw were. During a three-decades-long overlap in their jobs, Mack and McGraw compiled the leading statistics for managerial longevity and wins at the head of one team, marks that still stand.

Their temperaments were quite different. McGraw was combative, could be insulting, gave pep talks that berated players, and liked to be perceived as a tough guy. Mack was more gentlemanly. He wore a suit on the bench, which by the rules meant that he had to stay in the dugout, so he never approached umpires to question their calls by getting in their faces. He could be stern, but seemingly acted more like a concerned parent. He praised his players more often than not. Mack generally put on a positive face and did not often reveal his inner emotions publicly.

At least that was true when he was a manager in Philadelphia. Early on, in Pittsburgh as a player and a manager, he was more vociferous and less dignified, more profane and less likely to hide his displeasure. Mack had a temper and showed it then. It was later, as he aged, that he withdrew that behavior more from the public stage. Generations grew up thinking of him as kindly. By nature, he was, but by practice and through effort he had shelved some of his more undesirable traits.

Mack, who until then had dressed in the locker room with his Milwaukee players, realized he was steaming mad and likely to make a scene with a specific player and verbally assault him. He decided that he would

1. Connie Mack Becomes an Athletic

never again change his clothes where the players dressed. If he didn't wear a uniform, he didn't have to change at all. He figured that as long as he was no longer a player, he shouldn't dress like (or with) the players.

It was also Mack's personal preference to look snappy. For decades, he was not seen in public dressed in any other manner than a three-piece suit, with a tie and with a high collar. Not while working the bench, but when traveling, Mack also frequently wore a black bowler on his head. The only other well-remembered baseball manager to dress in street clothes on the bench is Burt Shotton, who led the Brooklyn Dodgers to the 1947 National League pennant. Shotton was 62 and retired when Branch Rickey begged him to fill in for suspended manager Leo Durocher that season, and when Shotton finally agreed to the cajoling, one condition of his employment was that he would not wear a uniform. Sometimes, however, Shotton did wear a Dodgers cap or jacket. It is Mack, though, who rates as the best-dressed manager in major league history.

When the Athletics were formed for the 1901 season, Mack owned about 25 percent of the club. As time passed and he was able to bank more money and his finances became more liquid, he was able to increase his investment. In late 1912, Mack's ownership stake increased to 50 percent when he bought out two partners. By then, Mack and the Shibe family were the only owners.

Certainly by then, Mack was purchasing from a position of credibility as well. His teams shined on the diamond and fans appreciated that. When Mack's Athletics won championships, some (perhaps too simply) assumed they were exemplars of clean living. Mack was the symbol of that. In 1913, *McClure's Magazine* singled out Mack to talk about "Clean Living and Quick Thinking," and he obliged.

The question of player drinking came up and Mack, who was not a teetotaler but drank in moderation, said he did not believe in players drinking. He said it was not a question of right or wrong, but of

> human efficiency. I don't want to put this question of clean living on the basis of morals for one minute. I'll leave preaching to the clergy. In our club we have rules about the players' personal habits. It is recognized that a major leaguer, with a career in front of him and really big money in his pockets, must cut out all bad habits. For if he doesn't the pace becomes too hot for him, the competition for a regular position too fierce.[8]

From that standpoint of efficiency, although he did not state so outright, Mack implied that players sometimes came to the ball park for games while hung over or when not completely sober. But he did refer to impaired judgment more than once, dropping hints.

Once, Mack slyly imposed a rule against drinking. That was during the Athletics' World Series against the Chicago Cubs in 1910. He gathered his men together and told them a story about a previous Series when rumors shot around that the losing team fell because it had been out carousing. Mack said he didn't want to hear any such tales about his team and made the players promise not to drink during the competition. "It would be bad enough to lose the championship, I reminded them," Mack said, "without having a bundle of regrets to pester you."[9]

It was not known if the A's abstained from alcohol during the 1910 World Series, but they did win it. It worked another time against the Giants, but Mack was certain that three players who did not take care of themselves well during the season in a different year cost the A's a pennant.

Mack encouraged marriage for players who had found the right girl. He encouraged players to save their money wisely. He liked having players with peace of mind so they had clarity of thought. He called it quick thinking and said that was needed on the field.

Pulitzer Prize–winning sports columnist Red Smith once said that no one, to his knowledge, disliked Connie Mack.

Still, all men are different, and it is difficult to believe that every player who played for Mack over a half-century either warmed to him or accepted all of his advice. Way back, during the 1910–1914 era, though, catcher Ira Thomas sounded practically brainwashed when he delivered a speech suggesting that not a single member of the A's $100,000 infield had ever taken a sip of alcohol. If that was overdoing it a little, at the least Thomas made clear how he felt about being one of the Mackmen. "We don't look up to Connie as a manager," Thomas said, "but as a father."[10]

Much later, the Connie Mack League was formed for teenagers too old for Little League but who still wanted to play ball, and it is still going strong. In 1948, the Connie Mack Sportsmen's Club of the Brookfields was already underway. Mack was still alive then and still managing.

As a member of Connie's Sportsmen's Club, a boy had to make a pledge reading,

> I promise to play the game to the best of my ability at all times; I will play to win, but if I lose I will never look for excuses which would detract from my opponent's victory; I will never take unfair advantage in order to win; I will always abide by the rules of the game on the diamond as well as in my daily life; I will always conduct myself as a true sportsman should on and off the ball field; I will always strive to play for the good of the entire team rather than for my own glory; I will never gloat in victory or pity myself in defeat; I will do my utmost to keep myself clean, physically, mentally and morally; I will judge a teammate as an individual and

never on the basis of his race or religion; Each player in order to be eligible must memorize and live up to the above pledge.[11]

The pledge was written by Mack.

To him they were rules not only to compete by but to live by, and although those guidelines were not written out for his Philadelphia Athletics teams of 1910–1914 to read and obey, anyone who knew Mack knew he believed in them and that such thinking colored his judgment in managing the major leaguers.

2

Rube Waddell and the Foundation

Connie Mack's boldness gave him the services of Larry Lajoie and some other ex-Philadelphia Phillies, if only for a little while. Mack's American League co-owners appreciated his efforts to raid the National League, and when the courts stripped him of those players, the owners stepped up to help Mack recoup his losses.

They gifted him with players to fill out the A's roster, and one of those guys was a future Hall of Famer. Pitcher Rube Waddell was definitely a mixed blessing as a player. When Waddell was good he was great on the mound, but when he was not on the mound he could drive even the most patient of men bonkers. Mack fit that category when necessary, and in his wisdom he promptly recognized that Waddell needed patient handling if Philadelphia was going to benefit from his talents.

If Mack had been a my-way-or-the-highway type of manager, Waddell's good will would have evaporated in less than a week with the A's. Realizing Waddell was a special case, Mack tried to tailor his planning around Waddell's strengths while minimizing his faults and their potential impact on the team.

Waddell was born October 13, 1876, in Bradford, Pennsylvania, and his name at birth was George Edward Waddell. The nickname of Rube came later because teammates thought it described his demeanor with regard to the sophisticated, wide world. He was 6-foot-1 and weighed just under 200 pounds. Waddell threw from the left side and he threw very well, good enough in the long run to win 193 big-league games with an earned run average of 2.16.

Between 1897 and 1901, Waddell pitched for the Louisville Colonels, then the Pittsburgh Pirates when they combined, and the Chicago Cubs. He did not burn up the National League, although he led that league with a 2.37 earned run average while somehow only going 8–13 in 1900. Waddell was a different pitcher for Mack and the Athletics.

Waddell led the American League in strikeouts six times, with batters hopelessly behind his fastball with their swings, and once in earned run average. In 1905, when he also led the AL in wins with 27, Waddell's ERA was 1.48. In 1904, he set a long-standing single-season strikeout mark with 349.

On paper, Waddell was a darling, a magnificent get for Mack. Off the field, not so much. Mack was going on talent alone when he first sought Waddell for his lineup. Almost as soon as he committed to him—traveling to pick him up in person, paying off his debts, and being told by town fathers that they were glad he was going—the A's magnate realized Waddell was going to be a handful. Usually talent trumps eccentricity, but in Waddell's case the balance was so out of balance those around him exceeded their limits of tolerance.

Waddell was a fun-loving dude, almost childlike in his approach to the little boys' game. He practically danced on the mound as if he were performing on the Broadway stage. He sometimes turned cartwheels when he retired the side. In his spare time, he rode fire engines or went fishing. He was neither punctual nor always reliable in showing up, which did drive Mack to distraction.

Waddell also chased fires. Once, arriving at the scene of a blaze and seeing nobody fighting the fire, he rallied a group of farmers to put it out. "I'm a peach at a fire," Waddell said. "There is nothing I like better than to fight fires."[1] Not even, apparently, whizzing his wicked fastball past hitters, though that did give Waddell a charge.

Mack believed himself capable of accepting and coping with whatever heartburn Waddell dished out with his periodic disappearing acts and regularly borrowing a few bucks from him. The fans loved Waddell's colorful behavior, and when he pitched he dominated and provided wins with his left arm.

Also, Mack was trying to build something in Philadelphia. He wanted a winner and he knew Waddell was a man who could win. So he put up with his shenanigans and generally got his money's worth.

In 1902, when the Athletics won their first pennant, Waddell went 24–7 with a 2.05 ERA and a league-leading 210 strikeouts. In 1905, when Philadelphia won the pennant again, Waddell was phenomenal with a 27–10 mark, that 1.48 ERA, and 287 strikeouts while pitching in a league-leading 46 games.

Waddell pitched his first game in Philadelphia on July 1, 1902, and faced just 27 men while striking out 13. He surrendered just an infield hit. When Waddell recorded the last out, he shouted to the fans, "It's all over, go home!"[2] Before departing, the spectators ran out onto the field and lifted Waddell on their shoulders.

Mack, who gained his first experience with Waddell while he was running the Milwaukee minor-league club, learned to coddle Waddell to earn his trust and get the best he could out of him. Once, after Waddell had pitched a complete game, Mack needed him in long relief a day later. If he would pitch again, Mack promised, he could take the next three days off to go fishing. Deal. Another time, Mack told Waddell that if he won a certain game, he could leave the team with his mother for a few days and go visit his sister. Waddell lost the game but left anyway and didn't communicate with the A's for five days.

Instead of berating Waddell when he reappeared, Mack gave him the ball, and he pitched an extra-inning shutout. After a day off, Waddell pitched and won again. Mack did not complain about Waddell's absence but just kept working him, and Waddell pitched four times in five days. Another time, on a whim, Waddell jumped the club, took a train to San Francisco and pitched a game there. Mack hired a Pinkerton detective to find him and bring him back. Because Waddell was susceptible, teams occasionally approached and tempted him with cash offers to pitch for them. Sometimes, depending on his mood, he was so inclined. Sometimes he had to be stopped.

"Rube had the mind of a child," Mack once said of his star pitcher, who very much possessed the powerful arm of a grown-up.[3] Waddell's antics were distracting and ulcer-provoking. He basically needed a full-time babysitter. That was one of Mack's duties, but he could only do it part-time. The rest of the time he was scouting, showing off his acumen in targeting talent. Waddell could be stupendous on the mound, but he did need teammates, and Mack was determined to build the A's into a regular contender.

Mack did so in an era of no-tech scouting, word-of-mouth reliability, and what he saw with his own eyes. While the Athletics did win pennants in 1902 and 1905 with Waddell the ace of the pitching staff, Mack kept busy changing roster pieces and adding keepers, men he felt could become cornerstones of the franchise. Waddell was young enough to stay around for a long time, but his temperament and Mack's need prevented the entertaining southpaw from sticking around until 1910, when the rewards began paying out in abundance.

Eddie Plank was already in place by 1901. Another extraordinary pitcher, Charles Albert Bender, joined the team in 1903 and helped turn the Athletics' staff into the best around. Jack Coombs came aboard in

2. Rube Waddell and the Foundation

1906. That group became fabulous, and when they overlapped with Waddell in Philadelphia in 1906 and 1907, it was arguably the greatest quartet of starters ever assembled. In 1907, Jimmy Dygert went 21–8, but he was a one-year wonder. The actual fourth starter by 1910 was Cy Morgan, not nearly as distinguished as the others but a key plus on the mound that season.

Unlike the modern era, where relief pitchers are as common as trees in a forest, when a team may well carry 13 pitchers at a time on its roster, only eight men threw the ball for the Athletics during the entire 1910 season.

Using five different men at one time or another, Mack had almost as many catchers as pitchers at his disposal that year. One of them was his son Earle, who was more coach than catcher since he appeared in just one game. Jack Lapp, Ira Thomas, and Paddy Livingston divided most of the load.

The core of the offense and defense was built around the $100,000 infield, which it could be said was discounted to perhaps $80,000 in value that year as Harry Davis at first base was nearing the end of his role as a starter. He was soon replaced by "Stuffy" McInnis. Frank "Home Run" Baker at third and Eddie Collins at second were on their way to the Hall of Fame. Shortstop Jack Barry became an esteemed college coach.

Rube Oldring and Danny Murphy were the hardest swinging outfielders, supplemented by late addition Bris Lord, reacquired in a trade after previous service with the team. The trade leaps off the printed page to historians and falls under the heading of "What was he thinking?" Mind readers of Connie Mack, viewed from the angle of the passage of a century, might dismiss his move as temporary insanity. They wonder just how great the dynastic Athletics might have been if Mack had hung onto to "Shoeless Joe" Jackson rather than giving him to the Indians for Bris Lord.

It is a worthy topic for discussion.

Before he even reached the majors, Joe Jackson had acquired the nickname "Shoeless." There really was a simple explanation of how he gained the moniker, one that was first obscured in some speculative comments. But Jackson set the record right. One day in the minors, he was breaking in new spikes in the field but they were too stiff and tight and left him with gargantuan blisters on both heels. The next day, when he suited up for another game, the shoes were so bothersome he knew he couldn't stand around in them, so he took the outfield shoeless.

"So the only thing for me to do was to take 'em off or die standing up," Jackson explained. The rest of the story is that a fan at the game in

Anderson, South Carolina, noticed and yelled, "Oh, you shoeless wonder!" Jackson's wry follow-up was, "I guess every baseball fan in the country heard him, for I have been called that ever since."[4]

Before Jackson ever reached the majors, he was already swinging with his favorite and famous bat, Black Betsy, a 36-inch-long, 48-ounce hunk of lumber dyed black with tobacco juice. Reportedly, Jackson kept the bat his entire life, until dying in 1951. In 2001, the bat was auctioned off for $577,610. The previous owner, a cousin of Jackson's widow Katie, said he had possession of the bat by inheritance since 1959 and kept it on a bookcase. A bat called Black Betsy came up for auction again in 2011 at a highly reputable auction house, and its appearance jump-started a dispute about authenticity. It was suggested this was a different, if truly Jackson-owned bat used after his big league career ended when he was barnstorming, though not Black Betsy, definitely the only bat kept by Jackson until his death. There was always some controversy brewing around Shoeless Joe.

Shoeless Joe Jackson is one of the best-remembered ball players of the early 20th century, for good reasons and bad, some of them myth, some of them truth. Shoeless Joe was probably born on July 16, 1887 (although some believe the year was off). There was no birth certificate handy to check, but his birth did take place in South Carolina.

As the oldest child in a large family, Jackson was expected to contribute to the family income, and he dropped out of school as a youth before he could be taught the fine points of reading and writing. While he loved playing baseball, he was very much motivated to achieve to make money. A homebody who married young, Jackson appeared on Connie Mack's radar screen because several scouts filed reports raving about his ability. Mack purchased Jackson from the minor league Greenville, South Carolina, team for $900.

Jackson was 20 years old in 1908 when he made his major league debut. However, a Southern boy who considered big-city Philadelphia to be as alien as the planet Jupiter, he was drastically unhappy. His cameo stretch consisted of five games. The 1909 season was similar. Jackson played in only five more A's games. He was happier playing in the minors in the South and sometimes jumped ship from the Athletics without any kind of approval.

Despite his raw talent, Jackson hit under .200 in both of those trials with the A's. Mack recognized his ability and wanted to see him succeed. But he believed he was at the helm of a ripening team that was a threat to win a pennant. Often in baseball, teams make the choice to play for a championship now and damn the future, giving up prospects for immediate help. In 1910, Jackson was back in the minors full-time, and after 136 games with New Orleans was batting .364. On July 23, feeling he needed assistance in the outfield to win a pennant, Mack traded Jackson to Cleveland and obtained Lord. Lord was a known quantity. He had spent the 1905–1907 seasons with Philadelphia. In 70 games with the A's in 1910, Lord did provide a spark, batting .280.

Although Philadelphia did win the pennant, Mack gave up on Jackson too soon. In 20 games with Cleveland that season, Jackson showed signs of becoming the Shoeless Joe Jackson, later regarded as the most natural hitter of them all. Jackson batted .387 in those few weeks' worth of games, and the next year, 1911, he hit a stunning .408, one of only a small number of batters ever to top the .400 mark.

Later, of course, Jackson was caught up in the Black Sox Scandal of 1920, when members of the Chicago White Sox were accused of conspiring to throw the 1919 World Series to the Cincinnati Reds. After 13 years in the majors, Jackson was one of eight players barred from baseball for life by new commissioner Kenesaw Mountain Landis. At the time of Jackson's banishment, his lifetime average was .356. There is much murkiness about the degree of Jackson's culpability in the fix, whether he was an innocent bystander who tried his hardest to win or was an unsavory beneficiary of payoffs. At the least, he had knowledge of the intended fix (although he said he tried to alert White Sox owner Charles Comiskey). Jackson's name was forever tarnished, though nearly a century later many believe he should be taken off the ineligible list and put on the Hall of Fame ballot.

Mack wanted Jackson to make good. But nothing in Jackson's attitude supported the notion that he was going to adjust to Philadelphia. He was unhappy in the big city and made it obvious. He missed his wife and wasn't ready to be separated from her in the North. Supposedly, teammates razzed him because of his youthfulness, Southern accent, and inability to fit in.

The owner-manager recognized Jackson's potential but did not think he would ever reach it with the A's. It wasn't even clear if Jackson would be willing to leave the South again for a major city in the majors. So Mack pulled the trigger on the trade for Lord with a go-for-it outlook that he hoped would pay off in a 1910 pennant. It did.

Mack said that he had offered to have tutors teach Jackson to read and write, but he turned him down. Instead, Mack, who often pursued college players because of their smarts and comparative sophistication in an era in U.S. history when higher education was much less prized and sought, said, "We arranged for a more literate boy to join the team at the same time to be sure that Joe would always have a pal and to read him the menus and also the reports of the games." Mack also said that when he traded Jackson to Cleveland, he told Indians (or Naps at the time) owner Charles Somers, "that Joe had the making of another great baseball player."[5]

Given that 1910 marked the beginning of a five-year A's stretch of domination in the American League, it is difficult to fathom just how good the team might have been if Jackson had been able to adapt to Philadelphia and if Mack had waited him out to take advantage of his final maturation into greatness.

Instead of becoming an Athletics stalwart, Jackson went on to fame in Cleveland and infamy in Chicago.

At one point, Ben Shibe, Mack's co-owner with the Athletics, was quizzed by a Cubs official impressed by Jackson. Charles Murphy asked Shibe how he ever let Shoeless Joe get away. "I guess Barnard must have hypnotized Connie," Shibe said of Cleveland vice president Ernest Barnard.[6]

It is worth considering that if Jackson had established his talent in Philadelphia, he might never have drifted into calamity in Chicago. Still, by 1915, when Cleveland traded Jackson to Chicago, Mack was dismantling the A's and might well have moved Jackson to Chicago without a major element of history being altered.

As it was, Mack had his hands full with Rube Waddell for six years. Maybe Waddell had exhausted him and made him less willing to work with a different set of standards for Jackson. Waddell was the king of disappearing acts. While Jackson's homesickness for the South and missing his wife seemed more legitimate than running off to pitch games for other teams or staying away from the park and partying, Mack wanted a cohesive unit and one he could count on to win big.

Even Waddell, whom Mack very much liked as a person, tested his boss one too many times. Mack certainly understood the depth of Waddell's talent, but on February 7, 1908, he sold him to the St. Louis Browns. It didn't hurt that Mack pretty much still had the best pitching staff in baseball, but parting with Waddell for no return said something about what a nuisance he had become.

Waddell had still been a 19-game winner in Philadelphia in 1907. And he turned in a 19-win season for the Browns in 1908. But that represented the end of his great run. By 1911, Waddell was finished at 33. Even more shockingly, less than four years later he was dead at 37.

In 1910, Waddell divorced one wife and took another. He announced that his new wife "would make a man out of me. I have stopped drinking and am in better condition than I have been in years."[7]

The final pitching stats in the record book next to Waddell's name read 3–1 with a 3.35 earned run average for the Browns in 1910. Early in the year, he was hit by a pitch thrown by Ed Cicotte, then of the Boston Red Sox. The ball cracked Waddell's left elbow, and his left arm was his pitching arm. He was sidelined from May to August, but while sitting out and recuperating, Waddell was drinking again. He did make a comeback before the end of the year, however.

Seeking a fresh start in the majors, in the minors Waddell worked his way into what he considered to be top, enticing shape to attract a new team. Although Waddell seemed to have the old pizzazz, the Browns no longer wanted him. He never would take a major league mound again.

As the 1913 baseball season was poised to begin, Waddell was living in Hickman, Kentucky, on the property of one of his old managers, Joe Cantillon. He had spent the winter hunting and fishing and was athletically trim. Terrific rainstorms caused flooding conditions, and Waddell pitched in to help during the disaster, winning him friends and fans in the area. He was stricken with pneumonia, however.

A year later, Waddell was still firm in his confidence, sure he was capable of pitching in top form again. Flooding attacked the Hickman area again, and once again Waddell turned in yeoman service helping people. But he suffered a recurrence of the pneumonia. Trying to fight through it, Waddell kept trying to play ball, seeking a spot with the Minneapolis Millers.

Waddell had lost his fitness, was battling pneumonia, and then, after being spiked in a game with a Northern League team, incurred blood poisoning. Pneumonia, pleurisy, and infection all plagued Waddell. Rather than rest, he kept playing baseball.

Somewhere along the way, Waddell shifted from Minnesota to St. Louis and perhaps back to Minnesota. As the winter of 1913–1914 unfolded, Waddell, who had spent all his money and was drinking, was diagnosed with tuberculosis. He ended up in a sanatorium in Texas, where ball players in spring training stopped by for visits as he weakened.

"On the hospital bed lay the shrunken figure of the once powerful athlete, who now weighed less than 120 pounds," said Mack. "His face was haggard. He could hardly speak above a whisper."[8] Mack reconstructed that scene in his autobiography. Waddell sent word to Philadelphia that he would like to see Mack one last time, but Mack did not receive the message until after Waddell passed away.

Rube Waddell died on April 1, 1914.

3

The Year 1910— The Beginning

The Mackmen were ready. It had been five years since Connie Mack's Athletics won the American League pennant, and now his scouting for talent paid dividends. By 1910, some of the regulars had been with the A's for years. Others were fairly new to the lineup. But this was a team poised to win.

The A's were terrific, going 102–48 for a winning percentage of .680. Anyone who got in Philadelphia's way that season was liable to be steamrolled. The Athletics were 14½ games better than the second-place New York Highlanders and 18 games better than the Detroit Tigers. They were 57–19 at home. Opponents were outscored 674–442. Philly could out-hit you and out-pitch you. Still, this was the Deadball Era, so the A's as a team hit just 19 home runs all season while stealing 207 bases.

Those 102 victories marked the first time an American League club had topped 100 wins in a season. The A's were so dominant it seemed Mack was silly to worry about copping a pennant and feeling as if he needed the reinforcements of Bris Lord while sacrificing Shoeless Joe Jackson's future.

The season began on April 14 with a 3–0 loss to Washington. The A's were in a tie for first place in the AL by April 25 and took over sole possession on May 6. There was a brief period of a few days when Philadelphia fell into second place, but by July 30, when Jackson was traded, the A's were six games ahead in the standings. They put considerable distance between themselves and the other clubs in August and September.

Mack knew entering the season that he had talent and depth on his roster. He felt the starting pitching rotation was set with Eddie Plank, Charles "Chief" Bender, Jack Coombs and Cy Morgan. In those days, if you had four quality starters you were in clover. Nobody stockpiled relievers, only emergency fill-in starting pitchers who could be used in occa-

3. The Year 1910—The Beginning

sional spots. The starting pitcher was supposed to be the finishing pitcher, going the nine-inning distance most of the time.

In 1909, Philadelphia did not win the pennant, but they won 95 games. The A's were a team on the rise, and it did not seem that much tinkering with the lineup was necessary. To Mack, that signaled the preparedness of his team for the next season.

"From the time we reported at Virginia Hot Springs for training," Mack said, "I felt we were pennant-winning material."[1] Nothing he saw once the 1910 season began changed his mind. "In essentials the Athletics were not much changed for the 1910 race," Mack said. "The Athletics of 1910 were off to a good start and while one or two rivals pressed us up to September, they gradually wore them down and won by a big margin of about 15 games over New York."[2]

Although Mack knew he needed stars to compete for the top spot in the league, sometimes it seemed he took as much pride in finding players in faraway places who could make the team as much as he did in nurturing other players to greatness. There was no organized scouting program in the early 1900s. There was no major league draft. If you found a player and could convince him to sign, then he was yours. It wasn't always easy to tell if some lad playing semi-pro ball in a farm town 300 miles away could do the job at Shibe Park, but Mack had a knack for sorting out the contenders from the pretenders. He had reliable sources who filled his ears and head with reports of players who could make it with the A's. Fortunately for him, they knew how to separate the wheat from the chaff, and when his guys in the field let Mack know about somebody, chances were that the guy could play.

It may be that they only turned out to be back-up players, but there were always diamonds out there waiting to be discovered as well.

The four mainstays of the mound in 1910 were superb. A couple had been with the team for years. Two made 1910 the best season of their lives. Together they overpowered the league. Plank and Bender had been A's forever, it seemed, Plank since 1901 and Bender since 1903. Coombs joined the A's in 1906 but was not generally mentioned in the same breath as Plank and Bender as a star. Morgan pitched for two other teams before coming to Philadelphia during the 1909 season. Although his career to that point was not special, when he was needed as a replacement for Rube Waddell, Morgan pitched better than ever before or after, over a two-year, 1909–1910 stretch.

When you have that kind of strength on the pitching staff, it takes a huge amount of pressure off of the hitters. If they can only string together

During the early Athletics dynasty, Rube Oldring was a regular outfielder for Connie Mack's bunch (Library of Congress).

a few runs at a time, easy wins follow. Of course, it was not so easy to run up the runs when the ball was lopsided half the time and the park's fences were so far away you needed a telescope to see them from home plate.

It was an anomaly of the age that the triple was a far more common weapon than the home run. No one on the A's stroked more than four home runs that season as part of that anemic total of 19. However, Philadelphia bashed 105 triples. Outfielder Danny Murphy slammed 18 triples, and second baseman Eddie Collins and third baseman Frank Baker each whacked 15. Outfielder Rube Oldring smacked 14. Substituting the triple for the home run as a concussive at-bat, the A's did show power.

Collins also ran like a deer. That season he stole 81 bases. Mack said,

> Eddie surely ran for me that season. We were still playing for that one run and if Collins got on and stole second or third, we had good men in Baker, [Harry] Davis and Murphy to drive him home. It was the kind of game I liked best. When the home-run era came in I adjusted myself to that kind of attack, but I derived much more personal pleasure out of directing a base-running offense.[3]

Those who have studied the Deadball Era know that such tactics were routinely referred to as playing scientific baseball. The true symbol of that style of play was the legendary Ty Cobb during his Detroit Tigers career.

3. The Year 1910—The Beginning 25

Accordingly, runs did not come in bunches, even for the best team in the league. In 155 games in 1910, the A's scored ten or more runs in a game only six times. They surrendered that many four times. Of the eight players who pitched in at least one game for the A's in 1910, the pitcher with the worst earned run average of 2.88 was Harry Krause, who went 6–6. Generally, that is an ERA to be proud of, not embarrassed by. Just as unusual was a true slaughter such as the 18–3 beating the A's hung on Cleveland on the road on August 16.

Not everyone on the roster became famous, received Hall of Fame recognition, or was well-remembered in the decades after retiring or dying. Yet they were keys to the A's accomplishments. Murphy was getting old, turning 34 that season. Born in 1876 in Philadelphia, Murphy broke into the majors in 1900 with the New York Giants, the year before there was an American League. Murphy was playing in Norwich, Connecticut, when Mack personally scouted him. By 1902, when he blossomed at the plate, Murphy belonged to the A's and hit .313.

Murphy stayed with Mack and the Athletics until he was 36, six times hitting over .300 for Philly and playing for five pennant winners. He was not a great fielder, with Mack saying he was not as smooth on the double play as he would have liked during the days he preceded Collins at second base, but fared better in right field. Murphy could always find his way on base. Murphy batted .300 for the 1910 club.

Murphy had forever endeared himself to Mack in his first A's game in 1902. He was so recently acquired that he did not make it to the ballpark in Boston on July 8 until the second inning. Pretty much a stranger to his teammates, never mind the opposition, Murphy cracked six hits that day, including a grand slam homer. One of the Boston pitchers who could not get him out was Cy Young, who gave up a three-run shot to the newcomer. Later, Mack was as bewildered as anyone else about the stunning situation in a 22–9 victory. "Goodness gracious, but we had a batting day that afternoon," Mack said. "I guess Jimmy Collins, the Boston manager, wondered how he was ever going to get Murphy, my new man, out."[4]

One of Murphy's outfield partners in 1910 was Rube Oldring, who batted .308 with 57 runs batted in. A 5-foot-10, 186-pound, right-handed thrower and hitter, Oldring was born in 1884 in New York City but grew up in Bridgeton, New Jersey, about 60 miles from Philadelphia.

This was Mack territory, but that's not how Connie got on to Oldring. Oldring was playing in the Southern Association in Montgomery for a manager Mack knew. Tom O'Brien tipped off Mack, who signed Oldring in September 1905. The A's won the pennant, but Oldring wasn't eligible to play in the World Series. Mack told him to go home and play semi-pro ball and make some money instead of sitting around.

Oldring went to New York, played a weekend on a local semi-pro team, and was spotted by the New York Highlanders. Future Hall of Famer Clark Griffith saw Oldring and signed him for $200 for the last few games of the season. Griffith did not know Oldring belonged to the A's. That's how Oldring ended up making his major league debut, eight games' worth, with New York. "I knew Connie Mack would get a good laugh at the idea that another Major League club was helping develop one of his own recruits," Oldring said.[5]

Or perhaps not. Mack may have choked on his bubblegum when this peculiar arrangement reached his ears. Anyway, by 1906, when he was 22, Oldring was patrolling the field for the A's. He spent most of his 13-year career with Philadelphia and batted .270.

Much later, in 1997, 36 years after his death, Oldring had a baseball diamond near Cooperstown, New York, named after him, honoring his efforts over the years of working in youth baseball. Cooperstown, best known as the home of the Baseball Hall of Fame, began ramping up efforts to attract youth teams to town over the summer to play in what was named Cooperstown Dreams Park. This was one of the fields in the complex.

In 1910, Oldring played center field until the end of July when the A's brought in Bris Lord. Oldring moved to left after that, but broke his leg in the stretch run to the pennant and missed the World Series.

Bristol Robotham Lord of Upland, Pennsylvania, nee 1883, stabilized the outfield in Mack's mind. Lord broke in with the A's in 1905 and played three seasons in Philadelphia before being traded to Cleveland and later back to Philadelphia. Generally, Mack adhered to a personal policy of never re-acquiring a player he had parted with, perhaps because there was always a reason behind that departure. He made the exception for Lord in the Jackson deal.

It was not as if Lord had distinguished himself the first time around in Philadelphia, batting .239, .233 and .182 before disappearing from the majors altogether in 1908. Call Mack a genius, but in 1910 and 1911, Lord hit better than he did back in Philadelphia than he did at any other time during his eight-year, big-league career.

Another reason Mack needed someone, if not Lord specifically, in the outfield, was the subpar play of Tully "Topsy" Hartsel. Hartsel turned 36 and in his 90 games batted just .221, the numbers clear signs that he was nearing the end of his career. In fact, after playing 25 more games for the A's in 1911, Hartsel was out of the majors. A player who broke into the

3. The Year 1910—The Beginning

big leagues in 1898, he had a lifetime .276 batting average. Four times he led the American League in walks for the A's, and twice he led with on-base percentages of more than .400. Hartsel also topped the AL in runs scored and stolen bases in 1902. Much of his effectiveness relied on his foot speed, and Hartsel had served the Athletics well, but it was apparent he could no longer help a pennant contender.

The one other outfielder in the mix, for part of the season, was Amos Strunk, a left-handed hitting and fielding native of Philadelphia who had been scouted by Mack personally. Strunk broke into the majors in 1908 with the A's as a 19-year-old, after Mack's wooing. Most of his 17-season career was with Philadelphia, but that included coming and going three times.

Strunk had just 23 games on his major league resume in two seasons prior to 1910, and he was a handy fill-in for 16 games during the pennant-winning season while batting .333. He seemed to have a knack for timely hits that year even if he was not heavily relied upon. Overall, Strunk was a good base stealer, a first-rate fielder, and batted .284 lifetime.

Strunk, Mack said, was "the most underrated outfielder in baseball." Mack meant that Strunk never got much attention from sportswriters who took him for granted and focused more on the exploits of the $100,000 infield. "Also, Amos made his job of playing center field look a lot easier than it really was."[6]

Renowned for his swiftness on the base paths, Strunk was known to score from second base on a bunt, almost running up the heels of a teammate headed home from third base. Mack, whose own nickname was "The Tall Tactician," employed the tactic of calling for a double squeeze play when Strunk was the trailing man. Mack loved to watch his men take extra bases. "It was a combination of speed and timing," Strunk said. "It grieves me to see so many modern players who are blessed with speed, but don't make proper use of it."[7] Among his exceptions of those with daring speed around the bases were Enos Slaughter, Jackie Robinson and Willie Mays. "Everyone knows about Ty Cobb," Strunk said. "He wasn't the only one who always raced at top speed. Connie's players, even some of the slower fellows, always ran as if the sheriff was after them."[8]

Interestingly, Strunk was insurance for Mack in 1910, and after he retired from baseball he became an insurance broker for 50 years.

The most unsettled position on the A's of 1910 was catcher. Mack had been a catcher in his big-league days, and if he wasn't too old he might have been tempted to suit up himself. Instead, he switched from catcher to catcher as the season progressed. Jack Lapp, who had been with the club since 1908, caught 71 games but hit a mediocre .234. Ira Thomas caught 60 games and hit .278. Pat Donahue caught 14 games and batted .143. Paddy Livingston caught in 37 games and batted .208. Mack's son Earle appeared in one game and went two-for-four at the plate. Even if Mack couldn't find the absolute correct answer to play behind the plate, he could field a basketball team of all catchers.

Thomas, who played ten seasons in the majors, was the most reliable swatter of the group and probably the best fielder, too. Above all, he was the best leader, was chosen captain, and remained with the A's and worked for Mack as a scout and in other capacities for 45 years in all. Thomas was known for his hustling, hard-nosed play. "How else could you get along during those days?" Thomas said of his playing career that ended in 1913.[9]

Lapp, from Frazer, Pennsylvania, spent eight years with the Athletics seeking the No. 1 catching spot and only once, in 1915, did he play more than 100 games in a season. Lapp did have some solid batting years for Philadelphia, though, once hitting .353 in 167 at-bats. In 1910, though, he hit .234.

Unlike the others, Donahue, from Springfield, Ohio, was only passing through Philadelphia. His 1910 season was wacky. Donahue, who was 25 that season, his last in the majors, started the year in Boston with the Red Sox. He became an Athletic, caught 14 games and batted just .147, then was shipped to Cleveland and finally back to Philadelphia for one more game before season's end.

Livingston was a fireplug of a backstop at 5-foot-8 and 197 pounds, and a life-long Cleveland resident. A career back-up, Livingston squeezed out 206 games of action over seven big-league seasons spread over 17 years, but out-lived all of his contemporaries to reminisce about the game and the old days until dying at 97 in 1977.

Livingston, who in his 80s urged the reintroduction of the spitter to the baseball pitcher's arsenal, displayed large hands and fingers, somewhat gnarled, from his playing days. "Too big to fit into a bowling ball," he said.[10]

It was strange that Livingston would lobby for the resurrection of the quirky pitch, since it was responsible for doing to so much damage to his hands due to its unusual dancing motion. For the most part, though, Livingston mastered its handling, and because he could control the uncontrollable pitch better than most of his contemporaries, the skill helped him stick in the bigs.

The premier base-stealer during Livingston's years in the majors was Ty Cobb. Cobb stole nearly 900 bases in between hitting .400 three times.

3. The Year 1910—The Beginning

He was brazen and could create havoc on opponents. Livingston had a strong arm and could gun down Cobb sometimes. He recalled one game where he threw out Cobb trying to swipe second against the A's, but Cobb spiked shortstop Jack Barry. Livingston said that later in the same game, Cobb cut third baseman Frank Baker on a slide. Fans made death threats against Cobb when he returned to Philadelphia for the next series, but Cobb shrugged them off. "Ty didn't scare," Livingston said. "They threw hats at him, but that was all. You had to admire the man."[11]

When Livingston took his first communion at age 11, he pledged never to drink or take the Lord's name in vain. He kept those promises for another 86 years. He frequently referred to the men he played with as gentleman, which was not the prevailing description elsewhere. The No. 1-rated gentleman in his eyes was manager Connie Mack. "Connie Mack offered me a job coaching, but as much as I loved that man I decided to quit to be with my family," Livingston said. "Mack was a wonderful man."[12]

Livingston played one game with Cleveland in 1901 and didn't play another game in the majors for five years, mostly working as a ship builder in between. Then he played 50 games for Cincinnati in 1906. Mack got wind of Livingston toiling in the minors and bought his rights.

On a frigid day in 1909 when a regular catcher wouldn't play, Mack inserted Livingston into a game. When Mack wished to speak to him afterwards, Livingston thought he was going to be released. Instead, Mack said, "You're a catcher." And from then on, Livingston was.[13]

Livingston, a carpenter for 43 years after retiring from baseball, remained a huge follower of the sport for the rest of his life. He thought managers and coaches over-coached players on the field. "We didn't have all that sign language going from the manager in the dugout to the coach to the batter," he said.[14]

Of course, one thing the A's did have was Connie Mack in the dugout, moving his outfielders around with his own signals, the players being waved into place by a shift of the rolled-up program in his fist.

The catcher who played the funkiest role in 1910 was Earle Mack. He sat in a squat behind home plate for one ball game, courtesy of his father. The younger Mack, born in 1890, actually appeared in just five games total in 1910, 1911, and 1914 combined with a batting average of .125. After collecting two hits in his one game in 1910, he did not get another.

Earle Mack was more of a coach and scout over the years for his father and ultimately was co-owner of the A's. As early as 1939, Connie Mack insisted that Earle would succeed him as manager of the Athletics.

The one catch was that if Connie ever retired. Earle, who had won pennants managing in the minors, was 49 at the time.

"Earle is going to be the next manager of the Athletics, if they ever have one," Connie Mack said, "and he'll probably do a better job than his dad."[15]

Earle never held the position.

4

Jack Coombs

For one season, Jack Coombs was a superman on the mound. His performance for the Philadelphia Athletics during the 1910 season was akin to magic. Up until then, the right-handed-throwing, switch-hitting batter was mortal. For one season he was so stupendous as to defy description.

Born in Iowa in 1882, Coombs went to high school in Maine and then attended Colby College, the school that contributed to his nickname of "Colby Jack." Connie Mack was partial to college-educated ball players as long as they had the right stuff otherwise, and Coombs did.

Mack's sources told him about the strong-armed hurler in Maine as early as 1903, and in a rendezvous in 1904, as Coombs was about to start his last year of college on his way to what he thought would be fulfilling his ambition to become a chemist, Mack offered him a contract. Coombs said no, he wanted to complete his studies. In December of 1905, Mack tried again, offering $2,400 to Coombs to take effect after he graduated. Coombs agreed. "It looked like a million dollars to me," Coombs said.[1]

The A's signed Coombs in 1905, and by 1906 he was in the rotation, going 10–10 as a rookie with a 2.50 earned run average. Coombs was a .500 pitcher for the Athletics for the next three seasons, sometimes flashing promising talent and other times getting pummeled, leaving Mack to wonder if Coombs would ever harness his potential. The 1909 showing of 12–11 with a 2.32 ERA was Colby Jack's best over those three years.

With Eddie Plank and Chief Bender being complemented by Rube Waddell through 1907, all of them Hall of Famers to be, Coombs was rightly overshadowed. As spring training unfolded for the 1910 season, with optimism rampant about a pennant for the A's, probably no one in the organization would have predicted that Coombs would produce one of the finest pitching seasons in major league history.

Coombs pitched in an American League-leading 45 games and went

Jack Coombs was the rare 20th-century pitcher who topped 30 wins in a season for the A's, though his career was later interrupted by a life-threatening bout with typhoid fever (National Baseball Hall of Fame Library, Cooperstown, New York).

31-9 (the most wins in the league) with a spectacular 1.30 earned run average and 13 shutouts. The shutout total not only led the league, it remains the single-season AL record 107 years later.

Coombs' parents were from Maine but sought farmland in Iowa the year before he was born. After spending several years in the Midwest, in 1887 they returned to Maine, and that was the child's true home.

A strong, 6-foot, 185-pound hurler, Coombs threw what is often called a heavy fastball. There are contrasting descriptions of how he delivered it, sidearm or overhand, or perhaps someone happened to see a day when Coombs fiddled around with his style. Although in the majors Coombs was nicknamed "Colby Jack," in college he had been more often called the "Colby Carbine." They both sounded a bit like gunfighter monikers.

Coombs made his major league debut on July 5, 1906, and threw a seven-hit shutout at the Washington Senators. His next big-league appearance was as a pinch-hitter. Although he gained a reputation as a pretty fair hitter, in reality Coombs' career average indicates he was just so-so, batting .235. He did drive in 100 runs in nearly 1,100 at-bats, though. But Coombs was paid to strike people out, not strike out.

A stunning game during Coombs' rookie year flabbergasted all of baseball and historians forevermore. On September 1, 1906, Coombs took the mound for the Athletics. Opposing him was another rookie, Joe Harris, of the Boston Americans, aka Red Sox.

Some 18,804 was the paid attendance in Boston that day for a game that nearly became the equivalent of three. The A's took a 1-0 lead in the third inning. Boston tied the game in the seventh. And 1-1 is where the score remained as inning after inning passed. The zeros stacked up on the scoreboard like cordwood piled up for the winter. Nine innings in, it was still 1-1. Eighteen innings in, it was still 1-1. In the top of the 24th inning, the Athletics scored three runs. Boston could not come back, and Philadelphia won the 24-inning marathon. Philadelphia put together 16 hits, as did Boston. A's third baseman John Knight collected five of those hits, an unusual suspect for such success since he batted only .194 for the season. For Boston, first baseman Moose Grimshaw struck three hits and had 25 putouts.

Later, Coombs said he was so new to big-league ball that he really didn't know how to pitch yet. He said the credit for the win should have gone to his catcher, Doc Powers, for the way he called the game. Coombs said he went to school on his own as a student with a college degree from Colby, but needed a master's in throwing. "I learned most about pitching by sneaking around and watching Cy Young and Addie Joss work out," Coombs said. "Those boys were smart. I had a lot of crude ability, but I was no pitcher until four years after that 1906 game."[2]

The game, which lasted 4 hours and 47 minutes, was notable for its length alone, but even more so because both starters, Coombs and Harris, went the distance in dual complete games, a remarkable 24 innings each, stressing their arms. While not so many years later Coombs was acclaimed as the best pitcher in the American League, Harris' entire career output was measured by a 3–30 record. His 24 innings thrown in a single game, however, is still the longest performance in Red Sox team history. Given the way such a game presumed strain on an arm that would now be viewed as insanity, it is not likely ever to be approached, never mind topped.

During Deadball days, when pitching staffs were small, relief pitching as a specialty was virtually unknown, and teams expected their starters to pitch as long as it took to get the job done, crazy things like the 24-inning showdown occurred. Coombs showed tremendous potential as a rookie, especially with the guts displayed in that lengthy encounter. But over the next two years his production dropped. Coombs finished just 6–9 in 1907 and 7–5 in 1908. He had a sore arm for part of 1907, and some wondered if he would ever blossom into a top-tier pitcher.

The answer came in 1910 when Coombs was fully healthy, an experienced 27-year-old, pretty much had his own personal catcher in Jack Lapp, with whom Mack felt he showed better control, and after a slow start seemingly could do nothing wrong for the last five months of the season. Coombs won ten games in July alone, all of them complete games and five of them shutouts. Both Eddie Plank and Chief Bender were off form, and Mack frequently handed the ball to Coombs on two days' rest. That was brilliant pitching, but Coombs was about to outdo himself.

There are a few contenders in baseball history for the greatest game ever pitched from both sides of the diamond. On May 2, 1917, Fred Toney of the Cincinnati Reds and Hippo Vaughn of the Cubs each threw nine innings of no-hit ball in Chicago before the Reds won in the tenth. On July 2, 1963, at Candlestick Park in San Francisco, future Hall of Famers Warren Spahn of the Braves and Juan Marichal of the Giants engaged in a 16-inning, 1–0 duel. They both went the distance, with Marichal victorious. That day the Giants ace threw 227 pitches, while Spahn, the Braves star who was 17 years older, threw 201.

Those games are at least contenders for best-pitched-game ever. But a nominee from the old days was Coombs' confrontation with the White Sox's "Big Ed" Walsh on August 4, 1910. Walsh, bound for the Hall of

4. Jack Coombs

Fame, threw a Herculean 464 innings in 1908 when he won a remarkable 40 games.

Walsh's pitching achievements left many historians agog, but in this game Coombs was also super-human, striking out 18 men and allowing just three hits. Naturally, given the year, the game began in daylight. It was actually quite sunny and a pleasant 70-ish-degree day. But on and on the game went, past nine innings in a scoreless tie and on to 16 innings, when the umpires stepped in and called off the proceedings because of encroaching darkness. There it was, 16 innings of superb pitching, a score of 0–0 with no winners or losers. Famed journalist Ring Lardner wrote of the game, "Perhaps it was not the best ever played, but don't try to tell anyone that there have been many better. And don't let us say that Walsh was better than Coombs, or that Coombs was better than Walsh. They were both just about perfect."[3]

Coombs, who had been so overpowering in July, seemed equally dominant in August and into September. This was one of the most famous no-decisions in history, but from mid–August to the middle of the next month, Coombs won all nine of his starts and never allowed more than one run in any game over the 30-day period.

The term "untouchable" is often applied to pitchers with hot stuff, but Coombs' stretch demonstrated what being untouchable at the hands of enemy batters is really all about.

5

Charles Albert Bender

If there is any record of anyone referring to Charles Bender as "Chuck" it is impossible to come by. Instead, pretty much like any Native American participating in sports anywhere in the United States during Bender's era, he was called "Chief."

Being born in 1884 was not the best time for an American Indian, though it was hardly the worst time. At least much of the persecution of Native Americans in terms of forcing them off tribal lands and killing them had decreased, if not ceased, in most parts of the United States. But it was not as if when a son was born that parents felt he was going to grow up in a land of opportunity, either.

Bender, a member of the Ojibwe tribe, was from Crow Wing County, Minnesota. He was dark-skinned, and if he had been classified as African American he would have been banned from Organized Baseball. Given the nasty and violent history with Native-Americans, it is somewhat miraculous to contemplate that the prejudiced baseball establishment, which did not allow African Americans in its ranks, didn't hold the same kind of grudge against Native Americans.

As often as not, Connie Mack called Bender "Charles," though sometimes when talking about him, he did refer to him as "the Chief." Glibly put, although Bender was subject to much discrimination in terms of fans shouting racial comments at him, whooping in parody of supposed Indian war-like behavior and having the appellation Chief attached to him, he was a chief on the mound. In the most respectful of ways.

In 1910, when Jack Coombs was dazzling the baseball world with his 31-victory season, Bender was performing at such a high level that on any other team, he would have been labeled the ace of the staff.

During a major league career that spanned 16 seasons, Bender won 212 games, compiled an earned run average of 2.46, and ended up in the Hall of Fame. His finest year was 1910, when he went 23–5 with a 1.58 ERA.

5. Charles Albert Bender

Author of a no-hitter and Connie Mack's favorite clutch pitcher, right-hander Charles Albert Bender was a Native American star nicknamed "Chief" whether he wanted to be or not. After winning 212 games, Bender was enshrined in the Hall of Fame (National Baseball Hall of Fame Library, Cooperstown, New York).

Coombs was great, but the A's would not have won the pennant without Bender.

The two most shameful episodes in American history were the enslavement of black people and the official efforts to annihilate Native Americans. By the time Bender reached the majors with Philadelphia, after attending the Carlisle Indian School in Pennsylvania where famed athlete Jim Thorpe also matriculated, the bloodshed was in the past, but the prejudicial feelings and scarred emotions were still raw.

It was stated that by 1890, the Frontier was closed. It took decades longer for harsh feelings about Native Americans to subside. Society was far different in the early 1900s from a century later, when multi-culturism is much more broadly embraced.

Against this backdrop, Bender became a marvelous pitcher, a linchpin of Philadelphia success, both when Connie Mack was building the Athletics' dynasty and when championships were claimed. Bender was just 19 when he stepped into the A's rotation as a rookie in 1903 and won 17 games. He contributed to the 1905 pennant and was around for the entire stretch in the 1910s when the Athletics ruled baseball. Nine times he won at least 15 games in a season for Philadelphia.

Mack scouted Bender in person at Carlisle, adding him to the roster the year after he brought in Eddie Plank from Gettysburg College. Something in their maturation and mental sharpness attracted Mack to players who attended college. He looked at those men as not only more seasoned on the field, but also having the smarts to make good judgments. Of course, he also signed Rube Waddell, the antithesis of the schoolboys. But in 1903, Mack made a conscious effort to research school ranks. "I had decided to scout the schools and colleges for potential material and I brought to Philadelphia a Chippewa boy, Chief Bender, from the Carlisle Indian School," he said.[1]

It is horrifying to review the types of racism Bender was subjected to by the newspapers of the time, enough to gag an independent viewer. Cartoonists had a field day lampooning him, although it seemed as if many of the images were drawn out of ignorance as much as malice, playing to stereotypes. The same could be said of sportswriters who employed the vernacular of the day by referring to Bender money as "wampum" and headline writers who always seemed to find a way to make some kind of Native American comparison (as opposed to just baseball) when Bender excelled. Bender mostly took this kind of abuse in silence. He always wondered whether his teammates sympathized with him, with the stereotyping, or were also bigots. But he did not rock the boat on the A's. He did his job and he did it very well.

There were other Native Americans in the majors and some that had passed through the ranks. Louis Sockalexis is often cited as the first Native American big leaguer, although other sources differ. He joined the Cleveland Spiders in 1897 and was the inspiration for the later American League team in Cleveland being called the Indians. An outstanding talent with a .313 career average, he was a popular player, though a shooting star, playing just three seasons.

Either Bender did not read the newspapers during his career or chose to take the path of least resistance, outwardly ignoring their crackpot commentary, as well as the insults hurled by fans, or otherwise he was residing in a dream world. One thing Bender recognized was that major league baseball gave him the opportunity to obtain financial security, and he was not about to jeopardize that for anyone. "The reason I entered baseball," Bender said, "was that it offered me the best opportunity both for money and advancement. There was so little racial prejudice in the game that there has been scarcely a trace of sentiment against me on account of birth."[2]

Still, at least once Bender was provoked by taunts sufficiently to walk over to the grandstand and, in one of the great retorts of all time from a Native American perspective, call the hecklers foreigners and asked when they were going to go home.

Whether those more delicate thoughts were dressed up or not, it was indisputable that Bender did develop a notable career and did make himself and his family financially independent through baseball.

To be blunt, although the nickname of Chief didn't sit well with Bender, it was complimentary compared to many ethnic epithets showered on African Americans, who were also being lynched in the American South. Any deaf-mute in baseball, such as William Hoy and Luther Taylor, was called "Dummy." For the next 100 years, and to some degree still today, professional boxing's ethnic nicknames were more pronounced. Lest people forget, in the movie "Rocky," the protagonist was referred to as "The Italian Stallion." Attempting to generate larger attendance, promoters routinely billed fighters as the Italian this or the Irish that in hopes of revving up nationalistic constituencies. So the application of an ethnic nickname did not necessarily connote an insult in the fight game. In retrospect, they may sound cringeworthy, but such references to heritages were not all used in a derogatory manner.

Bender won 18 games in 1905 when the Athletics won the American League pennant. He started two games in the World Series against the New York Giants. He pitched a four-hit shutout in the game he won, but also lost, 2–0, to Christy Mathewson, and the A's lost the Series. Between late June and the middle of August of the 1907 season, Bender threw 11 straight complete-game wins, a skein that included three shutouts. When he finally took a loss it was 1–0, and the victorious pitcher was named "Piano Mover" Smith of the Chicago White Sox.

Mack thought very highly of Bender and greatly respected his talent. He coined the phrase "money pitcher" for Bender because he always came through in the clutch for the A's. "Given proper rest, Chief Bender did not once fail me in a dozen years," Mack said.³

On one occasion Mack tried to motivate Bender prior to a World Series game against the Giants. He questioned Bender about how much money was left on his home mortgage, and when Bender informed him it was in the neighborhood of $2,500, Mack offered to pay off the bill if he won. "I knew then that the Giants were done for," Mack said.⁴

Quite a few teams were done for when Bender took the mound, a primary example being Cleveland on May 12, 1910. Bender threw a no-hitter as the Athletics won, 4–0, for their eighth straight win. Only one walk separated Bender from a perfect game. The club he handled included the great Napoleon Lajoie and future Hall of Famer Elmer Flick, who pinch-hit. The A's scored single runs in four innings. "There was nothing that looked like a base hit," said A's teammate Rube Oldring, who was also Bender's long-time roommate on the road.⁵

The losing pitcher was Fred Link, and Cleveland's walk was acquired by Terry Turner on a 3-2 pitch in the third inning. Later, Turner actually said, "I'm sorry I got that walk."⁶ He felt badly for ruining a perfect-game attempt.

Bender said he did not even consider the prospect of throwing a no-hitter until the ninth inning. He also ignored in-dugout commentary aimed at saving him from any jinx. When one player muttered something about a no-hitter in the offing and others told him to shut up, Bender didn't mind. He was focused on completing the no-hitter when Flick stepped in to pinch-hit. "Elmer Flick was the last man to face me," Bender said. "He worked the count to two balls and two strikes and then I turned loose with all I had on a fastball on the outside. He took a good cut, but lifted a foul behind the plate. Ira [Thomas] circled around it like a drunken sailor, but finally caught it. I breathed a big sigh of relief."⁷

Bender was a fast enough hurler, but he also threw a pitch which was called "the nickel curve." In the future it would be named the slider, and Bender may have been one of the first practitioners of the weapon. The slider does not quite come up to the plate as swiftly as the fastball does on the hitter, but it can break more dramatically than a curveball.

"I used fast curves, pitched overhand and sidearm, fastballs, high and inside, and an underhand fadeaway pitch with the hand almost down to the level of the knees," Bender said. "They are my most successful deliveries, though a twisting, slow one mixed up with them helps at times."⁸

Maybe Bender was just a good athlete. One of his favorite pastimes was shooting. In 1915, after the baseball season ended, Bender and some others went on tour, appearing in front of fans while trapshooting. Bender was joined by teammate Harry Davis, Giants star Christy Mathewson and Otis Crandall in roaming the East and Midwest. Bender topped the other contenders, hitting 1,658 targets out of 1,800 thrown.

The right-hander had the same kind of accuracy on the mound. Bender threw 3,017 innings in his career and walked just 712 batters. He posted seasons with 250 innings and 45 walks, and 250 innings and 47 walks. "Control is the greatest requisite for a pitcher," Bender said. "Without control you are like a ship without a rudder. No matter how much power or speed you have you are unable to get results. Speed and power with control, however, will make you a great pitcher."[9]

About 30 years after Connie Mack first said Bender was the greatest clutch pitcher he had ever seen, legendary sports columnist Grantland Rice contacted him to ask the question anew. Rice had been conducting an unscientific poll and had heard votes favoring Walter Johnson, Big Ed Walsh, Dizzy Dean and Carl Hubbell. Rice checked back in with Mack, and he hadn't changed his mind about Bender's status.

"Bender was unbeatable for more than 10 years in every important game," Mack said.[10] No fair-weather friend, Mack.

Bender may have accidentally explained the reason behind his success in those pressurized games even if he was referring to another topic. "Tension is the greatest curse in sport," Bender said. "I've never had any tension. You give the best you have—you win or lose. What's the difference if you give all you have to give?"[11]

Bender stressed relaxation to one and all, although not always in what some thought to be an appropriate setting. During a 1911 World Series game against the Giants, Bender purposely threw curveballs to first baseman Stuffy McInnis and second baseman Eddie Collins at their positions when he was fielding ground balls. They yelled at him to cut it out, but Bender just laughed. He said those teammates called him all kinds of names. "I'd like to tell you what they called me, but I'm afraid no paper would print it," Bender said.[12]

All he wanted the younger players to do was stay relaxed.

6

The 1910 World Series

> "Connie Mack owes part of the success of his team to keeping them well. They drink 'PUROCK.' Do you?"
> —Chas. E. Hires Co., 210 N. Broad Street, Philadelphia, Pa.[1]

So read a half-page advertisement in the ten-cent Athletics' World's Championship Souvenir, Shibe Park program for the 1910 World Series against the Chicago Cubs. Indeed, the product had Mack's endorsement. An additional paragraph followed of him extolling the virtues of the company's bottled water. In part, he said, "The water in several of the cities we play in has oftimes affected the playing of some members of the club."[2] So, you bet, Mack thought it was good for his guys to drink PUROCK instead of the local stuff.

As to whether or not the water helped the A's reach the World Series, well, that would be in the mind of the buyer.

The cover of the 5-×-7-inch program featured a grinning elephant, trunk in the air, lifting a smiling baseball player holding a bat and with what appeared to be a halo over his head, even if it was supposed to be a crown.

Other advertising of note included Chalmers Motor Cars, the company that awarded the leading hitter for average in the American League and National League an automobile and recognized the Most Valuable Players between 1911 and 1914; the *Philadelphia Evening Telegraph*, which touted its publication of the "Mutt and Jeff" comic strip; The Hotel Majestic, "a $3,000,000 home for anyone who chooses, home of the ball players"; and The White Company's "White Cars Like The White Elephants Are Incomparable."[3]

The advertising was wrapped around individual team biographies and photos, including owners Ben Shibe and Connie Mack, as well as players. Of team captain and first baseman Harry Davis it said, "Harry

Davis, who has been the mainstay of the Athletics' infield ever since he joined the team in 1901, is a Philadelphian born and bred." Davis, always appreciated for his acumen, was on his way out of a starting job the next season. Daniel Murphy was referred to as "hard-hitting Dan." Shortstop John J. Barry was called "Reliable Jack." Righty pitcher Harry R. "Cy" Morgan "is one of the iron men of the diamond, endowed with unusual physical strength, game to the core." Backup first baseman Ben Houser's nickname was "Smiling Ben." Houser was "one of the tallest men on the Athletic roster, standing 6 feet, 1¾ inches."[4]

Founded in 1901, the A's had won pennants in 1902 and 1905 under Mack. There was no World Series in 1902, and Philadelphia lost to the New York Giants in the second go-around. This time the Athletics wanted the top prize, and they had to get past the Chicago Cubs to capture it.

The National League team was a mini-dynasty in itself. The Cubs first reached the World Series in 1906, losing to "The Hitless Wonders," their rival Chicago White Sox from the south side of town. The Cubs

A view of the entrance to Shibe Park, home of the Philadelphia Athletics, the first concrete and steel ballpark when it opened for business in 1909 (Library of Congress).

bounced back and won the 1907 and 1908 crowns. Almost any serious baseball fan can quickly link the year 1908 and the Cubs together as the last time the north side team won the Series until 2016.

Naturally, that was unknown in 1910, and Chicago seemed to present a formidable obstacle to the Athletics winning their first World Series. The Cubs won the NL pennant with a 104–50 record under manager Frank Chance. Chance was the first baseman in the poetic tale of the double play, "Tinker to Evers to Chance" and the best hitter amongst the trio later enshrined together in the Hall of Fame.

All three were still in the everyday lineup, along with other notables such as catcher Johnny Kling and outfielder Frank "Wildfire" Schulte. Lesser-known Solly Hofman batted .325 that year, and semi-regulars Heinie Zimmerman, Ginger Beaumont and Jimmy Archer could be threats at the plate.

The Cubs had depth on the mound, though the No. 1 starter to be feared was Mordecai "Three Finger" Brown, renowned for his bat-paralyzing curveball. Brown, a future Hall of Famer, finished 25–14 in 1910 with a 1.86 earned run average. His distinguishing physical characteristic was the loss of two fingers on his throwing hand in a farming accident as a youth. Although Brown was a long-time stalwart for the Cubs, the next man up, and not nearly as well-remembered by posterity, was "King" Cole.

Cole, whose real first name was Leonard, went 20–4 with a 1.80 ERA in 1910, his second season, virtually equal to Brown's overall production. Cole's ERA was the best in the league that year amongst pitchers with the qualifying number of innings. His was a short career, however (18 wins in 1911) and he died in 1916 later at 29 after six years in the majors, the last several of them in decline. Cole was cut down by tuberculosis but found a modicum of enduring fame when the scribe Ring Lardner modeled his fictional short-story character of a ball-playing rube, "Alibi Ike," after him.

Besides their big two, the Cubs had four other pitchers who that season won 11–13 games, including Harry McIntire, Ed Reulbach, Orval Overall and Lew Richie. Overall had the distinction of being the man on the mound when the Cubs won the Series in 1908, making him a century-plus-old trivia answer amongst Cubs fans. He also went 23–7 with a 1.68 ERA in 1907. Between 1906 and 1908, Reulbach led the National League in winning percentage three times and went an aggregate 60–15. Jack Pfiester was there in 1910, too, in lesser action, but with a 1.79 earned run average, better than either Cole or Brown.

So the seasoned Cubs awaited the A's, ready to resume winning titles.

6. The 1910 World Series

There appeared no way Chicago would be a pushover when the Series began. Indeed, most observers gave the edge to Chicago on the basis of its pitching staff, even if Jack Coombs and Chief Bender were a superb one-two punch for Philadelphia.

The Series opened on October 17 at Shibe Park. Chance chose Overall as his starter for the first game, and Mack turned to Bender. He approached him the day before. "I'm looking for you to take charge of the Cubs in this important first game," Mack said. "Don't worry, Mr. Mack, I'm ready for them," Bender replied.[5]

He was. One thing that inspired Bender was a newspaper story from a road trip which insulted his skills. It read, "The Cubs will triumph over the Athletics and will have no trouble beating Bender." Bender was incensed, but quietly tucked it away for motivation. Before Game 1 of the Series, he pulled it out and re-read it. "I read that clipping just before I went to the box and had it in my hip pocket while I was on the mound. The fellow who wrote that story had no idea how much it helped me get set to win."[6]

The Athletics scored two runs in the second inning and one run in the third for a 3–0 lead, and Overall was pulled for McIntire. The 26,891 Shibe fans were giddy. Bender went the distance, allowing just three hits. The only run scored against him was unearned, and he struck out eight Cubs.

At the time Home Run Baker was known only as Frank, or sometimes J. Franklin Baker. But he emerged as the slugging hero of the game, going three-for-four with two runs batted in. Outfielder Danny Murphy knocked in one run, as did Bender with a hit. The Cubs got their lone run in the ninth after Philadelphia committed two errors. The run wasn't Bender's fault.

The choice of starters by both managers was intriguing. Mack could have gone with Coombs, who had a superior season, but he had grown to rely on Bender over a period of many years as an experienced hand who regularly came through. Chance viewed Overall likewise. Both Brown, the veteran, and Cole, the youngster, had better seasons than Overall, but he had a 3–0 record compiled over two Series. Still, he had had arm issues periodically.

Chance felt the problems were due to overuse and employed Overall cautiously at a time when other managers were drubbing the life out of aces' arms by piling up the innings. At the time, there was a famed arm specialist called "Bonesetter" Reese whom many pitchers visited for treatments. John D. Reese was a doctor in Youngstown, Ohio, who seemed to

Especially in the early days of the Athletics' dynasty, they were a major attraction for Philadelphia fans, who sometimes crammed Shibe Park to overflowing. In this photograph from the 1910 World Series, eager A's fans watch the action from the rooftops of houses located along 20th Street (Library of Congress).

have a special gift for curing ailing athletes, although that was not the primary source of his practice. Overall was one of those patients, and he felt Reese did help him, if only temporarily.

Overall, who stood 6-foot-2 and weighed 215 pounds, was a large man for the era and played offensive line for the University of California at Berkeley's football team before becoming a major league pitcher. He was born on February 2, and some observant and teasing folks called him "The Big Groundhog" because of that birthday. On this day, Overall apparently ducked back down the hole after seeing his shadow.

Actually, the circumstances were worse than that for Overall. He went 12–6 during the 1910 regular season, but following the Series his arm failed him completely and he was out of the sport for three years, frustratingly seeking medical help. In 1913, Overall returned to the Cubs to go 4–5, and then retired.

Overall, who died in 1947, remained a Cubs fan and famously said, "I hope I live to see the Cubs win another world's championship."[7] Overall was born in 1881 so he would have had to live 135 years for that to occur. It wasn't happening in 1910, at least.

"Three Finger Brown" and his baffling curve took the stage for the Cubs in the second game, going up against the sizzling Coombs. Partially due to what was perceived as his handicap from the farm machinery accident of his childhood, Brown began semi-pro play as a third baseman. One day the scheduled pitcher for his club failed to appear, and Brown was thrust into the spotlight. Almost immediately it became apparent that he possessed special stuff and that his pitches swerved so drastically they were difficult to hit.

That began Brown's mound career, one that led him to 239 big league victories, a lifetime earned run average of 2.06 (one of the best ever) and to the Hall of Fame in 1949, a year after he passed away. In 1910, Brown won 20 or more games for the fifth of six times in his career. He was less a strikeout artist than a hurler who coaxed batters into weak contact.

To their relief, the Cubs touched Coombs for a run in the first inning. Brown was reached for two runs in third inning and another in the fifth. In the top of the seventh inning, the Cubs added another run, so it was 3–2 A's going into the bottom of the inning. That's when it all fell apart for Brown. The great Ty Cobb, the player with the highest batting average ever, once said of Brown's curveball that it was "the most devastating pitch I ever faced."[8] Not this day.

The Athletics were on their way to a 9–3 victory with 14 hits. The bottom of the seventh began with Eddie Collins walking. Frank Baker singled, sending Collins to third. In the 2000s, a manager would stroll to the mound and chat with his starter, or even have his mind made up and yank him before damage could be done. Brown stayed in. Harry Davis ripped a 3–2 pitch to deep left field and it bounced out of play for a ground-rule double amidst the crowd of 24,597. Collins scored and Baker scooted to third.

Danny Murphy followed with his own ground-rule double to left, scoring both Baker and Davis for a 6–2 lead. Brown got his first out, but it wasn't a clean one. Jack Barry laid down a sacrifice bunt to send Murphy to third, a base-path advancement that proved critical when catcher Ira Thomas singled, sending Murphy home.

Coombs made the second out on a ground ball, although Thomas moved to second, another critical development since the next man up, center fielder Amos Strunk, doubled, and that brought in another run. Bris Lord lofted a fly ball to left that should have ended the inning, but Jimmy Sheckard made an error and Thomas scored, too. That was the last of six A's runs in the seventh. Game, set, match. Lew Richie finished the game for Brown, pitching the home eighth. The Cubs did pick off a final run in the ninth, but in no way fashioned a comeback against Coombs.

Coombs had started a bit shakily. He found it challenging to gain his groove after a layoff at the end of the regular season. At one point, when Mack thought his man's confidence was wavering, he said, "The only way you can lose is for you to beat yourself. I am satisfied they can't hit you effectively."[9] As he often was, Mack was proven correct.

There was a day off between Game 2 and Game 3 as the teams adjourned to Chicago by train. Observers were a bit skeptical of Mack's pronouncement. Rather than go with veteran star Eddie Plank or the more rested Bender for the game at the West Side Grounds in Chicago, he anointed Coombs to start again on just one day's rest. For some it was a baffling choice, but it certainly was a vote of confidence in Coombs, who after all had just recorded the best season of his life. Chance chose Reulbach, a veteran.

This was before the days of Wrigley Field, and the listed capacity of the West Side Grounds was 16,000. However, more than 26,000 fans crammed into the park on October 20. Friendly confines, indeed. If so, these were the very cozy confines, even claustrophobic confines. Chicago, players and citizens alike, was optimistic. Their Cubs seemed ready to bounce back. Coombs had to be weary, didn't he? Their prospects would be grim if they couldn't take advantage of him.

In fact, Coombs looked quite vulnerable in the early stages of the game. He surrendered one run in the first inning and two more in the second. It would have been swell for Chicago if Reulbach could have held the Athletics in check. But the A's scored a run in the top of the first, two in the second and five in the third. Reulbach was dead meat early, and Chance hurriedly replaced him with Harry McIntire, who was more arsonist than fireman out of the bullpen.

It might be said that the World Series was really won by the A's in the first three innings of the third game. In the first inning, Frank Baker singled Amos Strunk in with the first run to set a tone off of Reulbach. Strunk did not play much during the regular season, but filled in for Rube Oldring in the Series, the starter being out with a knee injury. The Cubs tied the game when Sheckard scored on a sacrifice fly.

Strunk did the job when called upon. He said the game was different when he played from the one he saw in future decades. He didn't think much of coaches constantly flashing signs to batters while they were in the box. "That's rubbish," he said. "A batter has enough to do to study a pitcher without looking down to third base. Hit the good pitch, whether it's the first pitch or 2-0 or 3-1. All the years I played with Connie [11 counting a return after his first 10], the only control he exerted over a batter was to call the play when the batter left the bench. If we wanted to tire a pitcher we didn't take good pitches, we'd foul them off."[10]

It wasn't as if the A's were wearing out Reulbach. He just didn't have his good stuff that game. Barry knocked in Davis in the second inning on a double and then scored on a Coombs double for two more A's runs off Reulbach.

The Cubs hung in there with retaliation in the bottom of the second. Frank Schulte's double was the key hit off Coombs, driving in Joe Tinker, the famed second baseman, and Ginger Beaumont, to make it 3–3. Schulte was an often-dangerous hitter in his 15-year career whose nickname was "Wildfire." Twice he led the National League in home runs, with 21 in 1911, a large number for the time, and once he topped the league in RBI. He also won a Chalmers Award.

After two innings, Mack's faith in Coombs did not seem particularly well-placed. He looked very much like a guy pitching on too little rest. While he never matched his normal regular-season proficiency, soon enough it did not matter because the Athletics went to town in the third, chasing McIntire, who lasted just one-third of an inning, and handling Jack Pfiester, who stuck around for the rest of the game, going 6⅔, but also allowing five more runs in the 12–5 defeat.

Coombs was not at his sharpest but pulled off the win for his second victory of the Series and pushed the A's to a virtually insurmountable 3–0 lead in games over the now-demoralized Cubs, who still had Game 4 at home.

For the fourth game, on October 22, Mack went back to Bender while Chance chose his young, 20-game winner, Cole, to start. This was a tight contest that went into extra innings. Bender gave up his first earned run of the Series in the first inning. The problem began with a leadoff walk to Sheckard. After stealing second, he raced home on a single to left by Solly Hofman.

Cole, who showed that perhaps Chance should have gone with him earlier, gave up a solo run in the third. His big mistake that inning was walking the pitcher, Bender. Strunk batted him home with a triple to make it 1–1.

The Athletics pushed across two more runs in the top of the fourth for a 3–1 lead. Eddie Collins singled and Frank Baker, who had another big game with three hits, lashed a ground-rule double to left field. There were men on second and third for Murphy, who doubled to drive in the two runners.

Three straight singles off Bender to open the bottom of the fourth by Schulte, Hofman and Frank Chance, sent Schulte across the plate. The A's still led, 3–2. Although this was not one of those days when Bender was extraordinarily sharp, he took that one-run lead into the bottom of the ninth with an opportunity to end the Series with an Athletics sweep. It didn't happen.

Schulte led off the inning with a double and was bunted to third by Hofman as the Cubs played for one run to extend the game. Then Chance came up big for the second time that day in his role as player-manager, belting a triple to center to drive in the tying run. But Bender kept the winning run from scoring.

Chance had lifted Cole after eight innings and replaced him on the mound with Brown, his old leader. The only baserunner against Brown in the top of the ninth reached on an error. He returned for the top of the tenth inning and safely pitched around a Harry Davis double.

There were two outs when Sheckard sent Jimmy Archer home with the winning run with a single to center. Bender lost this one and Brown got the victory. The teams stayed right there at the West Side Grounds for Game 5 the next day, October 23.

Apparently, the managers had limited trust in most of their pitchers because Mack went back to Coombs and Chance started Brown even after his two innings of relief the day before. This time the Cubs got a taste of the Coombs of the regular season. Brown was game and matched Coombs for most of the afternoon.

The A's took a 1–0 lead in the first inning. The Cubs tied it, 1–1, in the second and Philadelphia inched ahead, 2–1, in the fifth. The score stayed that way till the eighth inning, when they scored five runs to break things open. Bris Lord, Collins (one of his three hits) and Murphy were the key batsmen in driving in runs. The best the Cubs could muster after that was a single run in the bottom of the inning. The final score was 7–2, although each side notched nine hits.

It was over. The Athletics were World Series champions, 4–1 conquerors of the Cubs. It was the first world title in Philadelphia history.

In the end, despite some rough patches, the Series belonged to Jack Coombs, just as the regular season had. He went 3–0, the second pitcher in history after Christy Mathewson of the Giants to win three games in a seven-game Series. "It is gratifying to me that I was able to win the three games I pitched against the Cubs," Coombs said. "I got better as I went along and I never had any doubts about the results of the final game. I knew I was good and I knew the Athletics could hit any kind of pitching. I would have been happier if we had taken four straight, but I'm happy enough now."[11]

Philadelphia fans were virtually dancing in the streets in support of the A's. The team traveled home from Chicago by train, and it was estimated that about 10,000 fans met the squad at the station. The Athletics were taken by motorcade to the Bellevue-Stratford Hotel for a celebratory dinner. "They're a grand bunch of boys," Mack said. "I'm proud of them. They never quit. The first four games we only used 10 men. That speaks well of the way the boys work together."[12]

That was only the opening round of celebrations. The Athletics had another team dinner a few days later at the Hotel Majestic. As each player went home for the off-season, hometown fans tossed more galas to honor them with still more dinners and parties. They learned it was a big deal to play for a team that was a world's champion.

After Giants manager John McGraw attempted to insult the Athletics by calling them "white elephants" and Connie Mack's embrace of the name, the white elephant became a full-fledged, positive nickname. For decades, the white elephant remained a symbol of the team, and for most of a century, even after the team had departed for Kansas City and Oakland. Mack was pictured holding replica white elephants. The Philadelphia Athletics Historical Society even sold replica figures of white elephants.

From 1910 on, the white elephant certainly took on new meaning for the Philadelphia Athletics.

7

Infielders

Harry Davis was the first baseman when the Athletics won the 1910 World Series. He was established at the bag and regarded as an exceptional fielder, a smart player, and a solid hitter. Yet he was on his way out, about to be expelled from the $100,000 infield by Stuffy McInnis in 1911.

Davis was a Philadelphia guy, born in 1873, during an era when numerous players gravitated to their hometown team. Besides, before the era of widespread scouting, television and the like, it was much easier to learn about a player close at hand than one who played halfway across the country.

Connie Mack was a great admirer of Davis' style and intelligence and recognized he had the makings of a future manager. That's one reason why Davis became the A's captain when the team started up and through its early glory years. Mack often plumbed the college ranks for baseball talent, and Davis had attended Girard College, although he took a long detour between school days and the A's lineup.

Philadelphia connection aside, Davis was a veteran major leaguer before ever taking the field for the A's. Prior to joining the new American League outfit in 1901 for its first season, Davis had played for the New York Giants, Pittsburgh Pirates, Louisville Colonels and Washington Nationals.

Mack and Davis overlapped in Pittsburgh. Mack was ousted as manager as management sought to make numerous trades without consulting him. One of those trades shipped out stalwart Jake Beckley, later voted into the Hall of Fame, to the Giants for Davis. In the confusion of the comings and goings, Mack said, Pittsburgh fans blamed him for dumping one of their favorites. "I didn't make the deal for Davis," Mack said, "but I still recall people hollering at me from Pittsburgh windows: 'Why did you trade Jake Beckley?'"[1]

A couple of years later, after Davis injured a knee and was released by the Pirates, bounced around with a couple of minor league clubs and then retired to a job with the Lehigh Valley Railroad as an accountant in Philadelphia, Mack took over the A's. He tried to induce Davis out of retirement once and was turned down, then went back to him again with another offer. "I need you," Mack told Davis.[2] This time Davis said yes and returned to baseball.

Although the 5-foot-10, 180-pound, right-handed-hitting Davis was not a slugger by modern standards, he had some top-flight seasons at bat for the A's, hitting .306, .307 and .309. During the depths of the Deadball Era, he led the American League in homers four years in a row, from 1904 through 1907. Of course his totals were illustrative of the times, two of those seasons slugging eight and the other two years knocking out ten and 12.

Davis did make things happen, twice leading the league in runs batted in. Although he did it with Pittsburgh, Davis also led his league in triples one year with 28. More often he was a consistent banger of doubles, three times topping the league in two-baggers for the A's with a high of 47.

So Davis was no slouch at the plate, and Mack knew he could count on Davis to make good decisions in the field. Davis eventually became a Philadelphia city councilman after leaving baseball, although political cynics might suggest that offered no evidence about his brainpower.

Still, at times when Mack had to be absent from the team for business matters or to scout a prospect himself, he left Davis in charge of the club. As captain, Davis was supposed to represent his teammates, too. The necessity for a spokesman came up during the 1910 World Series when major league baseball, for the first time, sold film rights to the games. The players wanted a cut of the payout, even though the total payment was just $3,500. They chose Davis as the team leader to haggle on their behalf with officials. Administrative officials refused to grant them a share.

Davis served as team rep in other ways. Mack, who wore a trademark suit in the dugout rather than a team uniform, was not allowed to go out on the field to protest an umpire's calls. Davis did that work when called upon, once complaining about a call for eight minutes before being thrown out of the game.

When the Athletics won the 1910 Series and were celebrating, Mack graciously awarded considerable credit to Davis. "There was not a move made on the field that was not directed by Davis," Mack said. "He has not been appreciated to the extent his work merited by the Philadelphia baseball public."[3]

Davis was a key man in the Athletics' success that year, as a player and as a conduit between Mack and the troops. However, Davis was getting old for a full-time player and in 1911 turned 37. His mind was more agile than his feet by that point in his career, and he drifted to backup status. He appeared in just 57 games and batted only .197. He was replaced in the starting lineup by John "Stuffy" McInnis, though that was not preordained.

McInnis was considered a middle infielder. He had filled in mainly at shortstop, not first base. At 5-foot-9, he was on the short side for a first baseman. Normally, height is a prerequisite for the job so errant high throws can be grabbed. The man thought to have the inside track as the next first baseman was Ben Houser.

Houser was born in Frackville, Pennsylvania, and was named after one of Philadelphia's favorite sons, Benjamin Franklin Houser. He thought he was going to be Davis' designated successor. The story goes that both McInnis and Mack believed in his ability, but McInnis didn't see any openings coming up in the infield anywhere besides first base, so he bought a first baseman's glove and started practicing there.

Davis endorsed McInnis over Houser and another long-shot contender, Claud Derrick, saying, "[He] will get the high throws that any first baseman would get, and anyway our infielders will not make many high throws. All that I am worrying about is whether he will get the low ones."[4]

Houser saw his golden chance slipping away when McInnis began taking grounders and throws at first. At 6-foot-1, he was bigger and tried to elbow McInnis right off the field. "It was funny how Ben took it," Mack said later. "Every time Stuffy would go to the bag, Houser would come out from the bench and try to shove him away."[5]

During the 1910 season, Houser got into 34 games, but had just 69 at-bats while batting .188. After losing out to McInnis, Houser ended up with the Boston Rustlers (the team that became the Braves). He made a limited impact there and, after playing one additional season in Boston when he hit .286, was out of the majors. Houser made his largest contributions after he moved to Maine to become coach at Bowdoin College. Over the years he worked not only in government jobs there, but helped youth baseball organizations. For the last four years of his life, Houser was a scout for the Boston Red Sox. When Houser died in 1952, he was called "Maine's Mr. Baseball."

McInnis was barely more than half of Davis' age. A native of the Boston north shore community of Gloucester, a famous fishing town, McInnis made his major league debut at 18 in 1909. McInnis did not even finish his senior year at Gloucester High before joining the A's for spring training. Mack considered him a special talent, although very young. Mack

7. Infielders

Stuffy McInnis was one of the greatest fielding first basemen of all time, as well as being a lifetime .307 hitter. Many believe that he merits inclusion in the Hall of Fame (National Baseball Hall of Fame Library, Cooperstown, New York).

didn't want to send him to a minor league outfit and appointed the conservative, non-drinking catcher Ira Thomas as an unofficial guardian. Thomas took the job seriously and steered McInnis away from booze establishments.

While McInnis did not see much action that year, or even in the World Series-winning year of 1910, when called upon he produced. In 1910, McInnis hit .301 in 38 games as a 19-year-old. There was no way Mack could keep him on the bench any longer. By 1911, his and Davis' roles were reversed. McInnis was the starter, playing in 126 games while batting .321 with 77 runs batted in. It was now his time.

Although his family called him John, McInnis was bestowed with the nickname of "Stuffy" when he was still a kid. It wasn't his demeanor, but an offshoot from a compliment. McInnis' family boarded fishermen in Gloucester, and sometimes when he was a youth he played baseball with the older men. When he made a good impression, a good play, they would shout, "That's the stuff, Johnny." Soon enough they were calling him "Stuffy," and others chimed in with it as well.[6]

Later in life, McInnis became the baseball coach at Harvard University. Now Harvard was the kind of place where an outsider might glance at the atmosphere and call it stuffy. But it was also the kind of formal place where no person would be called Stuffy.

By the time McInnis was selected as Davis' full-time replacement, the other three positions of the Athletics' infield were set. Eddie Collins played second base. Jack Barry played shortstop. And Frank Baker was the man at third.

It wasn't until after McInnis was installed at first that the quartet was immortalized as "the $100,000 infield." It was a measure of respect that any players could be worth that much in trade value or however their worth was being measured. In the 1930s, the Newark Eagles of the Negro Leagues started a foursome termed "The Million-Dollar Infield," a sign not only of inflation, but appreciation. That group consisted of Mule Suttles at first, Dick Seay at second, Willie Wells at shortstop and Ray Dandridge at third. Suttles, Wells and Dandridge were all later elected to the Hall of Fame. Seay was known as an excellent fielder capable of turning a bunt into a serious weapon, but overall was not viewed as much of a hitter.

Jack Barry played college ball at Holy Cross in Worcester, Massachusetts, and after his playing career began a long stint as the baseball coach at the school. He remained close to the sport for the rest of his life and was amused by how the economics of the game changed in his lifetime. "It makes me laugh when I read where a club has given an untried youngster $50,000 or more to sign a contract," Barry said of the 1950s. "They called us 'the $100,000 infield' when I played with McInnis, Collins and Baker, but I'll bet it didn't cost Connie Mack more than $50 to land us all. I know that all it cost him to get Collins and myself was car fare."[7]

7. Infielders

One thing Barry was not was a great hitter. He made timely hits but didn't get a lot of them every day, finishing with a lifetime batting average of .243 in 11 seasons with the A's and Boston Red Sox. Barry was better afield, a spiderman fielder who it seemed could reach everything hit in his neighborhood.

Mack reveled in the compliments paid to his infielders and in 1950, when he wrote an autobiography after being around big league ball since before the turn of the century, he was as effusive as some of the fans. "Sportswriters began to talk about my '$100,000 infield,' Baker, Barry, Collins and Stuffy McInnis," Mack wrote, looking back. "I do not believe the game has ever seen anything better. Today, any one of these men would bring far more than $100,000 on the open market. They might even be called 'A Million-Dollar Infield.'"[8]

Jack Barry was the shortstop for the A's "$100,000 infield" and then coached college baseball for Holy Cross, his alma mater, for four decades (National Baseball Hall of Fame Library, Cooperstown, New York).

Bill James, the influential, expert baseball statistician and analyst, once ranked the 1914 infield of those four players as the best in baseball history. In pure current inflation dollars, the "$100,000 Infield" of 1914 would have been worth more than $2.4 million in 2016.

In terms of what Connie Mack was paying his esteemed infielders, salaries are not as readily available from the early 1900s as they are in the 2000s. Frank "Home Run" Baker made $8,000 from the A's in 1913. Eddie Collins made $4,200 in 1907 and $7,000 in 1913. McInnis made $5,000 after joining the Red Sox in 1917. No salary could be found for Barry.

These days, the highest paid individual at each infield position makes more than $20 million a year, including Detroit's Miguel Cabrera ($28 million) at first base, Seattle's Robinson Cano ($24 million) at second,

Toronto's Troy Tulowitzki ($20 million) at shortstop, and the New York Mets' David Wright ($20 million) at third.

Clearly the value of a dollar has changed, since two of the A's are in the Hall of Fame and only Cabrera in the modern group seems likely to become a Hall of Famer.

But $100,000 was a big deal in 1911, and it was after McInnis took over for Harry Davis that the Athletics' infield gained its appellation.

8

Eddie Collins

Collecting three hits and driving in two runs in the clinching game of the 1910 World Series gave Eddie Collins' reputation for being a clutch hitter a boost. Collins' nickname was "Cocky," and he now had a key performance to match the attitude.

Collins made his debut with the Philadelphia Athletics at 19 in 1906, but he had just missed the chance to participate in the 1905 Series and missed the 1902 pennant championship by a few years. So 1910 was his first post-season experience, and he came through when most needed.

Collins had been working his way to steady stardom over the preceding couple of years. He appeared in just six games in 1906 and 14 in 1907. He became a regular the next year, playing in 102 games while batting .273. Connie Mack liked his potential, but it had not truly unfolded yet.

Born in Millerton, New York, in 1887, Collins was another of those college men that Mack so liked. He graduated from Columbia University (too soon to be a teammate of Lou Gehrig's), but he mostly employed his Ivy League education in the baseball world. That was somewhat ironic because as late as his junior year in college, Collins still preferred football over baseball, although he didn't really have the size for that game.

In these days of the Internet and constant scrutiny through social media, it is nearly impossible to pull off the kind of scam Collins engaged in as a student at Columbia. He signed a professional contract with the A's while still a student and, perhaps uncertain of his future, sought to preserve his amateur status. So when Collins obtained some minor league experience while still a student, he competed under the last name of Sullivan.

Collins was 5-foot-9 and played in the majors at as much as 175 pounds. But when he was still a collegian and was offered a chance to play minor league ball in Plattsburgh, New York, under his fake name, he weighed just 135 pounds. His manager was an old friend of Connie Mack's, and he was the one who tipped off the A's boss about signing Collins.

Second baseman Eddie Collins was nicknamed "Cocky" because of his attitude, but he had much to be confident about, stroking 3,315 hits during a 25-year playing career (National Baseball Hall of Fame Library, Cooperstown, New York).

Meanwhile, Collins was trying to earn a few bucks from baseball whether it was legal or not under college rules. This was done more frequently than most fans knew at the time, but Collins, who was Columbia's captain, was found out. Mack played along, calling Collins "Sullivan." The player had signed for $400 a month, which was more than he could make playing summer ball elsewhere.

8. Eddie Collins

In practice, Collins endured a rude awakening, or rather a Rube awakening. Rube Waddell took the mound and blitzed three straight pitches past a befuddled Collins. "He threw me three curveballs that looked as if they had dropped off a table," Collins said. "I missed all three. I thought I'd never make good if they had that kind of pitchers in this league." Collins left the batter's box depressed, but Waddell, who indeed was telling the truth since he had set a record by striking out 349 hitters in a season, said, "Don't mind, kid, I do that to all of 'em."[1]

Collins appeared in six games for Philadelphia as Sullivan, but when he got back to the New York campus, it turned out Columbia officials had the goods on him and he was declared ineligible.

After those part-time, warm-up seasons with the Athletics, there was no doubt where Collins' career prospects lay. What wasn't clear yet was where Collins belonged in the pros' lineup. Mack already had a solid-hitting second baseman in Danny Murphy. But Murphy's bat sometimes overshadowed his off-days in the field. Topsy Hartsel and Amos Strunk held down outfield positions, but Mack believed the outfield could be upgraded and that Collins could slide in to replace Murphy at second. Murphy wasn't thrilled about the switch, but Collins' potential could not be denied. For a while he roamed the outfield at Shibe Park and didn't look very good doing it.

"It was a mean sun field," Collins said of having difficulty adapting to judging fly balls coming at him out of the glare of the sun, "and the sun glasses hooked to my ears kept sliding down my nose. Then a high, fly ball came soaring over near the line and I went for it. The glasses slipped. I stumbled, fell, and the ball whizzed past my ear to smack the earth. When I came in, Mack said, 'You better stay away from the outfield or you'll get killed.'"[2]

Not that even Collins knew he would find such comfort playing second base. It was not as if he lobbied for the spot with Mack, since he wasn't sure either where he best fit in on the diamond.

> It was in 1908 that I finally found my natural position. I wasn't a polished second baseman by any stretch of the imagination. But with Danny Murphy, whose position I usurped—let us say—tutoring me and with Connie Mack patiently laboring to develop my latent talents, plus some hard work on my part, I was gradually acquiring the first touches of polish.[3]

Collins and the A's matured at roughly the same time. In 1909, Collins batted .347 with a .416 on-base percentage, and it was clear his promise was about to be fulfilled. He burst out as a true star in 1910 and became probably the most valuable member of that $100,000 infield while holding down second base.

Collins had already shown he had good wheels with 63 steals in 1909, but the next season he led the American League with 81 stolen bases while adding 81 RBI and a .324 batting average. The stolen base achievement was significant, at least partially because in those days, the Tigers' Ty Cobb was about take ownership of that stat for a long time. Cobb won his first stolen base title with 53 in 1907 and he captured six steals titles between that year and 1917. In fact, when Collins broke in and was impressing baseball people with his speed, he was making Mack frown over his unimpressive sliding style. One day, Mack commented that Cobb slid into bases beautifully. Collins caught on and became an even better base stealer, looking better doing it and improving his efficiency. "You don't steal on the catcher," Collins said, something many fans don't realize because they watch the backstop try to gun down the runner. "You steal on the pitcher. Study every move he makes, particularly his feet. Never mind his hands. Watch his feet and hips."[4]

The creation of the All-Star Game lay a quarter of a century in the future, but Collins surely would have been an All-Star pick that year if the option was available. Eventually, Collins became a major figure in the discussion ranking the greatest second basemen of all time—and he remains high on anybody's list.

Collins was an extraordinary hitter. He studied pitchers from the time he was a youth and was difficult to fool, even by the best. His lifetime average was .333. Depending on how much weight is given to part-time seasons (a few of those thrown in), he topped .300 17 times when he played at least 95 games in a year.

Despite being a high-grade student of hitting, fittingly since he did graduate from a top university, Collins was superstitious. That let emotion get in the way of fact, but Collins couldn't help himself. One of his most unusual habits was parking his gum on the button of his cap until the pitcher had two strikes on him. Collins also adhered to some of the more widespread superstitions, such as avoiding black cats. The sight of barrels was something on his side. If Collins saw a truckload on the way to the park he felt he was due for a couple of safeties. A hairpin meant he would obtain a single, a double hairpin meant a double. Collins must have been doing something right, whatever was behind it, because he amassed 3,315 hits in his 25-year big-league career. (Anything credited to Eddie Sullivan was later converted.) More than 85 years after Collins retired, he ranked 11th on the all-time major league baseball hits list, first among second baseman. It will take some time before anyone else can surpass him.

Going back to superstitions, before he got married (to a woman he met through Mack), Collins lived with Harry Davis and his wife. One day, dessert was sliced pineapple. In that day's game, Collins stroked four hits. That turned pineapple into his favorite dessert.

Long after retirement Collins uttered a bold statement about where he ranked in the firmament of stardom during his playing days.

> In the face of being considered the supreme egotist, I want to say now that I always felt I would have been recognized as a much greater player except that the gigantic shadow of Cobb was spread across the American League diamonds during my best years as a player. That shadow eclipsed all who came into its orbit. There was never a more dynamic player than Cobb, and as long as it had to be a player of Ty's stature that dimmed my own shining star, I can't say I have any regrets.[5]

Mack wouldn't disagree. Connie's major league experience began in the 19th century and extended into the 1950s. It was an unparalleled involvement in the game, and when he penned an autobiography, he chose an all-time baseball team. Collins was his second baseman. "The greatest second baseman who ever lived," Mack said. "His fighting spirit was contagious. Eddie was a great base runner, as well as one of the top-notch hitters. He played baseball as it should be played, making the tough ones look easy. Eddie would be my team captain."[6]

Collins said spring training in New Orleans in 1910 helped him improve as a second baseman and denoted a turning point in the A's franchise. Calling it "a new era, it marked the surge of the A's as a Major League power. It marked the start of an era of greatness for Connie Mack and his subsequent teams."[7]

Whether he envisioned such a thing happening as a man turning from teenager to adulthood, Collins spent his entire life in the sport as a player, manager and general manager. From that vantage point of judging talent and watching ball players' salaries explode over the decades, in 1950 Collins said the $100,000 infield he was part of with Philadelphia would have been valued at $2 million by then.

"And it would be worth every part of it," Collins said.[8]

9

The Year 1911

The Philadelphia Athletics were on top of the baseball world and they liked the view. Rarely was there a team that had so much fun winning a championship.

One of the presents given to Connie Mack in gratitude for his helming the best club in baseball in 1910 was a huge chocolate elephant. A chocolate elephant, not white chocolate either, apparently.

This eye-catching sculpture made by the H. O. Wilber & Sons Chocolate and Cocoa Manufacturing Company was unveiled during a celebratory parade for the World Series champs. It weighed hundreds of pounds, but no specific figure was announced. From an artistic standpoint, the chocolate sculpture received rave reviews. It was not clear if food critics felt the same enthusiasm.

At that time, no one could match A's fans for enthusiasm anywhere in the big leagues. The Athletics led the American League in attendance in 1910 and again in 1911. Shibe Park was a popular place to visit.

In fact, the A's had so much fun winning the title in 1910 they decided to do it all over again the next year. It is said that the most difficult challenge for a team is to repeat. Typically, the hunger is sated by a first crown. Teams know how hard it was to win once and often they falter, unable to muster the same effort again immediately.

But the A's were the best team around, and the core of stars was almost identical. Stuffy McInnis had moved in at first base, shoving Harry Davis aside to the bench, but the mainstays of the pitching staff were the same and all of the other position players of note were back for another try.

Then, as now, pre-season predictions abounded. It was a logical and somewhat light-hearted way for sportswriters to kick off the season. A perusal of the A's roster helped experts come to a ready conclusion that the Athletics were again the finest team on the diamond. It was easy to keep the faith in Philadelphia. The Athletics appeared to have no weak-

9. The Year 1911

nesses. Ordinarily, Mack would be one of those managers who hated to build up his team too much before it accomplished anything. The problem was that the facts belied any poor-mouthing. The A's were loaded.

Yet Mack gave it his best to try to keep his players' egos in check and pick at their supposed vulnerabilities. "Can't let up," he said. "Other teams improved. [We were] lucky to escape injury last year."[1]

For all of their weapons, the Athletics did not get out of the starting blocks well. The Detroit Tigers, feeling frisky, raced to the front of the AL standings early in the season. Boy, the Tigers could hit. Sam Crawford batted .378 that season and didn't even lead his own team in hitting. Ty Cobb batted .420. After them came Jim Delahanty at .339. But Detroit did not have the pitching depth to match the A's. The Tigers' ace was George Mullin, who went 18–10. They had five other guys who won between ten and 13 games, but no true Mr. Reliable.

Still, by May 10 the Tigers' record was a blistering 21–2, one of the greatest starts in major league history. A month later they were 36–13. It took until July 4 for the Tigers to fall a half-game out of first place. On August 5, the teams were tied. But the Athletics dominated the home stretch, rolling to a far superior September and extending their final margin to 13½ games. Pitching, pitching, pitching is what did it. Detroit finished 89–65. Philadelphia finished 101–50. "It was the first time the Athletics had ever won two pennants in a row," Connie Mack said, "and Philadelphia realized it had a baseball machine that was going to last. Public sentiment and the opinion of the experts had greatly shifted in a year's time. Nobody considered our chances before the games with the Cubs, but it was different this fall."[2]

Although his earned run average spiked noticeably to 3.53, Jack Coombs' record was almost as good as it was the year before, when he won 31 games. This time he finished 28–12. Eddie Plank went 23–8, Chief Bender 17–5, and Cy Morgan 15–7. Harry Krause contributed at 11–8 as a fifth starter. Another of Mack's so-called finds (though one not nearly as valuable, as it turned out), Dave Danforth, went 4–1 in 14 games, mostly in relief, and made timely contributions. There was a bit of excitement when Mack signed Danforth since the boss' record was so good, and his talent whisperers as scouts said good things.

Danforth was born in Granger, Texas, in 1890 and acquired the nickname of "Dauntless Dave" from Eddie Collins. He was another college man, someone who put off joining the A's until July of 1911 so he could graduate from Baylor University in Waco. As a senior, the southpaw threw two no-hitters.

Danforth made the strangest of impressions after he reached the majors. Some thought he was a devotee of black magic and somehow used the secret of the dark arts on the mound. Batters thought he manipulated the ball with hocus-pocus, if not grease or other unusual substances, although Danforth always denied it. If he was such a genius of mysterious sources of power, it did not pay off that much for him in the majors. Danforth, who suited up for the A's for part of only one other season, split the rest of his career between the Chicago White Sox and the St. Louis Browns, going 71–66 lifetime.

It should be noted that doctoring the baseball was completely legal until 1920, spitballs included, and Danforth took credit for inventing the shine ball when he was sent to Louisville in the minors in 1915. One account relates that he was hardly secretive about gouging the ball, either. "He kept scratching the ball and roughing the surface until the visitors kicked about it."[3]

The shine ball was half shiny and half normal. At times, Danforth said the shine originally developed by accident when the ball rolled into some oil. Then he said the shine was really from a heavy-duty application of rosin. When Danforth returned to the majors, Ty Cobb became an especially vocal critic of what damage the lefty did to the ball before he pitched it. "I found that when I rubbed the oil and dirt off the ball into my trouser leg the unsoiled ball became real smooth and did some fancy hopping," Danforth said.[4]

While some said Danforth taught the shine ball to Ed Cicotte when they were teammates with the White Sox, other sources give credit to Cicotte for inventing the knuckleball and being the first genuine practitioner of seemingly mastering that tricky pitch. Throughout his ten-year big league career spread out between 1911 and 1925, Danforth was regarded as a controversial player because of his reliance on such juicy techniques, some admitted, some alleged. Danforth may not have had longevity with the A's, but his help over a couple of months was useful. The experience worked out well for Danforth, too. When the A's won the World Series in 1911, he used his winner's share to help pay for dental school at the University of Maryland. Eventually Danforth became a dentist and had less trouble pulling teeth than coping with accusatory baseball foes.

The Athletics were better hitters in 1911 than they were in 1910, and that helped all of the pitchers. As a team, Philadelphia outscored opponents, 861–602. The 605,749 fans, who again led the circuit in attendance, loved it. Even though the home run was still a rare weapon, the A's knew how to manufacture runs with singles, doubles and triples. And they did

9. The Year 1911

have the best home-run hitter in the American League, even if his total was puny by modern standards. Third baseman Frank Baker smacked 11 homers to lead the league.

It was the regulars' batting averages, though, that were impressive. Collins hit .365. Baker hit .334. Danny Murphy hit .329. McInnis hit .321. Bris Lord hit .310. Rube Oldring just missed joining them all at .300 with a .297 average. Ira Thomas hit .273, and shortstop Jack Barry, who never carried a big stick but carried his weight with his glove, hit .265. Catcher Jack Lapp was the only bench player who added much pop with a .353 average in 68 games. An unlikely source produced additional batting help. Jack Coombs batted .319 in 152 plate appearances and scored 31 runs. A pitcher in the 2000s would die for such stats.

Going back to that run-scoring, the A's scored at least ten runs in 22 games that season. All around, it was quite a collection of clout.

Although Harry Davis was aging, Mack still believed he had some good years left. Yet he also recognized he had to give McInnis more playing time. McInnis trained for the spot and took over at first base. Davis hit just .197 off the bench. It was time.

There was one special occasion in mid-season reminding fans of the glory of 1910. The championship banner was ready to be raised for all to see at Shibe Park on June 2. But when it was hoisted high, it was upside-down. If the superstitious read any kind of negative omen into that happening, such as a signal that team was in distress, it was an erroneous, hasty judgment. The A's got past the brief embarrassment.

Long after Ty Cobb retired from baseball in 1928, there was a vociferous dichotomy of opinion about whether or not he was a dirty player whose spikes extracted too much bloodshed while he ran the bases. One example pointed to as Cobb being Cobb was a June 7 A's-versus-Tigers game. Cobb could be ornery, and he always said he played his hardest to win, but without malice. During this game, Cobb and Baker had two confrontations at third base that might have erupted into fights. Once Cobb sought to kick the ball out of Baker's glove, but rather than yielding, Baker grabbed the Tiger by the ankle and twisted. On another play, when Cobb was leading off third, a pickoff throw to Baker resulted in them fully tangled on the ground.

In that era when fights were far more common than in modern-day Major League Baseball, it seemed almost a sure thing that fisticuffs would break out. But Baker just walked away. He respected Cobb. Most of the other big-name players understood Cobb's hustle, determination and pride. Likewise, Cobb tended to blow fuses more regularly than others, but also walked away. Cobb and Baker, and Cobb and Eddie Collins, played more like genuine rivals than angry foes.

After playing in just nine games in 1908, Baker became a regular in 1909 and hit .305 with a league-leading 19 triples. He had the look of a player who would stay around for a while. He dropped off a bit in 1910, but 1911 was the season when Baker stood out as a true star. He hit .334 with 11 home runs, but also knocked in 115 runs and stole 38 bases. And while no one realized it as the regular-season was unfolding, the best for Baker was soon to come in the World Series, occurrences that would change his image in the sport and for all eternity within the game.

By winning 31 games in 1910, Jack Coombs joined an elite fraternity. At the time, it seemed that the 30-win club would grow ever-larger indefinitely. That remained true throughout the Deadball Era. But once the game became much higher scoring and pitchers were asked to pitch ever fewer innings, down from the overbearing workloads they endured in the 19th century and the first 20 years of the 20th century, winning 30 ball games in a single season became something that almost never happened, and then faded out completely.

The last time a pitcher won 30 games in the regular season was 1968, when the Detroit Tigers' Denny McLain won 31. McLain finished 31–6 that year, nearly a half-century ago. The last time a pitcher won 30 games in the National League was in 1934, when Dizzy Dean of the St. Louis Cardinals finished at 30–7.

The sport was very different in the 19th century, and pitchers were not only expected to finish every game they started, but to pitch on only a couple of days' rest. The best pitchers won a truck-load of games. The top 23 winningest seasons were recorded before 1900. Jack Chesbro won 41 games for the New York Highlanders (forerunners of the Yankees) in 1904, the modern record. Ed Walsh of the White Sox won 40 games in 1908. The all-time winningest season was recorded by Charles "Hoss" Radbourn, who won 59 games for the Providence Grays in 1884. For decades Radbourn was credited with 60 wins, but revisionist research changed his total. Radbourn threw 678⅔ innings that year, a season after winning 48 games and pitching 632⅓ innings, all stupendous, nearly unbelievable totals.

John Clarkson of the Chicago White Stockings won 53 games in 1885, the only other big-league pitcher in history to crack 50 wins. Not including Radbourn and Clarkson and exempting Chesbro and Walsh, all other 40-win seasons were recorded before the turn of the 20th century.

Once the new century began, 30-game winners became much rarer.

9. The Year 1911

Coombs was in very elite company. Cy Young, who won 511 games, the most ever, won 30 in a season five times, the first three occasions in the 1890s and the last two in the early 1900s. The other 20th-century, 30-game winners included Christy Mathewson (37, 33, 31 and 30), Walter Johnson (36 and 33), Joe McGinnity (35 and 31), "Smoky" Joe Wood (34), Grover Cleveland Alexander (33, 31 and 30), Jim Bagby (31) and Lefty Grove (31).

The drift even farther away from even the prospect of 30-game winners began when teams began employing five-man rotations instead of four-man rotations.

However, Coombs nearly won 30 two years in a row, settling for 28 victories in 1911, again leading the AL in wins. After his 31-win season, Coombs was rewarded with a $5,000 contract for 1911, though it was not announced until close to the season. There were some suggestions in newspapers that Coombs wanted more money than that for his salary, but he put the kibosh on any rift between him and Mack, saying he had been too tied up on his farm to enter into contract negotiations. Coombs reported on time for spring training.

Coombs was also busy being a newlywed. He got married in the off-season after the 1910 World Series. Although Coombs did come around on the business side, the 1911 season did not begin nearly as auspiciously for him on the pitching side. On one play, he was hit in the head by a thrown ball and had to leave the contest. Opponents were hitting his best pitches with more frequency, sending him to a 3–4 start. Coombs had been spectacular the summer before, and anyone who puts together a long winning streak must have some luck. At the start of 1911, the scales were balancing and Coombs was having no luck.

Actually, Coombs' hard hitting came around before his pitching accuracy, and his own bat helped run up some wins. Then he fell into a groove and twice defeated Big Ed Walsh.

After setting the record with 13 shutouts in 1910, Coombs recorded just a single shutout the next season. However, he was on the mound when the Athletics clinched their second straight pennant—and got two hits to boot. Overall, Coombs was not as dominating, but the A's were equally dominating and no one was going to complain about a pitcher who won 28 times.

As the 1911 regular season wound down and the Tigers were in the rearview mirror, a different, yet familiar, foe loomed for a return trip to the World Series. John McGraw's New York Giants were back on the big stage. The Giants won 99 games that year, finishing seven games ahead of the Chicago Cubs, to earn their place in the championship series.

It was a sterling performance by New York, especially since at the very beginning of the season their home Polo Grounds was caught up in a fire that essentially wrecked the place. A blaze broke out on April 14, one for which a definitive cause was never found. The result was that the Giants had no home stadium. The New York Highlanders opened the doors of their Hilltop Park while the Polo Grounds was being rebuilt, and the Giants played there for two months.

If the misfortune was distracting, it did not show in the standings. The Giants seemed out of sorts in the early part of the campaign, but ran away with the pennant in August. New York won 17 out of 20 games from mid–August through the first few days of September. That took the Giants from 3½ games back to 3½ games ahead in the standings. Then they piled on a ten-game winning streak in September.

In 1905, the first year the Athletics won a pennant when there was a contested World Series, their opponent was the New York Giants, also then managed by McGraw. His star pitcher was Christy Mathewson, on his way to winning 373 career games. In 1905, Mathewson led the National League in wins with 31, in earned run average at 1.28, in shutouts with eight, and in strikeouts with 206.

Mathewson was at the end of a run during which he won at least 30 games for three straight seasons. He was the only 20th century-and-beyond hurler to do that. The Athletics had a right to be very afraid to face Mathewson again in the World Series, since in 1905 he pitched three shutouts, practically winning the championship on his own.

In 1911, Mathewson remained scary enough. He won 26 games and led the National League with a 1.99 ERA. But Mack spoke up, if only to try to demystify Mathewson for his team. He didn't want the A's to be psyched out before Mathewson even took the mound, something which could easily occur if they read too much praise of the man. "Matty is still a great pitcher," Mack said of "Big Six." "But he's six years older than he was in 1905 and I'm sure he's not as fast. And I think we have better hitters than we had in that earlier series."[5]

Was it false bravado or honesty? It was clear that the Athletics would receive a serious dose of Mathewson, but it was not quite clear whether they possessed the antidote to Matty's fabulous skills.

10

The 1911 World Series Foes

Connie Mack said he thought the fans had fresh, strong belief in his nine by the time of the 1911 World Series against the New York Giants because the A's already had that one title tucked away. "Therefore we had the confidence of the public," he said, "when we squared off to face the Giants that fall for the highest honors in baseball."[1]

One worrisome item was that first baseman Stuffy McInnis hurt his hand near the end of the regular season and could not play in the Series. So Mack, who had replaced incumbent Harry Davis for the 1911 season with McInnis, re-inserted the veteran as the starter.

Davis was soon to move on to full-time coaching and/or managerial jobs in the game and he did not thrive as a back-up that year, batting just .197 in 57 appearances. He was 37 years old and played like it. However, called upon for the short series versus New York, Davis responded. "Instead of being a hindrance to the young team," Mack said, "the veteran played some of the best ball of his career throughout the Series and his bat played a big part in our triumph."[2]

That may have been a bit sugary in describing Davis' contribution, though he did have his moments. Davis batted just .208, but drove in five runs. That was all still to come, though, as the pundits examined the match-up and predicted an exciting battle for the world's championship.

Giants manager John J. McGraw virtually strutted when he sat. He barked orders like a king and always fielded one of the top teams in the National League. Through the lens of history, Mack and McGraw, with their remarkable longevity in the dugout, are often spoken of in tandem as two of the finest managers in history.

They were easily contrasted, however, even if both men burned to win. The tall and slender Mack wore his suit in the dugout and essentially passed on his instructions with a wave of his program or by telling his uniformed captain what to do. McGraw brooked no middle men. Standing 5-foot-7 and weighing 155 pounds, he scowled as often as he smiled. It was no accident that McGraw's memorable nickname was "Little Napoleon."

Beginning in 1891, McGraw was a gruff and determined ball player, one good enough to bat .334 spread over parts of 17 seasons. The last few years with the Giants were mostly spent in charge of the club, not on the field. Between 1899 and 1932 McGraw won 2,763 games, ten pennants and three World Series.

Mack far outlived McGraw and managed by far longer than anyone else in history. But McGraw ranks second in wins. Perhaps early on the men were wary of one another, but as time passed and they outlasted all other managers, they built a mutual respect. A positive relationship existed, though maybe it would not have if they had played dozens of games against one another each season and fought it out for every pennant. Being in opposite leagues was likely much better for their dispositions—and their relationship. When they came together on the same field with the biggest prize at stake, it was important, but rare.

By 1911, it was possible that McGraw had reconciled himself to the existence of the American League and the realization that winning the World Series was important. No longer was being the boss of the National League sufficient when there was an additional, more prestigious crown to fight over. In 1904, McGraw had been powerful and arrogant enough to derail the young World Series. No more.

The first time the Giants appeared in a World Series was 1905. They met the A's, managed by Mack, vanquishing them in five games. This time it was a new generation of Giants, for the most part, not overlooking the still-spectacular Christy Mathewson on the mound.

New York won 99 games in 1911, and Mathewson was still the leader of the mound staff. He won 26 games but was ably backed up by Rube Marquard, who won 24. The left-handed Marquard was also headed to the Hall of Fame, winning 201 games. Doc Crandall added 15 wins, Hooks Wiltse 12, and Red Ames 11. Overall, the Athletics' pitching was stronger, though you could never underestimate Mathewson and what he might do by his lonesome. It was not beyond the realm of possibility that Mathewson could win three games on his own again.

Born in 1880 in Factoryville, Pennsylvania, Mathewson won 373 games with an earned run average of 2.13, and he pitched 79 regular-season shutouts while winning at least 30 games in a season four times. A religious man renowned as a gentleman, Mathewson did not pitch on

10. The 1911 World Series Foes

Sundays because of the observance of his faith. As a college man who attended Bucknell University, he was a man after Mack's heart, though his arm was coveted by every major league team.

Long before there was a National Football League (and before the turn of the 20th century) Mathewson played some pro football, specializing as a drop kicker. He also co-wrote a book called "Pitching In The Pinch" after the 1911 World Series and later wrote a children's book and a play. Mathewson served during World War I and suffered from inhaling chemicals, which may have contributed to his contracting tuberculosis and dying young at 45.

What Mathewson brought to the table in the 1911 Series was haunting memories from 1905, when he was so overpowering he nearly beat the A's himself. Mathewson threw three shutouts in that Series. Although Mack had stated that Mathewson was older and couldn't be as good as he was before, he did not overlook him as a threat. What Mathewson could do was the No. 1 concern of the Athletics. Since both teams were pulling away from competition on their way to their pennants, Mack quietly began thinking about Mathewson weeks before the October 14 Series opener.

Although Mack tried not to dwell too much on Matty as a superstar when he uttered the statement, there was no doubt that when it came to analyzing the hurler's talents, Mathewson had long before made a believer out of the A's manager. "Mathewson was the greatest pitcher who ever lived," Mack said. "He had knowledge, judgment, perfect control and form. It was wonderful to watch him pitch when he wasn't pitching against you."[3]

Mathewson was a known quantity, Marquard less so. It seemed as if he had parachuted into the Giants' rotation to win those 24 games. His major league debut occurred in 1908, but he did little to earn McGraw's confidence before 1911. His combined record from his first three partial seasons was 9–18. This year his .774 win percentage led the National League. A year later, Marquard set the all-time record by winning 19 games in a row, going 19–0 at the start of the season before losing 11 of his last 18 decisions.

Marquard and Mathewson were roommates on the road, and maybe a little of Matty's good stuff rubbed off on the young player.

> Matty was a remarkable man and athlete. I believe he could have been a champion at golf or tennis, as well as baseball. McGraw had a strict rule against playing golf, but he always overlooked it when Matty played between starts. He knew Matty was something special. I remember when I was rooming with him he'd be playing checkers in one room and be shouting out moves for a chess game in another room. And you know, he almost always won.[4]

Born in Cleveland, Richard William Marquard was no country bumpkin. His nickname of Rube was an homage to Rube Waddell, the ex-A's pitcher, chosen for Marquard because his style reminded a certain sportswriter of his predecessor. Marquard was not quite as colorful as Waddell, although he did perform in vaudeville with and marry actress Blossom Seeley. That marriage was its own story, and Marquard had two additional wives removed from the stage.

Marquard was headstrong enough to defy his father's wishes against him setting out on a baseball career, but McGraw ruled with an iron fist. He probably imposed harsher discipline than daddy. "He was a great manager," Marquard said. "You couldn't argue with the man. The first time I met him, he told me, 'Do as I say and you'll never be wrong.'"[5]

The third star on the Giants' staff, assuming McGraw wouldn't put all of the pressure on Mathewson and Marquard, was "Doc" Crandall, whose real name was James Otis (he was nicknamed "Doc" by sportswriter Sid Mercer, who said he was "the healer of sick ball games"). Crandall's record was 15–5, but the most distinctive aspect of his performance was that he was a regular coming out of the bullpen well before relievers were commonly used. Retroactive application of the statistic gave him five saves that season, but it was also noted on his record that Crandall was a late arrival on the mound 26 times in his 41 appearances. Sportswriters of the time gave him the moniker "Doc" because they looked at him as providing emergency assistance out of the bullpen for the Giants. An all-around player, sometimes Crandall played the infield or was a pinch-hitter. As a pitcher, Crandall, who was termed shy and unassuming, put together a 102–62 career record with a 2.92 earned run average. He also batted .285.

There was no stranger hurler attached to New York in 1911 than the peculiar Charles "Victory" Faust, whose personal big-league saga rates highly amongst the wackiest of all tales.

The Giants of 1911 did not start the season on fire and made so many mistakes that McGraw frequently seethed in their company. One day in late July while New York was in St. Louis and the Cardinals were on tap, the 6-foot-2, suit- and derby-wearing Faust appeared before McGraw. He was from the Kansas prairie and he was the answer to the Giants' prayers, he said, a personification of their destiny. Faust informed McGraw that a fortune teller had told him he would lead New York to the pennant, so he had come to fulfill the assignment.

If he hadn't been looking for a spark, McGraw might well have sent Faust away immediately. Instead, he grabbed a catcher's mitt and the alleged player threw to him. Faust's tosses were so lacking in speed,

10. The 1911 World Series Foes

McGraw began catching him barehanded. Faust took some strokes with the bat, hitting as ineffectually as he pitched. McGraw promptly recognized that Faust was going to be of no worth on the diamond, but the tale of the fortune teller's prophecy nagged at him.

McGraw gave Faust a uniform, told him to stick around, and the manager paid his expenses while the Giants immediately began playing superior ball and soon raced away with the NL pennant. Faust kept asking McGraw to play him, and he did appear in two big league games on the mound covering two innings while surrendering two hits and one run.

Faust did not actually pitch the Giants to a pennant, but as a mascot and good-luck charm he proved to be of estimable, if superstitious, value. Faust did not actually get off the bench during the World Series versus the A's except perhaps to cheer, though his presence hovered over the proceedings. Duty done, Giants champs, in mid–1912 McGraw cast Faust off. The man ended up in the Western Washington State Hospital for the Insane, where he died in 1915 at age 34, the period at the end of a somewhat baffling episode in baseball history.

Many years later, in an act of the type of graciousness he was little known for, McGraw wrote of Faust's contributions to the Giants. "Wherever Charley Faust is today, I want him to know that I give him full credit for winning the National League pennant for the Giants in 1911," McGraw said.[6]

Perhaps Faust was a human antidote to the voodoo magic that haunted Giants first baseman Fred Merkle, who in 1908 was guilty of one of the most highly publicized mistakes in baseball history. In 1911, Merkle was a New York regular whose statistics of 12 home runs, 84 runs batted in, 49 stolen bases and a .283 batting average represented powerful testimony to his recuperative powers after the 1908 gaffe.

The younger Merkle committed a base-running error, did not touch second base after a teammate apparently drove in the winning run in a showdown game against the Cubs. Fans thought the Giants won and mobbed the field. However, Chicago's Johnny Evers pointed out that Merkle did not touch the base, he was called out, and the score was turned back to a tie. As the pennant race unfolded, that lack of one victory loomed large. When a makeup game was played, the Cubs won and captured the pennant. Forevermore, the failure to run to second was labeled "Merkle's Boner."

Mack didn't care what Merkle did three years earlier, but he was worried about what he might do in the 1911 Series. Merkle never shed the nickname, but he didn't let it bother him on the field. The Giants had a whole group of solid hitters, including second baseman Larry Doyle and his .310 average.

Doyle won the 1912 National League Chalmers Award and a batting title in 1915, and was a lifetime .290 hitter. But he is best remembered for coining a phrase expressing his devotion to McGraw and the Giants. "It's great to be young and a Giant," Doyle said, and during the 1911 World Series he was both.[7]

Doyle's one on-field lament was not being in his prime when the lively ball succeeded the Deadball Era. But for a man who lived 87 years, his fondest memories seemed focused on the inexpensive cost of living of the early 1900s. He won a Chalmers automobile in recognition of his "most valuable player" achievement in 1912. "I can remember when I paid a chauffeur $25 a week to drive that Chalmers," Doyle said. "Prices were cheap then. I roomed with Fred Merkle … and paid $7 a week for a suite in the Braddock Hotel at Eighth Avenue and 125th Street. A big breakfast was 35 cents and a steak dinner 85 cents."[8]

In 1911 the Athletics and Giants were playing for a winner's share of $3,655 apiece. Even a loser's share of $2,426 would pay for quite a few whole cows before those dinners sizzled.

Not only did the comment about being young and a Giant stick to Doyle, his nickname was "Laughing Larry" because of his sense of humor. Doyle maintained that easy-going attitude during his 14-year career, mostly with New York,

Doyle, from Caseyville, Illinois, first worked in a coal mine, his father's profession, about 40 miles from St. Louis, and then joined the club baseball team. That's where he began playing for pay, and when he opened the envelope with his game-day reward it was $3.50. However, Doyle said being a true employee of the mine was worthwhile. "Working the mines is not the easiest pursuit for a lad, to be sure," he said. "But it certainly helped to fit me physically to play ball. I never regret the long hours I put in far below the earth, for it gave me strength, and when we lads did have the opportunity to play ball in those days we enjoyed it the more."[9]

There were a few steps in between, but being summoned to the Giants was the big one. He was a nervous wreck when the Giants obtained him. "I was scared to death when the Giants bought me in July of 1907 from Springfield of the Three-I League. Every ball player wanted to work for McGraw, but the thought of it terrified me. So did the prospect of being a teammate of Christy Mathewson, Iron Man McGinnity and the other heroes."[10]

When Doyle was trying to report, he couldn't find the Polo Grounds because he took a ferry in the wrong direction. "But I made it eventually," he said.[11]

"Eventually" was the key word because his fielding was quite poor when Doyle hit the big leagues, and he took considerable fan and newspaper abuse. McGraw ignored the criticism and stuck with Doyle until he improved. Then McGraw gloated because it vindicated his judgment. "I hung on to Doyle when the New York fans and critics were calling for his scalp," McGraw said, "and today I would not trade him for any man playing baseball. There is nothing like having confidence in one's own judgment."[12] And McGraw would tell you so himself.

Going into the World Series, the Giants may have seemed thinner than the A's in pitching, and they didn't have as many big guns at the plate. But whether it can be called a secret weapon or not, New York stole a flabbergasting total of 347 bases that year. No wonder Doyle could say, "In 1911, we stole our way to the championship."[13]

The swipes were spread around, too. Outfielder Josh Devore stole 61 bases. Fred Snodgrass stole 51, Merkle 49, Red Murray 48, Doyle 38, Buck Herzog 22, Art Fletcher 20, and Beals Becker 19. They ran other National League teams dizzy.

Another important Giants player was catcher John Meyers. Like Charles Bender, the A's pitcher, Meyers was of Native American heritage, from the Cahuilla tribe. Naturally, ball players and sportswriters also called him "Chief." Meyers was more outgoing than Bender and occasionally gave him tips about how to cope with a white world that so often stooped to making fun of Native Americans in newspaper columns, in cartoons, or verbally. Meyers was also darker skinned than Bender, and when McGraw brought him aboard some accused him of faking Meyers' heritage to slip a black player past them. At times, Meyers was even called "Nigger," a confused attack on him for sure.[14]

Meyers, who did speak of discrimination and Native rights more than the Athletics hurler, and Bender both, however, were regarded as role models for young Native Americans and attained significant cross-tribal support.

Although a little bit more out of the spotlight, Giants infielder Art Fletcher was a key contributor. Fletcher was not a full-time starter until early July, but hit .319 in 112 games. He was a savvy player who knew the ins and outs of the game and was counted on for field leadership by McGraw. Later, Fletcher was offered the manager's job of the New York Yankees and turned down the job. Despite the plum opportunity that few baseball men would have refused, he understood he did not have a managerial temperament. "I'm not the type," Fletcher said later. "I would have worried myself into the grave in two years."[15] And that was even when the Yankees were at the top of the class in the American League.

That type of thoughts didn't seem to intrude on Connie Mack's or John McGraw's thinking. In 1911, it was not clear that they would be the two greatest managers ever, but more than a century later the argument can be more forcefully made. They were going to match wits and strategy in this World Series, and for that alone it would be memorable.

There would be intriguing mound choices made and the two team leaders would be nonplussed by a six-day rain delay in the midst of the World Series that could have played havoc with any plans.

Beyond that, for all of the analysis, for all of the pitching comparisons and lineup study, the World Series would belong to one Philadelphia Athletics player. His name was Frank Baker when the championships began. It was "Home Run" Baker by the time the Series concluded.

11

The 1911 World Series Showdown

What began as a World Series showdown between the power team of the American League and the power team of the National League was later remembered for two distinctive reasons. In the middle of the Series, there was a six-day rain delay more fitting for the preamble to Noah's Ark ride than playing baseball. And before the Series was complete, one of the most famous nicknames in baseball history was affixed to a player.

Up until the 1911 Series, Frank Baker was sometimes known as J. Franklin Baker or just plain Frank. After the Series, and long after he died, Baker was better known as "Home Run Baker."

The World Series opened at the Polo Grounds in New York on October 14, 1911. As expected, the Giants sent Christy Mathewson to the mound, riding a 27-inning scoreless pitching streak dating to 1905, when he shut out several of these same Athletics in three straight games.

A's manager Mack countered with Charles A. "Chief" Bender, who finished 17–5 with a 2.16 earned run average that year. Connie Mack had his choice of Jack Coombs, who won 28 games, or Eddie Plank, who won 23, but leaned towards Bender. At times Mack told sportswriters he considered Bender to be his "money pitcher," or the hurler he could most count on.

The announced paid attendance for the opener was 38,281, which appeared to bulge the Polo Grounds to its seams. In those early days of new concrete and steel ball parks, this also marked the largest crowd ever to watch a ball game. However, some players felt New York owner John T. Brush lied about the attendance figure, underreporting it. Brush was one of the most vigorous opponents of the creation of the American League, although that had been a decade earlier. He was in poor health and died barely a year after the completion of this World Series.

What would have been Brush's motivation for misrepresenting atten-

Top and above: The A's in the 1910s were a hot ticket, as these photographs of prospective ticket buyers from 1911 (top) and 1913 demonstrate (Library of Congress).

11. The 1911 World Series Showdown

dance, in the minds of suspicious players? In those days, the players' shares were calculated by a breakdown of the attendance. Was it possible to issue a fraudulent accounting? Yes. Would there be motivation to do so in terms of financial gain? Yes. Would it be a dishonest approach bad for the game? Yes. Did it happen? Unproven.

For any sports fan who believes this is a modern invention of a football or baseball coach playing psychological games, Giants manager John McGraw changed his club's usual uniform attire. The players wore black uniforms with white trim, the same uniforms he briefly unveiled six years earlier in the previous Series between the teams. It would take more than simple good luck to beat either Mathewson or Bender if the men were in top form.

When Big Six set the Athletics down in the first inning, it added another shutout frame to his resume, and 28 scoreless innings established a World Series record. Bris Lord, Rube Oldring and Eddie Collins went down in order, the first two by strikeout. However, Matty did not extend the record any further, surrendering a run in the top of the second to Philadelphia. Baker singled and made his way around the bases, scoring on a Harry Davis single. That made it 1–0 A's, and it seemed significant because no one felt this was going to be a high-scoring affair.

The Giants tied the game in the home half of the fourth inning. Fred Snodgrass worked Bender for a walk and moved to second on a groundout. Buck Herzog's grounder to second did not appear to be dangerous, but Collins committed an error and Snodgrass came around to score the unearned run.

With one out in the bottom of the seventh inning, New York catcher John Meyers doubled to left field. A strikeout made it two outs, but Josh Devore also doubled, sending Meyers home with the go-ahead run.

Meyers, like Bender, was a Native American, and the two men were good friends. Meyers penned a ghost-written syndicated baseball column and sometimes commented on Bender's talents. "Albert Bender is a wonderful pitcher and had some of our boys standing on their heads," Meyers said. "I am glad to belong to the same race as that big fellow." At another point, there was a reference to "my Redskin friend," although that phrasing seemed alien to Meyers and more likely was contributed by a collaborator or an anonymous copy editor.[1]

Bender struck out 11 men in the game, frequently blinding Giants hitters with his fastball.

New York second baseman Larry Doyle, who collected one of the five hits Bender allowed, said the hurler's fast pitch "looked the size of a pea as it came over the plate."[2]

However, Athletics hitters had to have pretty good eyesight to decipher what Mathewson was up to as well. Philadelphia reached Matty for only six hits (two by Baker, two by Oldring), and the A's never could push across another run after the second inning. The fourth time around, the Athletics had actually scored against Mathewson, but not often enough. He stuck out five and walked only one. The final score was 2–1 Giants.

Even though Bender was the losing pitcher, he did not dent the faith Mack placed in him. For all of Bender's brilliance in a Hall of Fame career, all of the wins and spectacular performances, this defeat was often cited by Mack as Bender's best effort.

That artistic success aside, the opening-game loss made an A's victory in Game 2 critical. Falling behind 2–0 in a best-out-of-seven Series was tantamount to living on the edge. Rather than play two games in a row at the Polo Grounds, the Series shifted scenes to Shibe Park after a day off. It was easy enough for the teams to travel between the host cities since New York and Philadelphia are only about 100 miles apart, and even a century ago it didn't take inordinately long for the train to cover the distance. Shibe Park was not as large as the Polo Grounds, so the attendance was not commensurate with the enthusiasm. The second game drew 26,286 fans.

Mack started southpaw Eddie Plank, and the Giants countered with Rube Marquard. Gettysburg Eddie was terrific from the start. He was in command and struck out eight. The Giants couldn't handle his stuff. Not that the A's were all over Marquard, either, but they got to him just enough to eke out a 3–1 victory.

Plank had been a star for years for the A's, the most reliable big winner for the longest time. He had been so good for so long that 1911 was his sixth 20-win season for Philadelphia—and he was not done yet. This was a must-have game for the A's, and Plank was used to such circumstances. Because he got a late start in the majors, Plank turned 36 years old that season, but pitched like a younger man still in his prime with a stingy earned run average of 2.10.

Smarting from the close loss to Mathewson, the A's pressured Marquard from the start. In the bottom of the first inning, the first batter, Bris Lord, singled, then made it to second on an error by Murray and moved to third on Oldring's sacrifice bunt. Perhaps preoccupied trying to analyze what had just happened in the field, Marquard promptly threw a wild pitch, allowing Lord to score.

The Giants tied the game at 1–1 soon after, scoring in the top of the second inning when Buck Herzog doubled, went to third on a ground ball

11. The 1911 World Series Showdown

out, and scored on a Meyers single. Things remained knotted until the bottom of the sixth. Not only did the A's take over, but the first chapter of Baker's legendary Series was written.

After two quick outs on fly balls, Collins smacked a double down the left-field line. Baker was next up, and he powdered a two-run homer to right field to provide the A's with a 3–1 lead, which is how the game finished.

By today's slugger standards Baker was a small guy. He stood 5-foot-11 and weighed 173 pounds. Wielding a bat that seemed to rival the size of a telephone pole, Baker was a very solid hitter and sound in all aspects of the game. While he led the American League in home runs four seasons in a row between 1911 and 1914, the numbers, between nine and 12, seem insignificant in today's power-hitting world. It makes one wonder: if Baker had not been labeled "Home Run" as a nickname in 1911, what manner of thinking might have prevailed when Babe Ruth came along, by 1920 transforming the sport with 54 homers? Would it have been "Home Run" Ruth? But the name was taken, and a cross-section of nicknames applied to the home-run king became more famous.

More appreciation was lavished before Ruth on the men who helped fill the bases and drive home runs one at a time, but Baker's blow was a glimpse of the soon-to-come, big-bang world. When Baker cracked the home run to win Game 2, it was of multi-purpose value, providing the go-ahead runs, the eventual triumph, and a changing image of him as a ball player in the public eye. With 20–20 hindsight, it might also be said that when the Giants began picking on Baker, harassing him verbally, rather than rattle him, it focused him. When the Series began, McGraw was coaching third base for his team. Known as an active bench jockey, McGraw taunted Baker constantly. "You're a quitter," the New York manager accused Baker. "[Hughie] Jennings and the whole Detroit club told us so."[3] Such baiting was commonplace at the time, the hoped-for result being to induce anger and break concentration.

It didn't work at all. On the game-winning homer, Marquard had been warned by McGraw not to throw Baker pitches in that zone. Later, Marquard admitted he goofed by ignoring the advice during the at-bat because "I had one strike on him and he refused to bite on another outcurve, which was a little too wide. I thought to cross him by sending in a fast, high straight ball, the kind I know he likes."[4] The result was catastrophic for the Giants.

"Thousands of fans on their feet, hands waving, hats in the air, and shouting as you rounded second base is something a man never forgets,"

Baker said of the fan reaction to his big blow."[5] That was the end of the scoring. Plank was the victor in his duel with Marquard, and the A's evened the Series with the Giants.

The Polo Grounds hosted Game 3 on October 17, and attendance nearly matched Game 1 as 37,216 fans provided support for the Giants. It was an epic contest. Mathewson was McGraw's bread and butter guy, and he got a second start. Mack anointed 28-game-winner Jack Coombs for the mound work.

Few saw the likes of this one in a World Series. It was the pitchers' day. Coombs allowed just three New York hits. Mathewson gave up nine. At first that doesn't seem so impressive, but the game went 11 innings. Both starters went the distance. The duel went on and on.

New York scored first, pushing across a run in the bottom of the third inning. Meyers obtained an infield single. Mathewson singled to right field, sending Meyers to third. Josh Devore did not exactly belt the ball, but as the result of a third-to-second fielder's choice, Meyers scored for a 1–0 lead.

Mathewson befuddled A's batters after that, mowing down hitters with efficiency. As the game reached the ninth inning, New York was ahead and Mathewson was on the verge of hurling still another World Series shutout against the A's. No one would have been surprised, not the Athletics, not their fans. This was Christy Mathewson on the mound, and dominating hitters was what Christy Mathewson did.

Matty got the first out when Eddie Collins grounded out to third. In stepped Baker. Looking for a pitch that seemed hittable, Baker swung on a 0-1 count, sending the ball into orbit. The long blast to right field, taking the form of a vicious lined shot, gave him a home run and a nickname, and the Athletics a 1–1 tie to prolong the game. Extra innings.

Both starters remained on the mound, wanting to be the man who sent his team to a key World Series lead. The A's did not threaten in the top of the tenth as Mathewson set down John Lapp, Coombs and Lord. Coombs walked two in the bottom of the inning to flirt with trouble, but no Giant scored.

There was some drama, however. Snodgrass, willing to do anything to reach base, stuck his elbow out to get hit by a pitch. A Coombs throw did graze him, but the home plate umpire ruled that Snodgrass had not tried to get out of the way. Snodgrass did walk after that, though. A couple of batters later, Lapp dropped a Coombs pitch, and as soon as he saw that Snodgrass tried to steal third Lapp quickly scooped up the loose ball and fired to Baker covering the bag. Snodgrass led with his spikes, hoping to kick away the ball nestled in Baker's glove. Baker did not yield and, although disturbed, made the tag and held the bag even as Snodgrass drew blood by slicing open his arm and cutting his uniform.

Afterwards, Baker needed medical treatment for the inches-long arm wound between wrist and elbow and another cut on the right leg. Even Giants fans booed Snodgrass' actions, and the newspaper post-mortem was harsh to Snodgrass. "Yes, I believe Snodgrass spiked me intentionally," Baker said. "He jumped across the bag to get me. I was in my right position."[6]

In the top of the 11th, the Athletics put together a two-run rally consisting of three singles and two errors, to go up 3–1. The A's were on the cusp of a huge win. But they almost didn't get it. Buck Herzog, who was having a clutch Series, led off with a double to left field. Although Coombs got two men out, Herzog reached third. Beals Becker pinch-hit for Mathewson and reached on an error, with Herzog scoring. Becker tried to steal and was thrown out when Lapp fired the ball to second. Collins slapped the tag on Becker to end the game, 3–2 A's.

This time Marquard was writing a column and discussed what transpired conversationally between him and Mathewson. "It was the hardest game to lose I ever saw and Matty lost it the same way I did in Philadelphia," Marquard said. "When he came back to the bench I asked him what it was. 'The same thing you did, Rube. I gave Baker a high, fast one. I have been in the business a long time and I have no excuse.'"[7]

There was considerable discussion about Snodgrass' intent. Those on the Philadelphia side insisted the Giants' center fielder meant to harm Baker. New York players defended Snodgrass, including Mathewson, who said, "Snodgrass was only doing what he has a right to do. It wasn't dirty ball." Mack disagreed. "[They] can say what they please, but to my mind it was a deliberate spiking of Baker. They say Frank doesn't know how to tag a man at third. That is not true. Baker knows how to do it as well as any other third baseman in the business." More importantly, Ban Johnson, the American League president, sided with the Athletics' viewpoint, calling Snodgrass' act "one of the worst things I have ever seen on the ball field. There is no question in my mind it was done deliberately."[8]

Philadelphia led the Series, 2–1, and had all of the momentum after besting Mathewson. Going back to Philadelphia and Shibe Park for Game 4, the A's had home field, hot bats and optimism on their side. But not the weather. Suddenly, it was the monsoon season in Philadelphia. The scheduled October 18 Game 4 was not played until October 24. That is the second-longest delay between games within a Series in history.

The occasion for the longest delay was more dramatic and tragic. On October 17, 1989, the same two franchises, then representing Oakland and San Francisco, were about to begin Game 3 of the Series when the violent Loma Prieta earthquake struck Northern California, destroying infrastructure, killing 63 people and injuring more than 3,700. Baseball commissioner Fay Vincent halted the 1989 Series indefinitely out of respect for the dead and in acknowledgment of the chaos. Play resumed after a break of ten days between the second and third games.

Meanwhile, because of the long weather delay in 1911, fans, players and officials had plenty of time to talk about what had transpired thus far. That encouraged debate about the spiking and gave time for Baker's clouts to sink in. The train bringing the A's home was greeted by fans at the station, and Baker was mobbed by well-wishers once back in Philadelphia. People asked how he was feeling, and he downplayed the spiking injuries. When he was asked about his two critical home runs, Baker facetiously answered, "What home runs?"[9]

What home runs? Although there was no television or radio coverage of the World Series yet, the entire country seemed to know all about those home runs. Baker received bags of mail from fans all over the land, congratulating him on his blasts.

Seven soggy days after the A's took a 2–1 Series lead, play resumed in Philadelphia with Bender and Mathewson going head-to-head again, just as they had in the opener. The rain delays gave McGraw the opportunity to start Mathewson again. Bender was working on even more rest. His last start was ten days earlier.

When choosing Bender for the start after he lost the dismaying opener in tough circumstances, Mack included a pep talk. "I think you're going to win this one, Albert," Mack said. "I don't think we'll find Matty as effective as in the first game. He's very tired."[10]

Whether he was too rested or not, Bender was reached for two runs in the top of the first inning when the first two Giants rapped hits. Josh Devore singled to start the game and Larry Doyle tripled him home. Snodgrass' sacrifice fly to left brought in a second run.

It wasn't until the bottom of the fourth inning that the Athletics made Mack a prophet about Mathewson's possible fatigue. Whether he really was tired, the A's figured him out, or just what, Matty was unexpectedly vulnerable in that inning. Baker continued his power show with a leadoff double. Danny Murphy followed with another double. And Harry Davis contributed a third straight two-bagger. He also scored after a groundout and a sacrifice fly by Ira Thomas. The A's came out of the inning up, 3–2.

11. The 1911 World Series Showdown

In the fifth, Philadelphia added another run. Collins singled and Baker (who else?) pounded a double for a 4–2 lead.

As the game marched on, there was no additional scoring. In the top of the eighth inning, McGraw lifted Mathewson for a pinch-hitter, Becker again. He grounded out. Hooks Wiltse finished the game for the Giants, throwing the eighth inning with no misadventures. Bender went the distance for the victory. He allowed seven hits and two runs.

The Athletics had taken three straight from the mighty Giants and were on the verge of eliminating New York from the World Series.

After what seemed like a long vacation between the third and fourth games of the Series because of bad weather, there was a quick turnaround between Game 4 and Game 5, moving to the Polo Grounds the next day. Jack Coombs started again for Philadelphia, with Rube Marquard chosen for New York. Marquard had to perform. Mathewson had been beaten, and the Giants were on a precipice. If Marquard got in much difficulty, McGraw was not going to be patient with him trying to work his way out of it.

The A's put Marquard right into that trouble in the top of the third inning. Although it took only two hits, a single by Lapp and a homer by Oldring sandwiched around Coombs reaching on an error, Philadelphia scored three runs. That ended Marquard's outing. McGraw gave the ball to Leon "Red" Ames to save the day and the season. The right-hander went 11–10 with a 2.68 ERA during the regular season. He won 183 games in a 17-year career, relying heavily on a superb curveball that usually got the best of hitters. Ames pitched four innings in Game 5 and gave up just two hits and no runs, so he did his job.

New York pecked away at the lead. Fred Merkle opened the bottom of the seventh inning with a walk, moved one base at a time and scored on a Meyers sacrifice fly. It was a start.

During that inning, Doc Crandall was inserted as a pinch-hitter for Ames. He walked and stayed in the game to pitch. The A's did nothing more with Crandall's tosses than they had with Ames'. Over three innings, Crandall permitted two hits.

While the Philadelphia bats were flailing, the desperate Giants began hitting in the bottom of the ninth inning. Art Fletcher's double keyed a slow-motion rally. With two out, Coombs gave up a double to Crandall and a single to Devore, sending two men home and the game into extra innings.

In the top of the tenth, Coombs bunted for a single. Amos Strunk came in as a pinch-runner, but the A's could muster nothing else. Coombs had strained his groin in the sixth inning when he caught his spikes on the mound while throwing a pitch but had refused to come out of the game. That changed when Eddie Plank took over for Coombs for the bottom of the tenth and he ended up the loser as the A's fell, 4–3. Doyle doubled and eventually scored on a Merkle sacrifice fly.

This was an area of controversy. In those days, ball parks had no lights and many an afternoon game that ran long had to be halted because of darkness. The light was fading on this game when it concluded. Doyle slid home, and A's catcher John Lapp saw the play that way, a safe slide. The sharp-eyed may have noticed, however, that as both teams exited the field, home plate umpire Bill Klem had not made a safe signal. Good-looking slide aside, Doyle had actually missed tagging the plate, but no one protested and no member of the A's ran up to tag Doyle. That made him safe officially as everyone went home.

A Game 6, on October 26, would be needed at Shibe Park, the A's still having the Giants on the ropes, 3–2 in games. For all of McGraw's confidence in his Big Two, Mathewson and Marquard, he needed someone else to start this one. He chose Ames. Ames was regarded as a pitcher who could completely shut down a lineup with his curve when it was working, but when it was off target, he walked a large number of hitters. There was another interesting aspect to Ames' pitching. He threw his best in cold weather. That's why McGraw often used him in the season openers in April. In warmer weather, he wilted and pitched mainly in relief. This game was played in late October. Heck, it was almost November. McGraw likely looked at the calendar as a good omen for Ames.

However, the final day of the 1911 season did not play out that way at all, although things started just fine for New York. Larry Doyle's ground-rule double in the top of the first inning gave the Giants a man in scoring position almost immediately, and he scored later in the inning on an error. The 1–0 lead stood up until the A's half of the third, when Bris Lord's double scored Thomas, who had walked, making it 1–1.

The beginning of a rout and the beginning of the end for New York was spelled out in the home half of the fourth inning, when Philadelphia posted four more runs. Singles by Baker and Murphy started things. A convoluted play began with an attempted sacrifice bunt by shortstop Jack Barry. Two Giants errors and a wild pitch proved pivotal. Hooks Wiltse was in the game when things deteriorated further with a seven-run seventh inning en route to a 13–2 Athletics win.

By the end of the day, Murphy had four hits, Lord three and Baker two, and Bender owned his second triumph of this Series. And the

Philadelphia Athletics were world champions for the second year in a row. "Few World Series have resulted in keener batting than this one," Mack said. "Every game but the last one was close to the finish and two of them required extra innings to decide. Bender with his pitching and Baker with his winning home runs, were our heroes."[11]

Philadelphia was once again party central with fans celebrating in the streets and the team treated to more than one celebratory banquet after two straight World Series titles. During his speech at one victory dinner, Connie Mack said that he and Harry Davis had seen Doyle slide wide but had chosen not to protest the result on a technicality. Davis would have been the man to protest to Klem, but waited for a sign from Mack. No such signal was given. One reason was that thousands of fans at the Polo Grounds had poured out of their seats and flooded the field, creating mass confusion. Mack worried that a change of the decision from safe to out might have triggered a mass riot. "If any of my players had raised the point about Doyle's run I would have felt so sore that I believe I would have taken him by the scruff of the neck and thrown him over the grandstand," Mack said.[12]

The great mystery was what would have occurred if the run had been disallowed, the field cleared of spectators, and play resumed. In the long run, it did not really matter because the A's won it all anyway.

12

Home Run Baker

Before he matured into "Home Run" Baker, Frank Baker had a checkered baseball journey. Born in 1886 in Trappe, Maryland, he became a semi-pro player in his late teens, and his first paycheck from baseball was $5 a week. He moved around to other semi-pro teams, including a team called the Reading Pretzels, and flunked a minor-league tryout for the New York Giants organization. By then it was determined that he could not pitch at the pro level or master the outfield.

Eventually, Baker found a home at third base (he never played anywhere else on a big league diamond) and proved to early doubters that indeed he could hit. By 1911, when the Philadelphia Athletics won their second straight World Series crown, Baker was a member of that club's famous $100,000 infield.

> Yes, it was a great gang to be with. I can see Stuffy [McInnis] now, stretching out on his stomach picking up the low throws with that tiny mitt of his. And Collins, why, he is the undisputed champion among second basemen. Barry at shortstop was often mistaken for me. People would call Jack by my name and I'd get his. It got so we answered to each other's names. But Connie Mack never got us mixed up.[1]

Those who passed hasty judgment on Baker's ability later regretted it. Baker played 13 major league seasons with the A's and the New York Yankees between 1908 and 1922. He was an integral part of the Athletics' dynasty, but just missed staying around long enough to become part of the first Yankees dynasty. Baker retired at 35 and said the reason he did not try to extend his career any longer was that he was spending too much time away from family and his Maryland farm. Trappe was not a big place, population 272 in the 1950s, but it was always home to Baker.

Baker was not from the Trapp Family singers, but the Trappe farmers. He was ten when he decided his life goal was to become a professional ball player. The earliest edition of the Baltimore Orioles were prominent in the state. Among their stars managed by Ned Hanlon were Wee Willie

12. Home Run Baker

Keeler, John McGraw, Wilbert Robinson and Hughie Jennings. The roster included a solid, but lesser figure named "Boileryard" Clarke. One of Baker's oldest brothers may have been just as good at baseball, but when he tried out for a Philadelphia team he expressed disdain for the city. Ironically, that's where Frank enjoyed his greatest fame.

The most famous resident of the small community had roots deeply dug in Trappe. He noted that the family tree was planted there about 200 years previously. Baker said some members of his family on his mother's side went to Virginia and, through that side of the clan, he was distantly related to General Robert E. Lee.

Baker, whose full name was John Franklin Baker, though his signature often took the form of "J. Franklin Baker," was a .307 lifetime hitter. His highest single-season average was in 1912, when he batted .347. He led the American League once in triples and twice in runs batted in. More

Frank "Home Run" Baker, on his way to the Hall of Fame, was the Philadelphia Athletics' third baseman during the club's first dynasty, leading the American League in homers four straight years during the Deadball Era (National Baseball Hall of Fame Library, Cooperstown, New York).

famously, he led the league in home runs four times. Since this was still the Deadball Era, his league-topping totals ranging from nine to 12 seem ludicrous to later fans of the game.

In fact, Baker's lifetime total of home runs in regular-season play was 96. Often enough, the uninitiated wonder how in the world he received the "Home Run" nickname. The tale is then told of his successes in the 1911 World Series. He was elected to the Baseball Hall of Fame in 1955 while still alive. "I could see myself in a big-league uniform," Baker said upon his election to the Hall. "I dreamed of playing before big crowds. I dreamed of being a hero. But I never, never, never dreamed I would ever be in the Hall of Fame."[2]

Like the habit of throwing hats onto the rink in hockey when a player makes three goals, a long-forgotten practice of approval for baseball fans when a ball player smacked a homer was to sail straw hats onto the field. The straw hat was de rigueur for gentlemen at the park watching big league ball during the summer months—and only the summer months—though actually throwing them in celebration was not as common as heaving a mortarboard into the air upon a graduation. Still, a running joke with Baker was that a hat salesman in Philadelphia once measured the distance of a thrown hat following a Baker home run at 262 feet. It was declared a record.

Baker weighed 173 pounds as a grown-up, but at times he swung a 52-ounce bat, which may have been a different kind of record. Half the players in the big leagues probably couldn't lift it higher than they could raise a barbell. And another quarter of them probably couldn't swing it with any authority. Talk about carrying a big stick.

Leading up to the 1911 World Series, Baker recorded a breakthrough year for the Athletics. He batted .334, led the American League in homers for the first time with 11. On July 3, 1911, Baker batted for the cycle. Hitting for the cycle, a single, double, triple and home run, remains a rare baseball feat, but it was even more difficult to achieve during Baker's days because so few home runs were hit. Throughout major league history, a player hitting for the cycle has been about as common as a pitcher throwing a no-hitter.

Some other Baker contemporaries who did so include Danny Murphy, his A's teammate in 1910, and fellow Hall of Famers Tris Speaker and Honus Wagner in 1912. Baker was the only player in the majors to hit for the cycle in 1911. The Athletics beat New York, 5–1, that day. Baker also made an out during the game, going four-for-five.

Baker called his club "a man's-sized bat. "Up until I got too old to get around on good fastball pitching, I used a 52-ounce bat. Honest! You had to hit that ball fair and square and with some weight and power back of it to make it go over a fence. I won't take anything away from present-day players. They're fine boys and play good baseball. But the ball is different."[3]

There is no doubt about that. The "dead ball" was often battered lopsided. It nearly turned to mush on occasion. Unlike modern days, when a ball is replaced after many at-bats and sometimes seemingly after every other pitch, balls remained in use play after play during Baker's era. Often enough, the balls seemed way heavier than gravity.

"Why you know I've swung with all my might at a good fastball, hit it fair and square, and was lucky if it bounced against the fence," Baker said. "I hit the fence at Shibe Park 38 times one year. Eddie Collins told me if I had been hitting the ball Babe Ruth hit every one of them would have gone over the fence."[4]

Actually, between 1914, when Ruth first appeared in the majors for the Boston Red Sox, and 1920, when he first played for the Yankees, Ruth and Baker were hitting the same ball. In 1918, after Baker's run of home run titles had ended, Ruth won his first crown with 11 blasts. Ruth stroked 29 homers in 1919, the last of the deadball seasons.

Baker remained a fan of the sport and a close observer for his entire life. He mentioned attending a later Yankees game when star outfielder Joe DiMaggio was playing, and an event made an impression on him. DiMaggio was using a 35-ounce bat and in Baker's mind took "just an easy swing and hit the ball over the fence in right-center field."[5]

Baker got into nine A's games in 1908, but did not hit a home run. Jimmy Collins was 38 that season and near the end of the line, batting .217. Collins, who was the Boston Red Sox's first manager and ran the club as a player-manager from 1901 through 1906, did retire after that season. Baker's cameo session in Philadelphia did not make him feel secure about his baseball future, but Mack needed a new third baseman and liked Baker.

Baker's first career homer came the next season when he became a regular and appeared in 148 games. Philadelphia was playing Boston, and the Red Sox walked Danny Murphy to load the bases. The Sox wanted to put the rookie in a pressure situation. When Murphy trotted down the line to first, he spoke with Boston first baseman Jake Stahl and later told Baker what was said. Murphy told Stahl his team had just made a mistake because "that kid can hit the ball outta the park."[6] On the first pitch, Baker connected and ripped a grand slam over the left field wall.

Harkening back to that statistic of batted balls bouncing off Shibe's walls 38 times in a single season in 1913 when he also cracked 12 homers, Baker said that in a later era, after the ball had changed, he would have hit 50 homers. "You've got to figure just about every one of those as a homer with the lively ball," Baker said.[7]

It wasn't just the dead ball that made it hard on batters during Baker's day either. Pitchers had carte blanche to dirty, scrape, spit on, and rough up the balls in any fashion they pleased, all to the disadvantage of the batters. Many years later when he was talking about his life in baseball, Baker made sure to tell a writer that he was not in any way advocating that the spitball be legitimized again.

Reflecting about Baker's signature power in the 1911 World Series, Mack said two such game-changing home runs were remarkable at the time. "It was a big event in those days of the dead ball when a batter made a home run," Mack said decades later. "When Baker made two home runs in the 1911 World Series against the rugged New York Giants, it was more than an event. It was a sensation. It was a calamity for the Giants."[8]

When he was writing his memoirs near the end of his long big league career, his tenure in charge of the A's, and his life, Mack, who had an excellent track record of unearthing talent, listed several players whom he claimed as great discoveries. They were players either unknown to other teams, simply hidden gems his team of friends acting as scouts tipped him off about, or players he scouted by himself. "On their records," Mack said, "I think I have the right to feel proud of my discoveries. Look at Home Run Baker. We brought him to Philadelphia when other managers were overlooking him on the Reading team. In my opinion, he had everything."[9]

Baker, who later became a minor league manager in Easton, Maryland, discovered Jimmie Foxx, one of the greatest sluggers of all time. Baker spoke of how the Yankees passed on Foxx and he then sold Foxx to Mack's A's for $2,000. Easton management ended up firing Baker for not getting more money in the deal. Mack and Baker admired one another, though that business deal was not the reason.

Speaking of his early days with the Athletics, his rookie year and beyond when Philadelphia blossomed into world champions, Baker said, "Those next few years were some of the best years of my life. It was a real treat to play baseball for Connie Mack. He taught me more about baseball than any other man. He taught me more baseball than I had ever known. Connie developed me into a baseball player in almost every respect. Always patient, Connie was like a father to all of his players."[10]

Certainly, Baker was biased in favor of his choice, but in 1955, soon after he was chosen for the Hall of Fame and sportswriters paraded to his door in Maryland, Baker told anyone who asked what he thought of Mack. Always there were kind words and sentences tinged with gratefulness. "I think, with all due respect to the great baseball managers known to the game, that Connie Mack is the greatest of them all," Baker said.[11]

13

The Year 1912

Flush from capturing two straight World Series titles, Connie Mack began the 1912 season thinking this would be his most talented and productive team. That was asking a lot given the success of the franchise in 1910 and 1911. But there was no reason to think that the A's would not be able to earn a third straight American League pennant and move on to nab a third straight World Series.

All of the ingredients were in place. All of the key men from the year before were still active and seemed capable of turning in as fine a season as they had in 1911. Three pennants in a row seemed like a reasonable goal.

The $100,000 infield was intact with the usual suspects manning the spots. Harry Davis was gone, but Stuffy McInnis, Eddie Collins, Jack Barry and Frank Baker were going to play every day anyway. Jack Lapp and Ira Thomas were the main catchers. Bris Lord, Danny Murphy, Rube Oldring and Amos Strunk all returned for outfield play.

"That club had speed, hitting power, pitching skill, and more brains than one ordinarily finds on three clubs," Mack said. "There was talk of our having a monopoly on the pennant, like the later-day talk about the Yankees. The whole attitude of the league was that we would win again in a walk."[1]

If anything, the pitching had the potential to improve. The Big Three of Charles Bender, Jack Coombs and Eddie Plank were still kings of the hill. Cy Morgan, who had shown what he could do at his best, could be called on. Dave Danforth and Harry Krause were still around, too. Boardwalk Brown, who pitched in just two regular-season games in 1911, was ready for more action. Even more intriguing, though more so with the benefit of history and hindsight, was the addition of some fresh faces to the pitching staff. The Connie Mack talent evaluation machine had been working overtime.

13. The Year 1912

Joe Bush, whose nickname was "Bullet" because of the blinding speed of his fastball, made his first appearance in a game for the Athletics that season at the age of 19 before going on to win 196 games over a 17-year career. But he was a year away from contributing. Stan Coveleski was 23, also a rookie, but was also used minimally before becoming a star who won 215 games and was elected to the Hall of Fame. Just 18, Herb Pennock also arrived in the majors that year for 17 games before ultimately winning 241 games in a 22-year career.

The talent was so awesome on the A's that year this trio could barely crack the pitching lineup, though they were indeed young and inexperienced at the time. Coveleski and Pennock were both future Hall of Famers, and Bush later had a 26-win season, and yet they couldn't get off the bench. Byron Houck, less famous than all of the others and just 20 years old (and who had a much shorter career), actually contributed more to the team in 1912.

In 1912, Mack had 17 arms trying to impress him. In the modern era teams can easily use 17 pitchers in a season and sometimes managers are so quick to yank hurlers it might seem they use 17 in a single game of one-third of an inning each. In Mack's case, all of the candidates were starters because those were pretty much the only kind of pitchers there were in his day. "I considered the 1912 team the best I ever handled up to this time for the fact that by virtue of two straight World Series conquests the players had acquired the experience and confidence to win," Mack said.[2]

There was no doubt in Mack's mind when the team broke spring training that he was at the helm of another Athletics club that would win the American League pennant. How many managers are gifted with that bounty of talent at their fingertips?

There were not many such lucky bosses throughout the game's history. But 1912 happened to be a year in the AL when more than one team played superb ball. It was a season when more than one team had designs on first place and the goods to go for it. The Boston Red Sox and the Washington Senators made it a three-team race.

Like the Athletics, the Red Sox were one of the charter franchises of the American League in 1901. They were an early power, winning pennants in 1903 and 1904, and won the first World Series ever played in 1903. However, the Red Sox were the victims in 1904 when John McGraw's intransigence kept the Series from being played. The 1912 squad was the best Boston team assembled since those early days.

Although there have been several versions of the Washington Senators and Washington Nationals playing in the nation's capitol, the Senators of 1912 were also one of the inaugural AL clubs. This team of Senators was the forerunner of the Minnesota Twins. Between 1901 and 1911, Washington had never finished higher than sixth in the eight-team league and was last four times.

In 1912, the Senators were managed by Clark Griffith. Eventually enshrined in the Hall of Fame, Griffith, born in 1869, pitched long enough to win 237 games, managed four different clubs, and owned the Senators from 1920 until his death in 1955. Griffith Stadium in Washington, D.C., was named after him. His nickname was "The Old Fox," and for once, in 1912, he seemed capable of out-foxing Connie Mack to grab the pennant.

Of course, the No. 1 asset Griffith had working for him that season was Walter Johnson, the formidable contender for the title of greatest pitcher of all time. Johnson, called "The Big Train," threw a fastball that many batters claimed they could not even see. The right-hander's 417 victories are the second-most to Cy Young's 511, but Johnson had the misfortune of being shackled to a large number of lousy Washington teams. Not this year, though.

Johnson was in his prime at 24 in 1912. In a glittering career that saw him lead the AL in earned run average five times, in strikeouts 12 times, and in wins six times, this was one of his finest seasons. Johnson finished 33–12 with a 1.39 ERA and 303 strikeouts. It was a season to be framed behind glass and boasted about forever, though Johnson was not that kind of man (and besides, amazingly, his next year was even better).

It took some time for the Senators to unwind. They lost their first two games and hovered around .500 until early June. A 17-game winning streak that began with the second game of a doubleheader on May 30, Memorial Day, changed the complexion of Washington's season. A new winning streak of ten games in early July wiped out some previously erratic play and Washington stood at 48–31. The season played out in fits and starts for Washington. Several short losing streaks were mingled in as well, but a third notable winning streak of six games left the Senators at 72–44 on August 21.

Washington was not blessed with hard-hitting stars. Practically no one could hit home runs, and the team total for the year was 20. The two top hitters were first baseman Chick Gandil, who was later fingered as one of the ringleaders of the Black Sox Scandal, at .305, and outfielder Clyde Milan at .306.

The speedy center fielder, whose nickname was "Deerfoot," twice led the American League in stolen bases, with a career-high 88 that season and 75 the next year. It might be said that Milan was a deer with brakes,

13. The Year 1912

however, because he was caught stealing as many as 31 times in a year. A lifetime .285 hitter who played nearly 2,000 games for Washington during a 16-year career, he was long one of the most popular players for the franchise.

Above all, though, Walter Johnson was the weapon the Senators relied upon. "You can't hit what you can't see," was Johnson's philosophy.[3] He said that about himself, but others made numerous comments about how fast was fast. No one put it more vividly than Ty Cobb, the Detroit Tigers star of the same era. "His fastball looked about the size of a watermelon seed and it hissed at you as it passed," Cobb said.[4]

While Washington was making its case as a pennant contender, the Red Sox were feeling something special in the air, anxious to return to the top after nearly a decade's absence. They were 10–5 by early May, not bad, but certainly not running away with anything. They maintained that pace in May, again solid but not extraordinary, finishing that month at 25–13. But over a 17-day stretch in June, the BoSox won 14 out of 15 games. Now they were cooking, at 41–19. Another five-game winning streak as the month wound up made it clear that Boston was a team the Athletics had to fear. Then the Red Sox really revved up in July. The Red Sox took seven out of eight, beginning with the second game of a double-header on July 5, and tossed in a six-game winning streak later in the month.

By August 24, when the Senators were feeling pretty good about themselves, Boston was sitting at 82–36 and looking like a team that had no weakness. For starters, and the No. 1 starter was a key reason, this was the season of Smoky Joe Wood. Wood was 22 years old and in the midst of one of the single greatest seasons ever compiled by a pitcher.

Wood was 5-foot-11 and 180 pounds, threw from the right side, and his holy-moly pitch was a fastball that even Walter Johnson said was faster than his own (although Wood said Johnson was faster). Wood was born in Kansas City and even spent some time at the University of Kansas before making his first Boston appearance at 18 in 1908. In a now-hard-to-fathom situation, Wood actually first played for a Bloomer Girls barnstorming team; each one of those squads carried one male player when they met all-male clubs. The odds were good if you wanted to find a girlfriend, but perhaps not so great for career advancement.

After 1908, Wood improved in Boston each year following that 1–1 cameo. In 1909, Wood won 11 games. In 1910, he won 12, with a losing record but a 1.69 earned run average. In 1911, he won 23. And in 1912 he held the world in his palm, going 34–5 with a 1.91 earned run average. Wood threw ten shutouts that year. He was as close to unbeatable as a pitcher can be over 344 innings, over one stretch winning 16 times in a row.

Although Wood was doomed to a short career because of an arm injury that limited him to a lifetime mark of 117–57 on the mound, he was a sound enough hitter to make a comeback as an outfielder. But in 1912 he was without question the engine that made the Red Sox go.

Hugh Bedient (20–9) and Buck O'Brien (20–13) complemented Wood on the mound and contributed greatly to Boston's success, although in the big picture they were not nearly as well-remembered, even by the most devoted of Red Sox fans. For both men, it was definitely a passing season of big league glory.

In 1908, Bedient, who was from upstate New York, was pitching for a semi-pro team in Falconer, New York. On July 25, facing a team from Pennsylvania, Bedient struck out 42 batters in 23 innings of a 3–1 victory. Many years later, the achievement was publicized by Ripley's "Believe It Or Not." A rookie in 1912, Bedient's performance was his finest in a four-year career that concluded with a 59–53 record. He eventually jumped to the Buffalo Blues of the Federal League when that rival operation started business.

While Wood was playing with Bloomer Girls, O'Brien was a late bloomer. O'Brien, from the nearby Boston suburb of Brockton, was 29 when he reached the majors in 1911 and 1912 was his career highlight. The next year, 1913, he won four games and was out of the majors by the conclusion of that season.

Fenway Park opened on April 20, 1912, some might say a good omen for the Red Sox that season, and O'Brien was the starting pitcher for the home team in the first game played in the new digs. The players could not know that eventually Fenway would become as beloved as the franchise and endure for more than a century steeped in history, tradition and lore. Boston met the New York Highlanders (after an earlier exhibition trial run against Harvard University) for the official inaugural game at the park.

The opener was originally scheduled for April 17, but rain postponed the event three times. While there had been considerable excitement about the opening of a new ball park for the Sox, on April 15, the tragedy of the sinking of the *Titanic* in the North Atlantic after striking an iceberg cast gloom over the sporting contest. The entire nation was riveted to the drama as reports of who died and who survived came in, as well as details of the rescue operations.

Boston opened the season on the road with five games (including a two-game split with the A's) before winning the Fenway Park debut, 7–6,

13. The Year 1912

in 11 innings. Outfielder Tris Speaker knocked in the winning run with a single, the kind of play that was a habit with the future Hall of Famer that year.

While player-manager Jake Stahl held down first base and batted .301 and third baseman Larry Gardner hit .315, it was the Boston outfield that everyone raved about and worried about. Some say Speaker, "The Grey Eagle," was the best-fielding center fielder ever. He was at least as good a hitter, in 1912 batting .383 with 136 runs scored, 90 runs batted in, 10 home runs, 12 triples, 53 doubles and 52 stolen bases. He knocked out 222 hits and his on-base percentage was .464. Duffy Lewis drove in 109 runs, and Harry Hooper fielded like he owned the joint.

Players like Johnson, Wood and Speaker held the baseball public spellbound, but what of the Athletics during this stretch, the team of champions, the team that could not be beaten? Much to Mack's dismay, the A's were being beaten way too often. Boston and Washington were setting the tone in the American League instead of the A's. This very much annoyed Mack since he had been such a strong believer in the likelihood of sweeping to a third pennant in a row.

This was a veteran team. There were plenty of leaders who played the game the way Mack loved. His favorite competitors were Bender, Collins, Baker and Barry, but it was almost as if there was poison in the water slowing everyone down, distracting the team, blinding it. Attitude more than anything else bugged Mack. The A's seemed to be suffering from a malaise, a lack of hunger stemming from two straight seasons of accomplishing goals.

Through an accident of scheduling, Philadelphia met the two hottest clubs right away at the beginning of the season. The A's opened against Washington and won two straight. They split two with Boston and then split two more games with the Senators. So right away they learned what those teams looked like. In early May, the Athletics were 8–8. They were 19–19 on June 5, in sixth place. Pretty much the A's were running in mud, getting nowhere fast, stuck with a mediocre record. Mack tried to remain patient, but eventually grew angry at the lackadaisical nature of the team's approach.

> Why, when we got off to a poor start, they laughed it off. Nobody paid much attention to it and they took the attitude, "We'll win when we want to." I began to worry. I didn't like the attitude, but didn't say anything. Maybe I too was too complacent and thought the men would step up their pace when they saw they had a mighty good Boston club to beat. Then May slipped into June and June into July and still we weren't playing our game. By this time I was doing a lot of worrying and asked

them, "What's wrong with you fellows?" They still chuckled and replied, "We'll get going right along."[5]

For weeks in late May and into June, the Athletics resided in sixth, fifth and finally fourth place in the AL standings. They were a sailboat becalmed, a train out of coal, an automobile running out of gasoline. Yet judging by individual statistics, it wasn't easy to put a finger on the problem, to identify a slacker or a faltering player.

During the 1912 season, Home Run Baker had his best all-around year, batting .347 and driving in 130 runs. Collins batted .348 with a .450 on-base percentage. McInnis hit .327 and knocked in 101 runs. Oldring batted .301, Jack Lapp .292, and Amos Strunk .289, and even light-hitting Jack Barry reached .261. The only regular who slumped at the plate was Bris Lord, who dropped to .238. Although playing just 36 games, Danny Murphy hit .323.

Despite the plethora of arms, the pitching overall did fall off some. Coombs won 21 games, but Bender just 13. So did Boardwalk Brown. Cy Morgan dropped to 3–8, and that was basically the end of his run in Philadelphia. He pitched in just one more game the next year and retired. However, Eddie Plank was better than ever. The veteran lefty finished 26–6 with a 2.22 earned run average, one of the finest performances in the league. That was Plank's seventh 20-win season for the Athletics. "Eddie had one of his greatest seasons for me," Mack said.[6]

Although Plank never pitched an inning in the minors, coming straight to the A's from college at Gettysburg, he never seemed to miss that experience. He was an old rookie at 25 because of his campus stay but arrived as the mature product, stayed in the majors for 17 seasons and walked away with 326 victories on his resume. Never was he better than in 1912, and never was he more needed by a club seeking to make a late charge for the pennant.

Plank was an excellent pitcher, but his mound behavior also drove batters crazy. He received the throw back from his catcher and fiddled around, wasting time. He walked around on the mound, then fidgeted when he looked in at the plate and fidgeted some more before he threw another pitch. He was a great believer in taking his time and playing upon the impatience of frustrated batters anxious to hit.

As much as anything, where the A's fell down was in the field. This supposedly smart team made too many errors and too many mistakes of bad judgment. One time, Baker had the ball with an opposing runner ahead of him on the third-base line, but instead of firing it to catcher Jack Lapp, who was calling for it, Baker chased the runner, who out-ran him to become safe at home. "Lock the gates or he'll chase him out of the park!" yelled Mack, who could not abide such sloppy play.⁷

As days passed and Mack did not see any signs of his players wising up or shaping up following his team meeting, he called another meeting. He was even testier this time. "Two weeks later I called them together again and this time I really sailed into them," Mack said. "They were surprised to hear me talking like that and I think some of them really thought I was trying to frighten them into a pennant, but if they were impressed, it was too late."⁸

It was too late for the 1912 A's almost from the first month of the season, even if the players didn't recognize the threats and challenges of spring. By late summer, they were far in arrears as Boston kept up the pressure, thinking less about Philadelphia even than Washington because Washington was closer in the standings. Mack said it was almost embarrassing to face the Red Sox in August and not be viewed as a significant obstacle.

It was during the last few days of the month when the Athletics journeyed to Fenway Park for a three-game set. The A's were hopeful. They had upped their record to 73–47, and while they were still in third place and trailed the Sox by 10½ games, this was the time to mount an offensive, to chip away at the lead if it was ever going to happen. Boston brushed aside Philadelphia 8–1, 7–4, and 2–1, and the Athletics limped out of town 13½ games out of first.

"By August we were playing the Red Sox and they were already chiding us as the ex-champions," Mack said, "and we could do nothing about it."⁹

One thing Mack tried to do, early and late, was mix in some of the new blood on the pitching staff just in case a phenom would emerge to help immediately.

Pennock was just 18 and was from the Philadelphia suburb of Kennett Square. He was attending a boarding school in the area when he made the shift from playing the field to the mound. On the day he threw a no-hitter, his catcher was Earle Mack, Connie's son, which gave him an inside track to sign the player. When Pennock tossed another no-hitter, this time against a team of traveling African American players, Mack brought him to the A's.

Impressed by Pennock's raw talent, Mack sent him out for his major league debut on May 14. Pennock got into 17 games, mostly in relief, and finished 1–2. Pennock had good stuff and Mack pictured him as a star of the future. The A's manager was right about that, but except for an 11–4 season in 1914, Pennock never shone for the Athletics, and Mack traded him to Boston. The Red Sox subsequently sent Pennock to the New York Yankees, and that is where he produced his best seasons and shared in three World Series championships by 1932.

It may be argued that Mack parted with Pennock too soon. He did not like Pennock's work ethic and did not think he was mature enough. Still, Mack lost out on the services of a man who improved into a Hall of Famer.

Also in 1912, Mack thrust Stan Coveleski into the lineup for his major league debut on September 10. Coveleski, born into a Polish family in Shamokin, Pennsylvania, had the name Stanislaus Kowalewski on his birth certificate. He went 2–1 that season for the A's, but Mack did not keep him either. Coveleski, a spitball artist, spent three more years in the minors before reappearing in the majors in 1916. Most of Coveleski's success came with the Cleveland Indians and then Washington as he amassed 215 wins.

Although brother Harry, three years older, also came out of that coal country and won 20 games three times, he was often plagued by wildness. In all, Harry won 81 games, but also once walked 16 men in one game. Stan Coveleski might well have served the A's well as a long-term replacement once Plank, Coombs and Bender retired, but he went the way of Pennock and Shoeless Joe Jackson before he could become a major addition to the Athletics.

Of the trio that made a pitching debut with Philadelphia during the disappointing 1912 season, the one who became the most important asset later was Bullet Joe Bush. Bush's first game in the majors was the A's September 30 contest. From Brainerd, Minnesota, Bush was just 19 that day. He pitched eight innings and gave up ten runs, but didn't even take the loss. On one of the last days of the regular season, the Athletics topped New York, 11–10. Bush stuck around Philadelphia for several years and did make a difference in the rotation when Mack needed him.

Bullet Joe was actually christened Leslie Ambrose. Although his nickname derived from his fastball, Bush actually was credited with inventing the forkball, nowadays considered a very close relation to the split-fingered fastball. Of Mack's three pitching discoveries with such promise that season, Bush was the one who helped the A's the most and the one not chosen for the Hall of Fame.

In 1912, the Red Sox, with Joe Wood out-gunning everyone, played stupendous ball all year. Boston won the pennant with a record of 105–47, a winning percentage of .691. The distance between the Red Sox and second-place Washington, with 91 wins, was 14 games. Philadelphia closed to within one game of Washington, winning 90 games, a nice recovery after a slow start, but not within telescope range of the Red Sox.

As brilliantly as Boston played, the New York Giants were nearly as good in capturing another pennant in the National League. The Giants finished 103–48 with a winning percentage of .682. The World Series promised to be a high-class war.

For the first time in three years, the World Series did not include the Philadelphia Athletics. The A's players who excelled individually could take solace from that. All of them, though, were still probably shell-shocked, spending their autumn and winter wondering just how it came to pass that they could only finish third in the American League. If some looked into their souls and felt the accusations of complacency Mack sent out to sting them, then they knew what had probably occurred.

Meanwhile, the World Series was spellbinding. It actually took eight games to settle a seven-game series because the second game ended in a 6–6 tie after 11 innings. The Red Sox won the deciding game, 3–2, in ten innings at Fenway Park on October 16. Capping his spectacular season, Smoky Joe Wood won three times, besting Christy Mathewson in the last contest.

> "The Red Sox, winners in 1912, was a mighty club and deserved their honors," Mack said. "I don't want to take anything away from Boston because we did not happen to win. Washington also played brilliantly and finished second, while we had to be content with third place. Even if our players had attended strictly to business, it might have been possible for these two teams to have finished ahead of us."[10]

Mack may have been seeking to be gracious with that statement, but forevermore, for the last 40-plus years of his life, he lamented the loss of the pennant in 1912 as the one that got away.

14

Eddie Plank

"Gettysburg Eddie," as Eddie Plank was often called, was born in that Pennsylvania community a decade after the end of the Civil War, the event by which most people remember his hometown.

Numbering seven children, Plank's family inhabited a farm near Gettysburg, which was the center of their existence. Plank was a Gettysburg guy all of the way, including time spent at Gettysburg Academy for high school before the college recruited him to play baseball. Just why was not completely clear to everyone, since he had not played the sport seriously before.

In an as-told-to story in 1910, Plank made a little bit of fun of himself about his start in the game and his connection to Gettysburg.

> They all say I got my start the day of the Battle of Gettysburg, but they exaggerate somewhat. I was born in Gettysburg in 1875 and that gave the boys a chance to say things. I admit the 1875 without trying to get away and scalp half a dozen years off my age, as some of them do. At any rate, I am rather a freak as a baseball player because I seldom have heard of any case anything like my own.[1]

Plank said he played baseball growing up only on the Fourth of July or the occasional Saturday because it was very much play, and he did not follow the sport closely.

"Honestly, I never even read the scores, or knew who played in the big leagues until I was 20 years old," Plank said. "I didn't know a squeeze play from third base."[2] He thought the only reason he seemed to be an attractive prospect for the Gettysburg team and the majors was that he was older and strong. Nor did he claim to be especially gifted initially. "I was big and strong and fast and wild and inexperienced. I simply shut my eyes and cut loose and most of those who didn't strike out got base on balls." (Apparently before he joined the A's.)[3]

Plank was an outstanding pitcher from the start and went well beyond that status in the majors after Connie Mack brought him to Philadelphia for the A's in 1901. The southpaw became the first left-hander in baseball history to win 200 games and 300 games. Even now, a century after his career concluded, Plank is the third-winningest lefty of all time, his 326 wins ranking behind Warren Spahn's 363 and Steve Carlton's 329. It should be noted that Plank's total does include 21 wins in the Federal League.

Southpaw Eddie Plank broke into the majors in 1901, the year both the Athletics and the American League were founded. Plank was the first lefty to win 200 games and record 300 wins (National Baseball Hall of Fame Library, Cooperstown, New York).

Over his 17-season big-league career, Plank also recorded a 2.35 earned run average. At 25 he was an old rookie, but Plank stretched his big league playing days until he was 41. Later, fellow Hall of Famer Satchel Paige, who was considered an ageless hurler, titled his autobiography "Maybe I'll Pitch Forever." However, many years earlier than that, Plank pretty much predicted he would do that very thing.

Plank was in his forties when he made the proclamation, "I wouldn't be surprised if I would be pitching baseball when I am 50 years old."[4] It was a bold statement when he happened to be looking for a pitching job, but it was an aspiration that did not come true. When he did change his mind and actually retired at age 42, Plank said, "I am through with baseball forever. I have my farm and my home and enough to take care of me, so why should I work and worry any longer?"[5]

Plank specialized in a fastball and a curve, but also possessed a wicked change-up as well as accuracy. His excellent control kept walks to a minimum, kept runners off the base paths and kept his earned run average low. In his waning days as a big-leaguer, Plank did try to sneak more slow stuff past the best hitters. On one occasion he got Ty Cobb to swing at a waist-high pitch down the middle and he only got enough of it to pop out. Cobb yelled at Plank on the mound. "I ought to have my throat cut for hitting at that stuff," Cobb said.[6]

That was much later, after Plank had become one of the craftiest pitchers in the game, a learning experience that took a lot of time. Plank was actually slated to play for the minor league Richmond Colts in Virginia, but the team went out of business before he got there and instead he detoured to Philadelphia in 1901 to join the A's. Plank was so raw that he admitted he did not really know what he was doing on the mound. He merely tried to emulate his limited attempts at pitching at Gettysburg, considering that the wisest course of action. "Just wait till I saw the whites of their eyes and then shoot," Plank said. "I must say I got away with it luckily, especially after wounding a flock of ball players. Suddenly, I saw that there was more to it than throwing as hard as possible and curving them. I saw I would have to do some thinking and I began to study the game."[7]

Once he commenced his studies, Plank earned an A on his report card. "I worked and studied hard at the game," he said, "watched the other pitchers, picked up their tricks and began to pitch with much less exertion and strain and still get results. If I had gone on the way I started I would have been out of it in two seasons."[8]

Plank adapted pretty quickly since he won 17 games as a rookie. The next year, in 1902, he won 20 games for the first of seven times with the Athletics and helped carry Philadelphia to its first pennant. Over the following years, Plank threw for four more A's pennant winners, lasting longer with the franchise than any other teammate from 1901. Although he was not the best pitcher on the team every single season he was with the A's, Plank did stay around longer than Jack Coombs or Chief Bender, and he won more games than either of the other Philadelphia aces of the time period.

However, Plank was known as a hard-luck loser in four World Series for the A's. His career Series record was 2–5 despite his 1.32 earned run average. His biggest problem was running up against the Giants' Christy Mathewson when the New Yorker was throwing Series shutouts. In fact, the delightful poet Ogden Nash penned a short verse about Plank that touched upon this inconvenient situation of going head-to-head with Mathewson. Ogden wrote, "P is for Plank, The Arm of the A's; When he tangled with Matty, Games Lasted For Days."[9]

During his long career, Plank had just two years where his earned average climbed above 3.00. His 3.31 as a rookie and 3.30 as a second-year man would be regarded as just fine in the 2000s, but he kept getting sharper. Plank's best ERA of 1.76 was recorded in 1909. He was otherwise extremely consistent, almost always in the low 2.00s. Although he also won 26 games in 1904 (26–17), his best overall year was 1912, when the A's couldn't pull off that third straight pennant. Plank was the main man that year at 26–6. It wasn't his fault that Philadelphia did not return to the World Series.

Once Plank gained a pitching education, a policy he adopted was not to throw to bases to hold runners close to keep them from stealing. This was a risky practice during his day because many of the top base stealers of all time were active then and liked to run rampant on the base paths. Plank ignored them at his peril.

"I once heard Eddie Plank say, 'There are only so many pitches in this old arm and I don't believe in wasting them throwing them to first base,'" said Sam Jones, another top pitcher of the era who won 229 games in a long career.[10]

It seemed that after Plank earned his master's degree in pitching, he didn't mind sharing his knowledge with young Athletics pitchers. Bender was the same way and eventually became a long-term pitching coach paid to dispense such wisdom. Left-hander Rube Bressler joined the A's in 1914, and he was literally all ears (just ask him) when he overheard Plank and Bender talking. "I used to try to get near [them]," Bressler said, "and listen to what they were talking about and every question I'd ask they'd pay attention and tell me what they thought. I used to put sticks behind my ears so they'd stand out further. Boy, I wanted to hear what those guys had to say."[11]

Unfortunately for Bressler, he apparently did not have the ability to utilize all the wisdom offered. He was just 26–32 as a big league hurler, but did make the adjustment to become a successful first baseman and outfielder who posted a .301 lifetime average. It might have been interesting for Bressler to bat against Plank, but he never did because once out of Philadelphia, he spent the rest of his long career in the National League.

Plank was not as colorful as Rube Waddell nor as distinctive as Native American Bender. He never won 30 games in a season like Jack Coombs. The speed of his fastball was never compared to Walter Johnson's swiftest pitches. What Plank did for a long time was win. "Not the fastest," said teammate Eddie Collins of Plank. "Not the trickiest and not the possessor of the most stuff, but just the greatest."[12]

In a somewhat strange development, long after Plank's death, the baseball card featuring him from the 1909–1911 T-206 set with a white border has become both extraordinarily difficult and expensive to acquire. On the card, Plank is pictured bare-headed with wavy dark hair and somewhat sleepy eyes, with the collar slightly raised on his Philadelphia uniform shirt. The team's "A" is prominent on the left side of his chest.

The most valuable baseball card of all is the Honus Wagner card from this set. Wagner cards have sold for more than $2 million at auction. The prominence of the player, as well as the age of the card set, figure into this value, but the main reason it is so prized is its scarcity. The baseball cards were issued with tobacco, and when Wagner realized this he asked that his card be withdrawn from the market because he didn't want to be associated with luring children into trying tobacco.

Collectors eventually learned that the Plank card was also very rare, although there is no known reason like the Wagner tale. The fact that Plank is also a Hall of Famer of note contributes to the value. Depending on the expert and the condition (very important), the card has been valued at $188,000 at its best. There have been estimates that 100 such Plank cards exist. Not helping matters are other Plank cards from the time period featuring the same photograph of him. While also expensive compared to the average baseball card, some of those sell for anywhere from a few hundred dollars to many thousands of dollars. Someone who does not have tremendous resources may also pick up a reprint card of the original super-costly one for just a few dollars.

Baseball Reference's website can pinpoint only two years of Plank's salary with the Athletics at an estimated $1,000 as a 1901 rookie and $5,000 as a 1914 veteran. It would be interesting to hear the thoughts of the player upon learning that a small, cardboard image of his visage was worth so much money so long after he played the game. Perhaps Plank picked up a few of his own cards from that era and they remained in the family for a future generation to cash in.

There was never any indication that Connie Mack owned one of those cards either. But Connie Mack owned the genuine article on his team. "Gettysburg Eddie was one of our first big finds," Mack said. "He stands with the great mound generals of all times."[13]

15

The Year 1913

Connie Mack was disappointed with his team in 1912, but he did not institute a big shakeup. He believed the Athletics were the most talented team that season, so he did not wish to hastily dismantle the group that had provided Philadelphia with two straight World Series titles.

Mack had faith that the A's would rebound in 1913. The only key member of the roster who was aged was southpaw Eddie Plank, who was 37 in 1913. No other member of the pitching rotation or the starting lineup was older than 30, except for Jack Coombs, and he was a special case. Mack did not want to give up on his club prematurely only to see exiled players come back to haunt him with their achievements elsewhere.

So for the most part he stuck with many of the same guys who had taken the team so far in past years. Not completely, though. Some tweaking was involved, especially in the outfield, and with such a wealth of pitching it made sense for Mack to give some other hurlers a chance.

The big loss on the mound was Jack Coombs. Coombs was still with the Athletics, but Colby Jack couldn't pitch. He was felled by typhoid fever at 30 and appeared in just two games with a 0–0 record in 1913. It was testimony to the benefits of having young and hungry fresh faces around aching for a chance to pitch that resulted from Coombs' disability.

Coombs had spent the off-season in Palestine, Texas, with family. When Mack assembled the Athletics for spring training in San Antonio, it was merely a short trip for Coombs. He looked fine during the exhibition season and was chosen as Philadelphia's Opening Day pitcher against the defending World Series champion Red Sox. He did not pitch well, but alarm bells were not ringing loudly.

Mack started Coombs again two days later. This time it was obvious that something was seriously wrong with Coombs. He did not appear to have the physical strength to throw normal pitches. He was quickly yanked from the game. It turned out that those two were the only two games

15. The Year 1913

Coombs appeared in all season. He departed for the year (and some thought for good) with a 10.12 earned run average, throwing only five and one-third innings.

Coombs was diagnosed with typhoid fever, a killer across the United States and a common disease at the time. The illness is sparked by contaminated water or food and spreads salmonella bacteria throughout the body. It remains a potentially fatal disease in the 21st century. However, unlike in Coombs' time, antibiotics can cure typhoid fever and reduce the likelihood of mortality by 98 or even 99 percent.

Although Mack had rounded up a herd of pitchers in 1912 and hoped some would be ready by 1913, he was not confident about heavily counting on his finds just yet. He was counting on Coombs and now he didn't have him. Some younger pitchers would have to step up, and the team would have to count on them. When it became apparent at the start of the season

A collage of head shots of the 1913 World Series champion Philadelphia Athletics from the *Philadelphia Evening Tribune*. Top row, from left: Doc Lavan, Eddie Plank, Tom Daley, Jack Coombs, Connie Mack, Jimmy Walsh, Frank Baker, Billy Orr, and Chief Bender. Middle row: Harry Davis, Eddie Murphy, Amos Strunk, Byron Houck, Rube Oldring, Jack Barry, Danny Murphy, Stuffy McInnis, and Eddie Collins. Bottom row: Bob Shawkey, Boardwalk Brown, Herb Pennock, Wally Schang, Jack Lapp, Ira Thomas, Weldon Wyckoff, and Bullet Joe Bush (National Baseball Hall of Fame Library, Cooperstown, New York).

that Coombs was sick enough to be out for a long time, Mack tried to reassure the rest of the club. The best teams find ways to overcome injury and the loss of a player. The season was only days old, and Mack did not want the players' minds focused on the problem, but more on a solution. "We've got pitchers enough," he said. "We'll be all right."[1]

He was probably trying to convince himself as much as he was the boys. His confidantes on the team were told what Mack's strategy would be. He would try to break the newcomers in slowly at first. "An untried pitcher will learn more and gain more confidence by being in one inning nine separate games where the situation is apt to be different on each occasion than he will if he were to pitch nine consecutive innings and maybe get a good beating besides," Mack said.[2]

He imparted this philosophy to Harry Davis, who was much more coach than player by then, and veterans Eddie Collins, Ira Thomas and Danny Murphy. In fact, the only reason why Davis was around was because he had already been fired as Cleveland's manager after the Indians' 54–71 start in 1912.

The fellows Mack hoped would become stalwarts on the mound to aid Plank and Charles Bender included Boardwalk Brown, Joe Bush, and Byron Houck. Bush, at only 20, was quickly proving himself. Herb Pennock was there, but still young. The mid-season acquisition of Bob Shawkey did prove helpful.

Coombs was very much at risk, his life threatened, never mind merely his pitching career. No known source was pinpointed for Coombs' ailment, and after he was initially taken ill, he began bouncing back with some swiftness. As each week passed, Coombs kept informing Mack that he should be able to pitch again in a few weeks. He kept repeating that self-analysis. This situation persisted, though, for months, until it became clear as summer was nearing its end that Coombs would not pitch at all again that season despite such optimism.

Coombs had been overly optimistic about his recovery. He had lost more than 40 pounds during his illness and was down to 140, skeletal by his standards. The sports reporters of the time were not even sure of what ailed Coombs for months, speculating that he must have had the flu. Coombs was deluding himself if he believed he could come back to his team to play, although on August 4 he stopped at Shibe Park to mingle with the A's before they defeated the Cleveland Indians, 7–1. "I was a sick man," Coombs confessed that day, "so sick that more than one doctor gave me up. I was determined to live and get back once again with the boys, and although the fight was a desperate one, I finally succeeded in coming out victor."[3]

15. The Year 1913

A victor, yes, but not unscathed by the ordeal. Coombs' recovery to the point where he could once again compete in professional sport was a long time coming. When Coombs showed up in Philadelphia, he was once again predicting a comeback in the near future. He fully intended to pitch for the Athletics in September. To that end, he was working out on the field on September 1 when he collapsed and had to be rushed back to the hospital. Coombs did not leave the hospital again until after the season was over. In an act of generosity, Connie Mack kept Coombs on the team's payroll all season.

Mack coaxed some good work out of the majority of those seemingly spare-parts pitchers. For years he had relied on a Big Three of Plank, Bender and Coombs, who at various times had been supported by Rube Waddell and Cy Morgan at his best. During this time period, spaces on big league rosters were precious commodities, and pitchers were routinely overworked. Once a man was designated as a starter, he basically remained a starter. Only injury normally would enable others to demonstrate their stuff.

However, this year, Mack trotted out a whole crew of short-time wonders, shopping for one major find. Such pitchers as John Taff, Ensign Cottrell, Charlie Boardman, Pat Bohen and Dave Morey made cameo appearances so fleeting that if they had been appearing in a movie, they would likely have played uncredited war casualties on-screen for mere seconds. Taff made it into seven games and went 0–1 with a 6.62 earned run average. Only Cottrell, 1–0, recorded a winning record. He, Boardman and Morey made it to the mound only twice each for the A's. Bohen got into just one game.

Mack did not consider them keepers. That was the entirety of Taff's major league career. Cottrell, who had already pitched very briefly for two teams, spread his 12-game big league career amongst five clubs between 1911 and 1915. His Athletics victory was the only win of his career. Boardman was tried in two more games in 1914, then hooked on with the St. Cardinals, winning his only major league game with that club in 1915. Bohen pitched in one more game for Pittsburgh in 1914 and that was it for him. The 1913 games were the only ones of Morey's career.

It was a slightly different deal with Weldon Wyckoff. He pitched in 17 games with a 2–4 record, was back with the A's for a couple more stints after this season, and then later played for Boston, a major leaguer for parts of six seasons. Wyckoff must have showed potential, but Mack knew he couldn't count on him full-time in the rotation in 1913 if he wanted to win a pennant.

Unlike all of those others, Bush was already entrenched, even at age 20. Bullet Joe went 15–6.

Mack very much wanted to prove that the A's being nudged aside by the Red Sox in 1912 was a fluke. He had not anticipated the loss of Coombs, however. What he did to counter the uncertainty of his gang of young pitchers was to rely on Eddie Plank and Bender even more than usual. There was no such thing as pitch counts or, for that matter, innings barriers, in 1913. Managers often thrust starting pitchers back out on the mound after just two days' rest. What they did not very often do was take them out of games before nine innings were up and replace them with a fresh arm. The relief pitcher was almost non-existent at the time unless a field boss thought he needed to pinch-hit for the moundsman and was then forced to replace him on the mound.

What Mack chose to do was lean on Plank and Bender as more than just starters. Plank went 18–10 with a 2.60 earned run average. Bender went 21–10 with a 2.21 ERA. That was normal enough for the big guns. Bender pitched in 48 games and Plank pitched in 41 games. That was because Mack regularly used them out of the bullpen when one of the young pitchers was weakening.

The "save" in baseball, credited to a reliever who comes through at the end of the game to preserve a victory, was not implemented by major league baseball until 1969. Formal criteria for awarding a save were created by long-time baseball writer and historian Jerome Holtzman in 1960. Baseball statisticians have retroactively assigned saves to pitchers dating back more than a century. Although Plank and Bender went to their graves unaware of how much they had accomplished in that manner, their records now include saves. Plank saved four games in relief in 1913. Bender, in addition to his 21 wins, was credited with 13 saves. If it seemed as if those two hurlers were on the mound for a part of a game almost every day, there was good reason for that impression.

> Never in my career did I lean heavier on two pitchers than I did on Plank and Bender that season. Before I hardly was aware of it I found that I was starting a game with one of my young pitchers and finishing it with either one of my veterans. Substitution was almost a daily occurrence at a time when pitchers were not shifted as frequently as they are today. It did not seem that we had a juvenile curver who could go over two or three innings.[4]

There were a couple of major pitching success stories in 1913 from amongst the group of newcomers who had been briefly tested in 1912. Boardwalk Brown started 35 games, went 17–11 with a 2.94 ERA and threw 11 complete games. Byron Houck went 14–6, although his earned run average was an unsightly 4.14, especially for the Deadball Era.

Brown was a right-hander born in Woodbury, New Jersey, not much farther from Philadelphia than some of his teammates born in Pennsylvania. His name was Carroll William Brown on his birth certificate. Mack first became aware of Brown when he was playing sandlot ball in Atlantic City—hence the nickname Boardwalk.

Brown, just 24 that season, was one of the young pitchers Mack was addressing when he took the group aside and warned them what was to come during the season, being lifted at any time for another man. He told them not to take it personally. "Now I don't want any of you to feel bad, or to think I am not satisfied with your work in the box, if I suddenly take you out and put in another man," Mack said. "What I want you all to bear in mind is that we have a lot of capable pitchers right here and I want each of you to go at top speed and give us all you've got when you are in the box. If it is only for three innings, or only one, or even to one man, pitch your hardest."[5]

Fast-forward a century or so and that would be understood by pitchers. It's just that no one else was playing the game quite that way in 1913 besides Mack and the Athletics.

There were a couple of times when, as alien a concept as it may have seemed, Boardwalk Brown would have appreciated the hook a bit earlier. In April, when Mack was off scouting, he left Danny Murphy in charge of the team for an exhibition game and was appalled to learn that Murphy let Brown pitch 18 innings.

Once, during the regular season in a game against the Detroit Tigers, Brown walked 15 batters in seven and two-thirds innings. Even he must have been astonished to be left on the mound in the face of such erratic doings. Mack at last yanked him in the eighth inning. "I noticed he was slowing up in the eighth," Mack said, as if he had not noticed anything else amiss before that. "Any time you see a pitcher ease up in order to get the ball over the plate it's time he got out. It's no wonder, though, Brownie was slowing up. He pitched about four games out there this afternoon.[6]

The only problem with all of that was that by the end of the season, Brown was pitching with a sore arm. He blamed the 18-inning stint in April for his woes. He was never the same again, either, finished within a few seasons of this glory year.

The other young pitcher who got some serious work was Houck, who was only 21, just a year older than Bush. He did not pitch an insane number of innings, just 176. And he was important to the 1913 A's success, but he never had any more and was out of the majors after four years.

Shawkey was the intriguing story. He was just 22 in 1913 and, while his record of 6–5 was not distinguished, his earned run average of 2.34

was excellent. He blossomed the next year, but Mack couldn't figure out why he did not sustain his flourish of excellence and gave up on him too soon.

Although Coombs' sad condition forced Mack into making some of his unorthodox moves with his pitching staff, if he really believed the veteran A's had become complacent, he did make a few additional roster moves that affected the position players.

He pretty much felt that Murphy's main contributions from then on (notwithstanding the foolish move of keeping Brown in an exhibition game for 18 innings) were going to be assisting him on the bench in a coaching capacity and only sometimes getting out of the dugout as a backup.

Murphy had been a major contributor to several top-notch Philadelphia teams since 1902, but he turned 37 years old in 1913 and Mack did not feel he was any longer an everyday player. A broken kneecap had slowed Murphy the year before and probably permanently limited his maneuverability. Murphy appeared in just 40 regular-season games, but he did bat .322 when he was out there. Murphy was a fine all-around player, a good fielder and knowledgeable about the game, as well as a lifetime .289 hitter. Murphy was also renowned as an expert stealer of other teams' signs. Still, during that era, with that group of Athletics, he was overshadowed by other stars.

Danny Murphy was a reliable .300 hitter for Philadelphia, but when Eddie Collins came along he was shuttled from second base to the outfield because of the newcomer's fielding prowess (Library of Congress).

Although he was not a full-time starter in the outfield, playing in 94 games, Amos Strunk was still around and doing some damage. He hit .305. Rube Oldring was still patrolling the pasture of the outfield and hit .283. But the guys standing out there with him were new fellows. Eddie Murphy, 21, out of Villanova, batted .295 and stole 21 bases. He had earned respect from Mack the year before when

15. The Year 1913

he played in 33 games and hit .317 as a part-time rookie. He did his job in 1913, also accumulating a .391 on-base percentage and scoring 105 runs in 137 games. The other outfield regular was Jimmy Walsh, who played about the same amount as Strunk. Walsh made his major league debut in 1912 and hit .252 in 31 games as a 24-year-old. He hit about the same, .254, in 1913, and only once again in a six-year career hit that well again. Outfield slugging was not the Athletics' forte that season.

One thing that Mack did have going to for him was a motivated, intact $100,000 infield. Home Run Baker led the American League in four-baggers again in 1913 while driving in 117 runs and batting .337. Shortstop Jack Barry, who was almost always the weakest hitter in the A's lineup, batted a career-high .275. Collins was still Collins, hitting .337. And Stuffy McInnis at first base ripped the ball at a .324 clip, knocked in 90 runs and had a .382 on-base percentage.

Some question why McInnis is not in the Hall of Fame. In a 19-year career, he batted .307, topping .300 12 times including partial seasons. He collected 2,405 hits in 2,128 games. McInnis came to bat 8,637 times and struck out just 251 times.

He was such a terrific fielder, McInnis once handled 1,700 chances without an error, a record for a first baseman that lasted until 2008. He played on five World Series winners. In different seasons, McInnis recorded fielding averages of .996, .997 and .999. In 1921, when he posted that latter stat, McInnis made just one error all season in 152 games. That average remained the single-season American League record 95 years later. McInnis' lifetime fielding average was .991. During his playing days, even sharing the spotlight with such stars as Baker, Collins, Plank and Bender, McInnis was considered the most popular player with the Philadelphia fans.

There was one more new face amongst the position players. For years, Ira Thomas and Jack Lapp had pretty much platooned at catcher. Lapp played in 82 games in 1913, a typical season for him. In nine years in the majors, he never caught as many as 100 games in a season. By 1913, Thomas was running out of juice and played in just 22 games.

They had to reckon with another catcher whose skills showed he was ready for more playing time. Rookie Wally Schang was at the beginning of a 19-year career during which he batted .284, although many of his finest seasons were turned in for clubs other than the Athletics. Schang, who was born in South Wales, New York, was a switch-hitter. Eventually, Schang hit .300 or better six times, but he was just starting out with Philadelphia. Mack thought he was on to someone special when he signed

Schang, saying he was as proud of obtaining Schang as any player he brought to Philadelphia.

Schang was from a farming family and when he took up baseball had no plans to become a catcher. However, his brother Bob, the catcher in the clan, got injured, and Schang was inserted behind the plate in sandlot play. Schang was playing for a team called the Buffalo Pullmans when George Stallings, infamous later with Philadelphia fans for his handling of the Boston Braves, discovered his talent, though he ended up with the A's. Schang made his major league debut in May of 1913.

In an off-beat anecdote, when he was a young catcher, a bad dream Schang had in a hotel while visiting upstate New York on a bowling trip became legendary. Apparently, Schang had a very specific nightmare. He dreamt he was playing against the Detroit Tigers and their exceptional base stealer Ty Cobb. Schang's nightmare consisted making a play on Cobb only to have the star called safe.

Schang began bellowing in his sleep, "He's out! He's out! I touched him when he was two feet off the bag!" Schang, still supposedly napping, was sharing a room with his brother and grasped him around the neck in anger. Schang was so loud that other members of the bowling team broke down the door, demanding to see what was amiss. They perhaps rescued Bob from a nasty fate. Further explanation of the dream by Schang informed the curious that he was yelling about Cobb because he was worried about a double steal, and sure enough Cobb barreled in to the plate. "I was crazy and I guess I would have choked Bobby to death if you boys had not come into the room," Schang said. "It was one of the most real games I ever played."[7]

One thing Connie Mack could be sure of was that Wally Schang was going to give his all blocking the plate. On a less dramatic but more genuine note, one day in 1915 Schang threw out six base runners attempting to steal in one game against the A's.

The Athletics opened the 1913 season in Boston on April 10 against the Red Sox. Eddie Plank got the victory in a 10–9 game. The next day at Fenway Park, the A's won again, 5–4, and Plank got the win again. The same teams moved to Philadelphia for a fresh series and the A's won their third straight, with Joe Bush getting the victory. Philadelphia got off to a good April. The A's went 9–3 in the month, and Plank had three of the wins. Then Philadelphia got hot as May began, ripping off six wins in a row over the New York Yankees and St. Louis Browns.

With a 15–3 start, the A's were proving to Mack that they were not going to be complacent or lackadaisical again. It was not going to be 1912

15. The Year 1913

all over again. After that, several losses were mixed in until the A's put together a season-defining streak. On May 27, in the first game of a doubleheader, Plank shut out the Washington Senators, 8–0. The Athletics did not lose again until June 11. During that stretch, Philadelphia won 15 games in a row. At that point, the A's were 37–10, but had only a four-game lead in the American League standings.

The streak began with two victories over Washington, continued with four wins over New York, and then included two more wins over Washington. A four-game sweep of Detroit followed. The A's took three straight from the Browns before losing the fourth game of the series, 10–4. Bender won five of the 15 games.

Winning streaks of 15 games in baseball are not common. The only time the Athletics topped that number in franchise history was in 1931. Connie Mack had built a second juggernaut in that era, and the A's won 17 straight games that season between May 5–26.

The 15-game streak made a statement, but the A's couldn't take for granted that it gave them the AL pennant. The Red Sox had dominated in 1912. There was no reason to believe they would yield easily a year later. But they did. The setback to Smoky Joe Wood, who could not come close to replicating his 34–5 record of the previous season, helped ruin Boston's year. The Red Sox started slowly and replaced manager Jake Stahl after 80 games when the club was 39–41. They finished just 79–71 and placed fourth in the league.

The Washington Senators, who couldn't even get support in their hometown, were in the hunt. The Senators drew just 325,000 fans that year, even with a gate attraction like Walter Johnson. That season represented the pinnacle of greatness for the great Johnson. He went 36–7 with a 1.14 earned run average in 1913. The Senators weren't even hot yet. The Cleveland Indians were playing at a 35–15 clip and trailed the A's by three games on June 11.

Philadelphia didn't mess around this season. The team put on small bursts of winning ball to pull away steadily from the competition and hang on to first place. The A's had another four-game winning streak in late June, won another four straight between the last day of the month and the first week in July and mixed in two additional three-game winning streaks in that month. Two four-game winning streaks in August and another in September kept the A's out front. The one stumble at the very end of the season was a six-game losing streak when Mack relied on several of those young pitchers. Boardman twice, Shawkey, Wyckoff, Bohen and Houck all took losses.

In a season where the A's outscored the opposition by more than 200 runs, 794 to 592, they spent just four days of the regular season out of first place and never again dropped as low as second after April 23. There may have been more of a juggling act with personnel than in the other recent successful years, but Philadelphia had returned to the top of the American League in 1913. It was a satisfying achievement for Mack, especially with a creatively functioning pitching staff.

The Athletics' record was 96–57. Washington finished 90–64 and Cleveland 86–66. The Red Sox finished 15½ games behind in fourth place.

Even more dominating in the National League were the good old New York Giants. John McGraw's club had its way with their foes, finishing with a 101–51 record. The Philadelphia Phillies took second place with an 88–63 mark. The Chicago Cubs also won 88 games but had 65 losses.

Many of the Giants' usual suspects remained in the lineup, including John Meyers, Fred Merkle, Larry Doyle, Art Fletcher (now a starter), and Fred Snodgrass. Tillie Shafer was in at third base and hit .287. George Burns, a new outfielder, batted .286.

The same anchors held down the pitching responsibility. Christy Mathewson was 32, but hardly over the hill after going 25–11 with a 2.06 earned run average. Rube Marquard, at 23–10 and 2.50, was his usual self. Doc Crandall, Red Ames and Hooks Wiltse were lesser contributors, but two new starters had taken spots in the rotation since the 1911 World Series. Al Demaree went 13–4 with a 2.21 ERA, and Jeff Tesreau was the new stud on the staff with a 22–13 mark and a 2.17 earned run average. The Giants did not score as much as the Athletics did in 1913, but the pitching staff allowed fewer runs with 515.

Demaree was a 28-year-old right-hander born in Quincy, Illinois, who had just an eight-year, big league career with 80 victories. The 1913 campaign was one of his best. The preceding July, the Giants had obtained him from Mobile of the Southern Association for $7,000. That was after the St. Louis Browns and Detroit Tigers passed on Demaree. They didn't realize his spitter was going to be so effective, a late addition to his repertoire.

Although his name was really Charles, Tesreau was called "Big Jeff," at least partially because he stood 6-foot-2 and weighed 218 pounds in an era when that was roughly equivalent to 6-7 and 250 pounds today. He could have been Big Charles or Big Chuck, but a sportswriter gave him the other label when he was still in the minors.

Tesreau threw right-handed and made a big impact instantly upon arrival in the bigs in 1912. As a rookie at 24, Tesreau went 17–7 for the

Giants with a National League-leading earned run average of 1.96 and also pitched a no-hitter. In 1913, Tesreau started 38 games, the most in the league. He was still on his way up, even better in 1914 with a 26–10 mark and a league-leading 41 starts and eight shutouts.

Although Tesreau's career was over by the time he was 31 with 119 victories and a 2.43 ERA, he was on top of the world as the World Series beckoned after the Giants copped the 1913 pennant. Tesreau departed the majors in the middle of the 1918 season after an argument with McGraw, saying he would never play for the Giants again. McGraw refused to trade him. It was a strange way to go out. Tesreau retired to become the long-time baseball coach at Dartmouth and at one time expanded to more than 300 pounds in girth. "It looks like the job might be permanent," Tesreau teased after 26 years as the Ivy League school's coach.[8]

That was a problem for the future, though. At the moment, in the fall of 1913, Tesreau was Connie Mack's problem.

16

The 1913 World Series

When the New York Giants clinched their third straight pennant in 1913, it was acknowledged that John McGraw had assembled a powerhouse. McGraw liked to go around saying that he had the best baseball team in the world. But for all of their National League muscle flexing, New York had been defeated in the previous two World Series, first by the Athletics and then by the Boston Red Sox.

While the fact that the Giants did monopolize the NL was indisputable, it wasn't as sexy to go around boasting that they were the second-best team in the world. McGraw dearly wanted to capture this Series championship. So did Mack after his team's letdown of 1912. The Red Sox were at last in the rearview mirror, smarting from their so-so season, the firing of Jake Stahl and the health problems of Smoky Joe Wood.

On deck were the Giants. The way Connie Mack juggled his pitching staff to get through the 1913 regular season might not work best in a short series against New York. Clearly, fans believed, Eddie Plank and Charles Bender would get as many starts as was practical. The hope for A's rooters was that those two would pitch complete games. Once the Series unfolded, it appeared that Mack pretty much agreed with the supporters. He wasn't ready to trust Byron Houck with a start and not even Herb Pennock or Bob Shawkey, who seemed on the cusp of stardom.

Mack burned to win as much as McGraw, although he was a bit calmer about the way he went about it and less acerbic in public utterances. The gratification of World Series victory was not so far in the past that the glow had worn off. Mack remembered how it felt to be a winner, to be celebrated by the team's home community, to be feted at banquets. He was not the kind of man who generally thrived on such showiness, but it was symbolic. For two years, 1910 and 1911, quite recently, he had managed the greatest ball club in the world. He wouldn't mind hearing others say that about his Athletics once again.

16. The 1913 World Series

New York and Philadelphia had met in the Series in 1905 and 1911. The Giants won it all the first time, the A's the second time. There had been much roster turnover between 1905 and 1913, but one intriguing angle to the showdown was that Eddie Plank was still there pitching for Philly and Christy Mathewson was still there pitching for the Giants. Between them they won 699 games in the majors, 373 by Matty and 326 by Eddie. In the modern, multimedia era, one can only imagine what level of attention would be focused on such a World Series match-up.

It was not an everyday match-up to see two such accomplished winners going head to head. In the modern era, when fewer pitchers even have the prospect during their careers of hitting the 300-win plateau because they are relieved by the bullpen much more frequently, start on five days' rest instead of four or three, and are not asked to pitch complete games, the likes of Plank versus Mathewson in the Series is unlikely to be seen again.

One might be tempted to say that the duo's victory total was exceeded by only Cy Young against another veteran hurler. Young's career covered a dozen years before the World Series began, but he did pitch in the inaugural one in 1903. Young ended up with 511 victories. Deacon Phillippe, his Pittsburgh Pirates counterpart in 1903, concluded his career with 189, giving them 700 wins between them, or one more than the Plank-Mathewson duo. Young and Phillippe faced one another twice in that Series won by Boston. Also, Young started another game, this one against Brickyard Kennedy, who won 187 games in his major league career.

The Senators' Walter Johnson won 417 games, but during his lengthy career his club reached just two World Series, in 1924 against the Giants and 1925 against the Pirates. In his first Series game ever, Johnson went up against Art Nehf and his 184 wins, then faced Jack Bentley (46 wins) twice. In 1925, Johnson met Lee Meadows (188 wins), Emil Yde (49 wins) and Ray Kremer (143 wins).

Although many players on the Giants' roster were well-known to the A's from recent confrontations, there was one additional man on the club that year that was well-known for things beyond baseball. Although this sport was not his best, there was still room for Jim Thorpe. The man who was eventually voted the greatest athlete of the first half-century in 1950 won the Olympic decathlon at the 1912 Summer Olympics in Sweden, was a tremendous football star later enshrined in the Pro Football Hall of Fame in Canton, Ohio, and he also dabbled in major league baseball.

There were suggestions that Thorpe, the first Native-American to win a gold medal for the United States, could do everything well in sports, and when confronted with any kind of challenge he pretty much proved it. That is, with the possible exception of hitting the curveball with regularity.

Born in Oklahoma in 1887, Thorpe later attended the Carlisle Indian School in Pennsylvania. Thorpe got into 19 games for the Giants in 1913. He played six seasons in the majors and batted .252 in 289 games. Thorpe's best season was his last, in 1919, when he hit .327 for the Boston Braves. Among his pro football teams in the early days of the National Football League were the Canton Bulldogs and the Oorang Indians.

Thorpe's roommate with the Giants was catcher John Meyers, a fellow Native American. He once recounted how emotional Thorpe became upon having his Olympic medals stripped from him because he had violated the strict amateurism rules of the day, even though he had made only a few dollars.

> Jim was very proud of the great things he'd done. A very proud man. Very late one night Jim came in and woke me up. He was crying and tears were rolling down his cheeks. "You know, Chief," he said, "the King of Sweden gave me those trophies. He gave them to me. But they took them away from me. They're mine, Chief. I won them fair and square." It broke his heart and he never really recovered.[1]

Thorpe had fans in many places and in many sports. As talented and adaptable as he was, track and field may have been his best sport. "He was the greatest athlete who ever lived," said Abel Kivat, 1912 Olympic silver medalist in the 1,500 meters for the U.S. "What he had was natural ability. There wasn't anything he couldn't do. All he had to see is someone doin' something and he tried it … and he'd do it better."[2]

Thorpe did not get into the World Series against the A's in 1913, but he did appear in a single game against the Chicago White Sox in 1917.

Series tickets cost $2, and the opener was scheduled for the Polo Grounds on October 7. There was huge demand for the ducats, with people standing in line in the street overnight waiting for the box office to open the next morning. It was estimated that thousands of would-be attendees were turned away when the sellers ran out.

Intriguingly, McGraw and Mack chose different starting pitchers for Game 1 than most people expected. They each held back, saving Plank and Mathewson for Game 2. Instead, the Giants went with Marquard and the A's went with Bender. While each man was a 20-game winner that season (Marquard won 23), neither player was at his sharpest for the opener before 36,291 fans. Most of the scoring was clustered in the middle innings.

16. The 1913 World Series

The Giants reached Bender first in the bottom of the third inning, pushing across a single run. Fred Merkle led off the inning with a single. Marquard bunted him to second. After a fly out to center, Larry Doyle singled to right to drive Merkle home.

The Athletics did not stay down for long. In the visiting half of the fourth, they retaliated with three runs. Eddie Collins, who had one of his best days ever in a World Series game, tripled as the leadoff man, rifling the ball to deep right-center. Home Run Baker settled for a single that didn't leave the infield but scored Collins anyway. The game was tied. Both Collins and Baker had Marquard's number this day, each stroking three hits. Baker collected three runs batted in. The A's were not finished that inning, either. A double by Jack Barry and a triple by Wally Schang sent two more runners home. It was 3–1 Philadelphia for the moment.

New York did nothing in the bottom of the fourth inning, but the A's continued to beat on Marquard in the fifth, piling on two more runs for a 5–1 lead. Collins walked, the perfect table-setting, and Baker belted a two-run shot, clearing the right field fence. The same two Athletics kept picking Marquard apart.

That was enough bad news for McGraw. He realized Marquard didn't have his best stuff and pinch-hit for the hurler in the bottom of the fifth inning after Merkle singled off Bender again. McGraw sensed the Giants might get something going, and he couldn't afford to wait around for Marquard to get in his groove. The choice of Moose McCormick to hit for Marquard worked out, McCormick singling. Doyle reached on an error, Art Fletcher singled, and a George Burns groundout scored a run. New York was back in it, trailing 5–4 as Doc Crandall relieved Marquard. Marquard was gone after allowing five earned runs. It was up to Crandall to cool off the A's.

In a rarity, Bender had some shaky moments, but as the game turned to the sixth inning, he was still leading. In the bottom of the sixth, it was three up and three down for the Giants. No threats.

In the top of the eighth inning, Philadelphia added another run, making it 6–4. Collins and Baker each singled again, and Stuffy McInnis promptly doubled. That was it for Crandall, McGraw replacing him on the mound with Tesreau. Tesreau got out of the jam, but although Bender permitted two singles in the New York seventh and one in the eighth, the Giants did not come close to scoring.

The only thing Tesreau yielded in the A's ninth was a walk. Bender did him one better, wiping out the Giants on three straight batters. Game 1 went to Philadelphia. "Two men beat us yesterday—Baker and Collins,"

Doyle said. "Somebody told us they couldn't hit left-handers. I wonder what left-handers they have been facing."[3]

Marquard actually accepted the blame rather forthrightly, saying he was too on edge emotionally and too wild on the mound, not bringing his best control up against the batters. He did walk only one, though, so he must have been referring to pitch placement. "I alone lost the first game for the Giants," he said. "I make no apologies or alibis. If I had had control, we would have won the game."[4] And maybe if Eddie Collins and Frank Baker had stayed home.

Although Bender did allow 11 hits, Mack noted that he had only been hit hard in one inning. That was the fifth, and Bender improved once he survived that shaky frame.

With Bender on the mound for Philadelphia, Thorpe on the bench for New York and Meyers behind the plate for New York, it was remarked upon that this was the first time three Native Americans were competing for a World Series title. Although history would prove him wrong since the game never quite took hold in the manner he anticipated amongst Native Americans, Meyers made a thoughtful observation that seemed promising for the moment. "If my race continues to devote the same attention to the diamond game that it has in the past few years, there will soon be a pretty large tribe in organized baseball," Meyers said. "The national pastime has opened a profession to the Indian in which he can best employ those natural senses that centuries of life in the open have endowed him with."[5]

Meyers did overlook the fact that both he and Bender had been bestowed with the same nickname, "Chief," because of their heritage. Depending on who was doing the talking, that was either a derogatory appellation or it was complimentary, if condescending. While there have been quite a few prominent players with Native American blood, the nation's first peoples never did challenge for overall supremacy in the game. Beside the trio of players who overlapped in this Series, some other well-known Native American baseball contributors include Louis Sockalexis, Jacoby Ellsbury, Allie Reynolds, Rudy York, Joba Chamberlain and Zack Wheat.

Game 2 provided the mound match everybody wanted to see, Plank for Philly, Matty for New York. This was the fourth year Mathewson would pitch for the Giants in a World Series and the third Series for Plank. Although the location shifted to Shibe Park in Philadelphia, no travel day was provided for, so the second game was on October 8. The contest did not draw nearly as well as the first game did in New York, with just over 20,000 people in the park. Shibe was smaller, but it wasn't filled.

16. The 1913 World Series

The Giants were desperate for a win. They feared falling behind, 2–0. But they couldn't have found a better hurler to count on than Mathewson, New York fans figured. Everyone remembered those three brilliant shutouts he tossed against the Athletics in 1905. They tended to forget that his Series record had not been quite as good since. Of course, that would have been virtually impossible. When Mathewson lost in a World Series, it seemed it was mostly because of a bad break or because his mates did not score for him. It was not because he got hit hard. His lifetime World Series earned run average was 0.97, yet he somehow lost five games. Just the year before against Boston, Mathewson went 0–2 in the Series, but with an ERA of 0.94.

This Plank-Mathewson showdown was a doozy. Inning after inning passed with the pitchers baffling the hitters. One, two, three innings gone by for Plank against the visitors. Nothing doing on the scoreboard. One, two, three innings gone by for Mathewson. All zeroes. The same again in innings four through six on both sides. They continued to battle, throwing their best stuff, setting the best hitters down. They repeated the performance one after another again in innings seven, eight and nine. Plank and Mathewson had a double shutout going.

A long-distance view of the action during Game 2 of the 1913 World Series between the A's and the New York Giants at Shibe Park on October 8, 1913 (Library of Congress).

It wasn't as if the pitchers were in much jeopardy, either. The A's got a man to third base in the first inning. They advanced a man to second in the fourth inning. Philadelphia got a single with no advancement in the fifth and seventh, but generated a little bit of excitement with two singles in the eighth. Two singles and two fielder's choices produced no score in the bottom of the ninth, when the A's might well have sensed victory.

The Giants managed two base-runners in the third inning, their first off Plank. An error put a man on in the fourth, but a caught stealing ended that inning. New York put two men on with a single and a walk in the fifth. Plank kept the bases clear in the sixth, seventh and eighth innings. Two New Yorkers reached base in the ninth, but didn't get anywhere.

Hungry for a bottom of the ninth inning win, the A's got the crowd revved up when Amos Strunk and Jack Barry singled. So it was two men on, nobody out—and the rally fizzled. Strunk made it to third base, and when Jack Lapp slapped a grounder to first base, he ran for it. Hooks Wiltse, who had replaced the injured Fred Snodgrass, threw him out at the plate, catcher Larry McLean tagging Lapp. On the play, Barry raced to third. Rather remarkably, the next play was almost identical. Plank, periodically an okay hitter, batted for himself. Plunk hit another ground ball to Wiltse, who picked it up as Barry sought to end the game by attacking the plate. Barry, too, was tagged out.

Mack took some heat from sportswriters who wondered why he did not pinch-hit for Plank. It's doubtful that anyone foresaw a double fielder's choice scenario with two men thrown out at the plate, but that's what happened, and Mack got testy when he was criticized for letting Plank stay in the game. "That's your job," Mack responded to writers. "That's what your paper pays you for, to criticize these days. Now go ahead and do it and don't ask me to help you."[6]

Nobody would have said a word if the A's had scored a run in the ninth and avoided extra innings. Plank would have been the hero of the day for his superb pitching. The failure of the Athletics to convert one of those chances may well have exhilarated the Giants. They jumped on Plank immediately in the tenth, spotlighting the A's coming up short in the ninth. McLean singled to right. Eddie Grant pinch-ran for McLean. Grant moved to second on a sacrifice bunt, and then Mathewson hit for himself, too. His single to left-center scored Grant. An ill-timed error put Buck Herzog on base, and then Plank hit Doyle with a pitch. Fletcher singled, and before the inning ended New York was up, 3–0. The A's had one more chance, but Mathewson never let them sniff a convenient pitch, retiring three straight. The 3–0 score was the way it stayed, and the result tied the Series.

Back the teams went to the Polo Grounds for Game 3 without a day off, scheduled to play on October 9. The Internet is regarded as the speediest form of communication man has invented, sometimes resulting in email exchanges seconds apart. In 1913, long before the computer age, when games were yet to be broadcast on radio or shown on television, the impact of the daily newspaper stories was surprisingly swift. Before Game 3, Mack said he was the recipient of more than 100 demeaning telegrams "from fans advising me to resign as manager because I was no longer capable of handling a ball team. Most of these messages came collect."[7]

After using the heck out of his top two pitchers to start the World Series, Mack had to come up with a fresh face to succeed Plank and Bender for Game 3. His choice was Joe Bush, who as a 15-game winner had produced as well as than any of the other hurlers during the regular season besides Boardwalk Brown. But Brown's arm was ailing. This could be a tipping point game in the Series, and McGraw, who liked the way Tesreau looked in relief in Game 1, selected him to start Game 3 at the Polo Grounds.

Spitball or not, the Athletics seemed not at all intimidated by Big Jeff, perhaps because they had seen him throw before, or just because the batsmen came ready to swing. For either reason, Philadelphia pounced on Tesreau from the game's start. The top of the order was particularly unfriendly as the A's rung up three runs right away. The A's made it seven men deep into the batting order in the first inning, likely dizzying Tesreau with developments and driving McGraw wild.

Leadoff hitter Eddie Murphy started with a groundout (although he would get two hits this day). Rube Oldring singled, Eddie Collins singled and Frank Baker singled. Oldring scored on Baker's hit. No doubt alert to any distraction or frustration exhibited by Tesreau after this unnerving start, the A's promptly threw on a double steal with Collins going to third and Baker grabbing second. Their advancement into scoring position was critical. After Stuffy McInnis struck out, Amos Strunk reached on an error, by Fletcher and both Collins and Baker scored. In later years they called that "small ball." But small ball was the way of life in the Deadball Era, and the A's had just manufactured three runs with speed and by taking advantage of the opponent's mistakes.

The Giants had nothing to offer at the plate, and the A's came right back and added to the lead with two more runs in the second inning. Three singles and another stolen base brought home the additional scores.

Collins drove in Murphy and Oldring. Collins was on his way to a three-hit, three-RBI, two-run game. Oldring scored three times, Baker had two hits and two runs batted in, and Tesreau was reeling.

Meanwhile, Bullet Joe Bush, just 20 years old, was living up to his nickname and reinforcing Mack's faith in him. The Giants, who collected just five hits in the game, finally reached Bush for a run in the fifth inning. Larry McLean knocked in Red Murray with the run, but two stolen bases also factored into the threat against Bush. Mostly, expect for rare lapses, Bush was throwing bullets.

It was a big stage for Bush to perform on with his minimal experience and with his youth possibly showing through. McGraw and right-hand man Wilbert Robinson talked trash incessantly. Robinson, a teammate of the Giants' boss with the old Baltimore Orioles, and later manager of the Brooklyn Dodgers, hoped to shake up Bush. Bush looked worried for a moment in the first inning after Doyle singled and he plunked Art Fletcher with a pitch. There were two men on, but they weren't going anywhere. Bush escaped the inning without any damage, except perhaps to his hearing.

The gentlemanly side of Mack made him usually refer to players by their formal, given names rather than their more down-to-earth, ball park nicknames. He called Bender "Charles" or even "Albert." This time he called Bush by his birth certificate name of Leslie. "That's the boy, Leslie," Mack said after the inning. "Nothing to it now."[8] That might have been an oversimplification, but apparently Bush relaxed after the mini-crisis and pitched the way he was capable of for the rest of the day.

The Athletics stretched their lead to 7–1 in the top of the seventh inning. Murphy picked up his second hit, Oldring forcing him at second but scoring on a Collins triple. Baker followed with a single and presto, there were two more runs to make things easy for Bush. He did allow a second Giants run in the bottom of the inning, though, when Tillie Shafer doubled and Murray singled. McGraw had given up on Tesreau before the end of the A's seventh, lifting him for Doc Crandall. The Athletics greeted Crandall rudely in the eighth when Wally Schang ripped a solo home run.

Bush went the distance and Philadelphia won, 8–2, to go ahead two games to one in the Series, with the championships returning to Shibe Park for Game 4 on October 10. Once again there was no day of rest between games.

Al Demaree was John McGraw's Joe Bush that season. He was the man chosen to fill in between Marquard and Mathewson with the hope he could stave off the Athletics' surge. Trailing two-one in games, the Giants very much needed a victory. Demaree was older than Bush at 28, but he was no more experienced since he also broke in during the 1912 season. This was his chance to solidify his reputation and ensure his future with the Giants. Although he had his moments over the rest of his career, it turned out that the 1913 season was Demaree's high point in New York. It didn't help any that he was going up against Bender, the hurler Mack most wanted to use in a pinch.

Although this did not turn out to be one of Bender's best games, for the first six innings he completely controlled the Giants. He allowed just two singles through that point in the contest. Meanwhile, the A's were mistreating Demaree, although not through the bats of the Series' early run producers. Philadelphia scored one run in the second inning, three runs in the fourth and two more runs in the fifth. Demaree departed after the fourth in favor of Marquard, but he too was at the mercy of a slick A's offense.

On a day when Collins and Baker each went oh-for-four, the rest of the lineup took over and made things happen. McInnis ignited the offense with a single to lead off the bottom of the second inning. He moved to

Athletics ace Charles Albert "Chief" Bender is on the mound, preparing to pitch to Giants pinch-hitter Doc Crandall in Game 4 of the 1913 World Series (Library of Congress).

second on a sacrifice bunt by Amos Strunk and scored the game's first run on a double off the bat of Jack Barry.

The next onslaught came in the bottom of the fourth inning. Strunk, Barry, Schang and Oldring all singled, and a Giants error and a passed ball all helped propel them around the bases for three runs. Demaree was toast, and McGraw pinch-hit for him in the top of the fifth. Although New York worked Bender for a single and a walk in that inning, he got out of the jam without much trouble.

Marquard, who was unhappy about his first-game performance, was no more scintillating this time, promptly being touched for two more runs in the bottom of the fifth. All of his difficulties emerged after there were two outs, too. Strunk walked, Barry doubled, and Schang, who had a tremendous day, drove both of them home with a single. He had two hits, knocked in four runs and scored a run in Game 4.

Until then the A's were on cruise control, Bender his usual self in charge. All of a sudden the complexion of the game changed in the Giants' half of the seventh. Finally, they reached Bender and began a gradual comeback. George Burns and Red Murray singled, which wasn't all that worrisome until Merkle blasted a three-run homer to left field. That gigantic A's lead was not looking quite as secure at 6–3.

The Giants also weren't quitting. Whether Bender was wearying, or new optimism seized the New York batting order, the eighth inning more resembled the seventh than Bender's mastery in the first six innings. Buck Herzog singled, but two groundouts put Bender into commanding position to get out of the inning without damage. He did not. A Burns double brought home Art Fletcher, and Shafer followed with a triple. The A's pain eased there after two New York runs, but suddenly it was a one-run game.

All Bender had to do was to hold on for one more inning. In the 2000s, a manager would have taken him out before that and absolutely would not have let him come out to pitch the ninth inning. But Bender stayed in. It was his game to win or lose. In Mack's mind, he had seen Bender come through so many times he had to figure the odds were with him to get three more outs without surrendering a run.

McGraw sent in pinch-hitters twice in the top of the ninth, but Bender, vindicating Mack's belief (he didn't want any more telegrams telling him he couldn't manage), breezed through the side, one, two, three. The A's won, 6–5, and with victories in three of the four games played were in striking distance of another world championship. This was the pins-and-needles and bite-your-nails game for Athletics fans.

As the scene shifted to the Polo Grounds on October 11, again with

16. The 1913 World Series

no day off in the Series, all of the pressure was on the Giants to salvage something with a win. All of the momentum was with the Athletics. Naturally enough, with everything on the line, McGraw went back to Mathewson. Similarly, Mack sent out his well-rested Eddie Plank.

The great Mathewson did his best, but it wasn't good enough this day. The A's didn't exactly light him up, but with Plank pitching with the same authority he showed in Game 2, simply scratching out one run loomed as a difference maker.

The Polo Grounds gang was probably shocked when Philadelphia reached Mathewson for a run in the opening frame. Eddie Murphy led off the game with a single. Oldring bunted, but New York gunned down Murphy with Oldring safe at first. A Collins single sent Oldring scurrying to third, and Baker brought him in on a sacrifice fly for the 1–0 lead.

Even more surprising to the suddenly quieted fans, the A's added two more runs in the third inning. There were no big clouts, but Murphy again started things off with a single. This time Oldring reached on an error. A Collins bunt moved both of the runners ahead to second and third. This was a common style of situational baseball at the time. Surveying the lay of the land, Frank Baker stepped in. His single scored Murphy, and McInnis' sacrifice fly scored Oldring. The game was only a third old and Philadelphia led, 3–0.

Meanwhile, Plank was mowing down all comers to the plate. He put down the side in order in the first, second, third, and fourth innings. With one out in the fifth, after the first 13 Giants were retired, Shafer received a base on balls for his team's first base-runner. An A's error and a single by McLean produced a New York run. It was 3–1 Athletics halfway through the game.

Though no one knew it, that was pretty much it. No more runs scored. The only other hit off of Plank was a single by Mathewson in the sixth (and he was erased on a double play). Mathewson allowed just one more single, too. If Mathewson was thought to be invincible, the A's proved otherwise. He was still a star, but human after all.

The Philadelphia Athletics disposed of the New York Giants in five games. Baker batted .450, Collins hit .421 and Schang hit .357. For the third time in four seasons, the A's were World Series champions. The result made Connie Mack the first manager to win three World Series.

It was after this World Series that Mack gave Bender a $2,500 bonus to pay off the mortgage on his house.

The city of Philadelphia was prepared to throw another party to fete the Athletics. However, the 13-year-old son of A's mainstay Harry Davis died suddenly, of no known cause, just a few days after playing ball on the field at Shibe with his dad and teammates. Naturally, Davis and his wife were crushed, but so were the players who knew the lad. The members of the $100,000 infield served as pallbearers. Plank called off a celebration in his honor in Gettysburg. The Philadelphia's A's celebration was postponed until October 28.

17

The Federal League Forms

As giddy Philadelphia Athletics and their fans reveled in capturing the 1913 World Series over the New York Giants (the brash opponent likely making it even more satisfying), the baseball world of the American League and National League was quietly being undermined.

It would also not be very long before the world at large would undergo much more seismic shifts, as a by-product affecting major league baseball, too. By the middle of the 1914 season, World War I would be under way, and eventually it would dramatically change elements of the sport. But that lay a little while in the future.

The major element confronting the established big leagues was the creation of the Federal League, a third professed major league, formed to compete against the AL and the NL and determinedly willing to fight in the trenches by stealing established players from those leagues.

To a large extent, the American and National Leagues ignored the Federal League in 1913 when it was starting up as a minor league, but that approach did not last long. While most average baseball fans are likely unaware of any other big league in the past, since all they have known for a century has been the AL and NL, in 1913 the American League was just a dozen years old. And baseball historians do categorize the statistics and records of selected other competing leagues from the 19th century as big league. So if it seems foolhardy to the uninitiated, the Federal League could draw upon precedent without thinking it was embarking on a hopeless mission.

The history of professional baseball in the United States dates to 1869, when the Cincinnati Red Stockings were formed and became the first touring team on which players were paid for their performances. They were true pioneers and included such key individuals as brothers Harry Wright and George Wright, both of whom were selected for the Hall of Fame.

The National League commenced business in 1876. Two teams established in that year, the same year of General George Armstrong Custer's last stand in Montana grasslands, remain active in different forms today. The Boston Beaneaters evolved into the Boston Braves, transferred to Milwaukee and are currently the Atlanta Braves. The Chicago White Stockings became the Chicago Cubs. That's some longevity. In 1883, the New York Gothams, forerunners of the New York Giants, now San Francisco Giants, were organized. The Philadelphia Phillies also began play that year.

In 1882, the American Association was founded to compete with the National League. That league played ten seasons, dissolving after 1891. No doubt Federal League founders were encouraged by the Association's somewhat successful run. Some members of the league were the St. Louis Browns (though that Browns club became the St. Louis Cardinals), an earlier Philadelphia Athletics, the Pittsburgh Alleghenys, who eventually became the Pirates, and the Cincinnati Red Stockings, who are the modern-day Cincinnati Reds.

Another fledgling league called the Union Association gave it a go in 1884. Henry V. Lucas of St. Louis was the impetus behind the establishment of this league, and he ran the St. Louis Maroons. Lucas had inherited $1 million from his father and wanted to spend some of his fresh cash in this manner. Some of the other teams in that ill-fated proposition were the Wilmington (Delaware) Quicksteps, the Altoona (Pennsylvania) Mountain Citys, the Kansas City Cowboys and the St. Paul (Minnesota) Apostles (who also went by Saints). The league was in trouble almost from the moment it formed. Lucas' St. Louis team won the championship, and then he produced a $2,500 franchise fee to join the National League, leaving the others behind, saints and sinners alike.

It was generally conceded that the Union Association was an inferior league since few of its alumni made an impact playing elsewhere after its demise. Fred Dunlap, who led the circuit in batting with a .412 average for St. Louis during that single season, was an exception. Dunlap, who also led the league with 13 homers, enjoyed a lengthy playing and managing career, and his lifetime average was .292. Historians also credit him with being the best second baseman of his time.

Some years after Dunlap's retirement, John Montgomery Ward, a Hall of Famer who was a pioneer labor activist for ball players in the Players' League, which followed the Union Association, wrote glowingly of him as a fielder. "Fred Dunlap was the king," Ward said. "[He] was the personification of ease and grace. He was something of a grandstand player

17. The Federal League Forms

because of his tendency to make one-handed catches and stops, but he got there just the same and was a big favorite wherever he showed."[1]

A group of unionized players created the Players' League in 1890. However, that league lasted just one season. Some well-known players competed in the Players' League, including Pete Browning. During his 13-year career, Browning batted .341 and won three batting titles, two of them in the American Association, the other in the only year of the Players' League's existence. Browning, who was from Louisville, Kentucky, and spent most of his career with the Louisville Eclipses, gained the nickname "The Louisville Slugger." He is regarded as the first player to have his bats personally made and was the inspiration for the Hillerich & Bradsby Company in Louisville to begin manufacturing baseball bats in the 1880s.

Roger Connor was a large-for-his-time first baseman and third baseman at 6-foot-3 and 220 pounds, and a power hitter when practically no one else was. When Connor retired after 18 seasons, he had clouted 138 home runs. It was Connor's career record that Babe Ruth broke. Connor was chosen for the Hall of Fame in 1976.

Ward the player batted .275 in 17 seasons as an infielder, but for the first seven years of his career he was also a pitcher who won 164 games, threw a perfect game in 1880 and won 47 games in 587 innings with the Providence Grays in 1879 when he started 60 games.

After attending Columbia University, Ward went to law school at Penn State and became an attorney. He was in on the ground floor of the Players' League, encouraging players to defect from the National League and American Association. The Players' League had a profit-sharing plan for those on the roster and notably had no reserve clause binding a player to one team. Ward was way ahead of his time in attempting to abolish the reserve clause. Ward also became a Hall of Famer in 1964.

Given its brief existence, the Players' League was influential, but the National League outlasted both that organization and the more stable American Association. The American League was better funded and had more staying power. Once the AL arrived on the scene in 1901, it was not going anywhere. Since the Players' League and American Association had been run out of business, it was easy for the AL and the NL to think that the Federal League should not be taken seriously either. As for the founders of the Federal League, they could take heart from the decade-long challenge of the American Association or could look at the Players' League and see how easy it would be to fail.

There were, however, some men with money who were willing to bet on the endeavor that the United States needed more baseball and was ready to accept and embrace it. In fact, quite a few of them were waving cash around. A United States Baseball League was formed in 1913, but lasted about a week on the field. A second group had more success that year. More big league baseball—that's where chief founder John T. Powers was coming from. He set out to sell the concept of the Federal League.

Powers was a promoter who in 1912 started something called the Columbian League. That attempt to create a new baseball league failed without playing a single game. Powers was sidetracked when a key investor backed out, but he had sought out other money men who wanted to own baseball teams. The Federal League replaced the Columbian League in 1913.

That season, Powers served as league president. It was his baby, and he wanted to lead the assault on the existing major league clubs. Powers realized that he needed backers whose pockets were so deep that they didn't merely make deposits in banks, they told banks what to do. More or less, anyway. One such investor was Harry F. Sinclair, the founder of Sinclair Oil. Sinclair was a sports fan and viewed himself as a sportsman. In addition to taking this run at baseball team ownership, he was a prominent figure in thoroughbred racing, and some of his horses from the Rancocas Stable won Triple Crown races. One of those horses, Zev, won the Kentucky Derby and the Belmont Stakes in 1923. Sinclair's team in the Federal League was the Indianapolis Hoosiers (which moved to Newark in 1915).

Even in 1913, the Hoosiers had some talent. Edd Roush, the talented center fielder and future Hall of Famer, was on the club, and although his lifetime average was .323 it did not include statistics from that year because the Federal League was not judged to be a major league until 1914. Bill McKechnie, later a highly regarded manager, was still a player when he appeared with the Hoosiers that season.

Phil Ball, who made his money in ice at a time when American refrigeration was at a premium, operated the St. Louis Terriers in the Federal League. Besides the Hoosiers (the champs with a 75–45 record) and the Terriers, other teams in the Federal League in 1913 included the Pittsburgh Rebels, the Chicago Whales, the Cleveland Green Sox, and the Covington (Kentucky) Blue Sox. Covington surrendered its team in mid-season and became the Kansas City Packers.

Few of those teams are remembered at all today except for trivia buffs. But as with any new venture, there is always optimism at the start. Organizations do not begin with gloom on the mind, believing they are fated to fail. Neither did the Federal League. In fact, the Federal League under Powers took cautious baby steps initially. While the owners did field teams in 1913, they did not pretend they were of major league caliber at first. It was a get-the-feet-wet season. Big league leadership was aware of the Federal League, of course, but since it had not even proclaimed itself to be anything but a minor league, the newcomers were dismissed as an outlaw league.

At the time, baseball did not have a commissioner. The appointment of Judge Kenesaw Mountain Landis was to follow the Black Sox Scandal of 1920. The overseer of the game was the National Commission, a three-man body consisting of Ban Johnson, president of the American League, Garry Herrmann, president of the Cincinnati Reds, and Thomas Lynch, the National League president who was replaced late in the 1913 season by John Tener. Johnson and Herrmann said they weren't worried about the Federal League as long as its representatives did not sign players protected by the reserve clause. They would soon see how that turned out.

Cleveland Indians president Charles Somers had a different take on the upstarts. He was wary of the Federal League from the beginning. "We'd better give them real consideration right now, before this matter goes to a point where we'll be forced into some ugly position," Somers said.[2]

In 1913, the Federal League played a 120-game season. The teams had acquired enough ball players to compete, but at what level? That was uncertain. Even the honchos of the Federal League considered it to be more or less a practice league. It was like opening a play Off Broadway, far off Broadway.

Following the conclusion of the 1913 World Series, while the Athletics were celebrating, major league baseball embarked on a lengthy world tour. New York's John McGraw and Chicago White Sox owner Charles Comiskey colluded on the plan to bring baseball to far-off lands, make an international splash, and make some money, too, no doubt. They buttressed their own rosters with several other stars and, after barnstorming across the United States as a tune-up, climbed aboard ship to explore China, the Philippines, France, Egypt and other ports of call. The tour began in the fall and ran into the new year.

At the conclusion of the 1913 Federal League season, Powers was ousted as president, and James Gilmore of Chicago replaced him. Gilmore wanted the league to go big-time, as in big league. Forget this minor league stuff. Gilmore made the pronouncement that changed the landscape. The major change after this debut season was the manner in which the Federal League clubs sought talent. While acknowledging the reality that many of the players in the American League and National League were under contracts to their teams, Gilmore said it was well known that many others had played out their contracts and were only being protected by teams because of the reserve clause, held in limbo until they signed new deals.

To Federal League teams, Gilmore said, that meant those players without contracts were fair game, free to sign with anyone they wished. That's the way 1914 lined up, a war on the baseball front almost simultaneously sparked at the same time that the World War I conflagration ignited.

One of the first players to jump to the Federal League was Joe Tinker, a member of the Chicago Cubs' Tinker-to-Evers-to-Chance literary combination. Tinker had agreed to a contract extension managing Cincinnati, but then was fired. The Brooklyn Dodgers coveted his services and promised him $5,000 for the 1914 season. But Tinker wanted $10,000. When they reached an impasse, the Chicago Whales of the Federal League stepped up and made a three-year, $36,000 deal with Tinker as player-manager.

Soon enough, Tinker began recruiting big league players for the Federal League, even sending telegrams overseas to star players on the World Tour, urging them not to sign their 1914 contracts just yet.

One other development was bugging the majors in the fall of 1913. Dave Fultz, a former player who had even competed for the Athletics, went from playing pro football to major league ball to coaching the University of Missouri football team. He graduated from law school, became an attorney and then helped organize the Base Ball Players' Fraternity. One of the chief aims of that union was to abolish the reserve clause.

This played into the hands of the Federal League, although the reserve clause was not actually eliminated from major league baseball until 1975.

Fultz had numerous other demands for the owners to improve the conditions of players, but for the most part it wasn't until the 1960s, when Marvin Miller took over as executive director of the modern Players Association, that players gained equal footing with owners at the bargaining table.

How all of this potential turmoil would affect the World Series champion Philadelphia Athletics during the 1914 season, as they sought to win their fourth title since 1910, was an open-ended question. Connie Mack had favored the Players' League's existence when he was a player. He was a key character in the success of the American League in 1901. In both of those cases, he was on the side of the rebels. Now Mack was the establishment. When questioned as to how concerned he was about losing A's players to the Federal League in 1914, he told sportswriters he was not worried.

"There isn't a chance for any member of a championship outfit to desert to the outlaws," Mack said.³

Could he really be that naïve? Mack was a believer in loyalty and trust, and felt it was a two-way street with his players. He thought of the Federal League as an iffy proposition at best, so perhaps he could not envision any of his guys throwing away security with the Athletics.

At least one of Mack's players, however, went public with his support for the Federal League. Star second sacker Eddie Collins recognized that if the Federal League succeeded, the competition for players would likely result in across-the-board salary increases. "Personally, I would like to see the undertaking a success," Collins said, "as I think it would aid the player in the long run. Whatever happens, the player has everything to gain and nothing to lose."⁴

What Connie Mack did not anticipate was that the Federal League would become one of the biggest headaches of his long tenure running the Athletics. As the 1914 season approached, he could not have foreseen a future that would dramatically alter his fortunes, create complete upheaval within his team, and propel him into making some of the most drastic personnel moves of his life. The series of moves he made, mostly because of the rise of the Federal League, would be remembered forever, dissected and analyzed by historians and despised by Athletics fans.

18

The Year 1914

The principals were the same, with some minor shifts in the lineup and some pitchers coming of age.

That was the way the Philadelphia Athletics looked on paper at the beginning of the 1914 regular season. Connie Mack's club, winners of three of the last four World Series, was still loaded. There also seemed to be able replacements who gained experience in 1913 and moved smoothly into full-time roles the next year.

Nothing ever goes exactly as planned during a long baseball season. Surprise showings of age and unexpected injuries can derail even the best of teams. Mack had been wise to integrate some younger players into his lineup gradually and especially in 1913, so when he needed several of them the next season, they were already seasoned.

With a team earned average of 2.78, the A's allowed only 529 runs in 158 games that season, the front-line pitchers either doing what they always had done or the younger ones now being counted on to fulfill their promise. The one exception was poor Boardwalk Brown, so important in 1913, whose arm seemed so used up after that season that he finished 1-5 in 1914.

Jack Coombs was still sidelined after his bout with typhoid fever, not ready to resume arduous, full-time athletic work just yet. His body had been weakened far more than either he wanted to believe or acknowledge. There was much chatter about whether he would ever again play big league ball. Coombs had wanted to return to the A's in time for the 1913 World Series, but was disappointed when his body let him down. He was 31 years old in 1914 and desperately wanted to resume his career as one of the key arms for Philadelphia. His attitude over the winter was simple and straightforward.

"Will I play with the team next year?" Coombs said of 1914. "If God gives me the strength I will. The rest has done me worlds of good. And

18. The Year 1914

let me whisper this softly. I feel that I could clout a ball from here to next week."[1] The more compelling question was whether he could throw a ball 60 feet, 6 inches with authority. Doctors predicted by June that he would be able to, and that's what Coombs set his sights on. It was not clear exactly whether Mack thought this was possible, but in reality, although Coombs, who spent his free time scouting for the A's, was around and available, he was not counted on by Mack. Mack had plenty of healthy pitchers, and he only used Coombs in two games that season, in the waning days of September. Coombs finished 0–1 on the year.

One can only wonder whether Mack truly had Coombs' best interests at heart, or his belief that Coombs was not yet his old self mattered less because the A's did not need him back in 1914 for them to win.

Mack was optimistic from the start and after a sluggish start, including losses in their first three games, the A's began to click. A 12-game winning streak in July began putting distance between the Athletics and other American League clubs. "We started off with a mighty flourish and headed

Left to right, members of the 1914 Philadelphia Athletics: Billy Orr, Herb Pennock, Weldon Wyckoff, Bullet Joe Bush, Bob Shawkey and Amos Strunk. The A's won the American League pennant that season, but lost the World Series to the Boston Braves (Library of Congress).

for the pennant early in the season," Mack said. "In the first half of the race we were 12-to-15 games ahead. Everything pointed to us winning the championship without ever being challenged at any stage for the fight."[2]

It wasn't quite that easy for the A's. By July 21, they were 51–32 and led the standings by 4½ games. Their bulge did hit double figures, though, on August 10.

Mack spread the mound work around. For a time he had relied on a trio, Coombs, Eddie Plank and Charles Bender. This year he built the staff around Plank and Bender and turned loose the young pitchers who had seen limited action a year before. Plank showed his age a bit, but at 38 he still finished 15–7 with a 2.87 earned run average. Mack used Plank more judiciously than he had in 1913, when he also pitched often in relief. The difference now was that Mack trusted the young arms more than he had the year before.

In some ways, Bender, who turned 30, was never better, even though he too had his workload reduced. The veteran right-hander went 17–3 with a 2.26 ERA while starting just 23 games and appearing in 28. In fact, given the many innings thrown by Plank and Bender over the years, Mack used them cautiously during the first month-plus of the season because of cold temperatures.

Bender threw just 14 complete games and 179 innings in all that season, a puny amount by standards of the day. "I never asked to be taken out of a game," Bender said.[3] He meant ever.

One problem that Mack deflected with Bender and other members of the team was their feeling that they were underpaid by the standards of the sport and particularly given their accomplishments. Bender was not a vocal complainer, but he was disgruntled about that topic. He was paid $2,400 in 1914. "The greatest pitcher in the big leagues when working right," Mack said.[4]

Mack paid off his stars with flowery words to the sportswriters and to their faces. Such praise made them feel good, but not rich, and the annoyance was beginning to mount up.

So as usual as the 1914 season dawned, it was Bender-Plank 1-2, or Plank-Bender 1-2. Otherwise opportunity was available for the pitcher who could seize it. Bob Shawkey, Bullet Joe Bush, Weldon Wyckoff, Herb Pennock and Rube Bressler, just 19, thrust themselves into the picture. Mack gave them all a decent number of starts, though holding back a little bit for Bressler and Pennock, just 20, because of their ages. Mack was known as "The Tall Tactitian." While he hadn't grown any, he did have to pull off some intriguing tactics in 1914 in deploying his pitching staff.

Shawkey, then 23, had matured quite a bit from the erratic first impression he had made with the A's in training camp before making his 1913 major league debut. He depressed even himself when he couldn't find the plate. "I was wild as a mountain goat," Shawkey said, "and my fastball was whistling by the ears and ankles of the batters, while my curve kept breaking into the dirt."[5] He asked Bender for some pointers, and the ace who later became an expert pitching coach straightened Shawkey out.

Bush had already established himself in the rotation the year before and was solid again in 1914, going 17–13 with a 3.06 ERA. He was still just 21. Plank was the only aging pitcher on the staff, and he was more than counterbalanced by the youngsters' promise.

Pennock, like Shawkey, had the makings of a major star and would indeed fulfill that potential, although primarily elsewhere, not for Philadelphia. He was darned good when needed in 1914, though, during the A's hunt for the pennant. Pennock went 11–4 and also kept his earned run average low at 2.79.

Although less heralded and less well-remembered, Weldon Wyckoff turned in his best year at 11–7. In fact, 1914 was the highlight of his short career. A year later, in 1915, Wyckoff was a miserable 10–24, the latter number leading the American League in losses. He never again played a full season after that, gone from the majors by age 28 with a lifetime mark of 23–34. After he retired with the Boston Red Sox after being sparingly used, Wyckoff operated a taxi cab business in Williamsport, Pennsylvania.

Bressler was the surprise, and this was the beginning of an interesting major league career. Born in 1894 in Coder, Pennsylvania, Bressler was a southpaw. Earle Mack, Connie's son, found him for Philadelphia. In 1914, on limited experience, Bressler went 10–4 for the A's with a 1.77 earned run average. He started ten games and completed eight of them.

Despite that rather wondrous start, one that certainly bespoke of a good future on the mound, Bressler quickly faded as a pitcher, compiling a record of just 26–32 overall. The very next season, Bressler could not get anybody out. He finished 4–17 with a 5.20 ERA. For different reasons and with somewhat different results—although they were not bad— Bressler followed the example of Babe Ruth and switched to the field. In a career that he extended for 19 years with several teams, Bressler batted .301 as a first baseman and outfielder. Over three straight seasons in the 1920s, Bressler hit .347, .348, and .357 for the Cincinnati Reds.

Bressler did not agitate for the change, nor was he particularly comfortable making the switch to the outfield pastures at first. Sensing his unease, future Hall of Famer Edd Roush offered to help. "I'd never played the outfield," Bressler said. "Edd Roush said, 'Let me know if I can give you any tips.' That was pretty good, I thought—Roush merely the greatest outfielder in baseball asking if he could help a guy who's never played outfield before. There was plenty he could tell me."[6]

While for Bressler that was a comparative lifetime away career-wise, in 1914 Mack could be forgiven for thinking he had discovered another hot pitching prospect who could serve the A's for years.

When it came to making out the lineup card for the position players, Mack very rarely had to stretch his brain. If he had to make calculations to figure out which pitcher to rely on which day, there was no such problem with the other eight slots. Wally Schang had taken over the regular catching duties, as anticipated, and hit .287 even though his greater contributions were as a take-charge man behind the plate. There was remarkably little to choose between in the trio of regular outfielders. Amos Strunk, Eddie Murphy and Rube Oldring all hit between .272 and .277. They all drove in between 43 and 49 runs, and the fewest games any of them played was 119. Mack did not wear out many pencils making lineup changes in 1914.

Also, the $100,000 infield was intact (and boy, wouldn't those four guys have been thrilled to have their salaries add up to $100,000). Stuffy McInnis hit .314 at first base, Eddie Collins hit .344 manning second, and Frank "Home Run" Baker still operated at full speed at third and hit .319. Jack Barry was still slick at short, though he batted only .242, not that uncommon for him.

Larry Kopf, who played in just 37 games and hit just .188, was a substitute infielder. He weighed only 120 pounds when he signed his first professional contract, which may be why he didn't have much pop in the bat. As the all-around fill-in for the $100,000 infield, some clever newspapermen said the infield was worth $125,000 when Kopf was around. The value must have been placed on his fielding. He was a full-timer the next year while hitting only .225. Kopf performed better with his next team, Cincinnati. In fact, he was inducted into the Reds' Hall of Fame. Unlike some of the cameo Athletics of the season, Kopf's career did not peak in Philadelphia, and he was part of the 1919 Reds World Series champs.

Shag Thompson of Haw River, North Carolina, did not have a long career, but he did have a long life, and one of its highlights was spending three seasons in a Philadelphia A's uniform as a backup outfielder. Thompson, whose given name was James, shagged flies in no more than 17 games in a season, and his lifetime average was .203. But he appreciated being around such greats.

18. The Year 1914

Thompson was born in 1893 and lived to be 96 years old. He was the last surviving member of the 1914 A's, and he reveled in being asked about his stretch in the majors, even if he got into only 48 total games for Philadelphia. One favorite story was about facing Walter Johnson, a fate few wished on any hitter. In his commentary, Thompson comes off as the noble batsman, but inevitably fails against the Big Train. "Mack sent me up to hit for Bender one day against Johnson," Thompson said. "I fouled off 17 pitches before he struck me out on the 18th."[7]

There were some cup-of-coffee guys with the A's of 1914 besides Thompson, players whose careers lasted oh-so-few precious games in the bigs. One of those was Billy Orr, a backup infielder. He had been around for 30 games the year before and batted .194. He appeared in only ten games in 1914 and hit .167. And that was the end. That may have been a dream fulfilled for Orr, those brief appearances in the majors. But he did not disappear from baseball. He also played in the Pacific Coast League and coached the Stanford University baseball team. Known for his assistance with the local Northern California Little League where he lived, Orr was called upon to throw out the first pitch for the kids each season.

In all, 16 other players competed in fewer games for the A's in 1914 than Orr. The most prominent among them was coach Ira Thomas, the former regular, who was used on the field by Mack in two games, former star Harry Davis, who showed up in the box score five times, and Mack's son Earle, who got into two games.

There were also some players whose careers were so short that Connie Mack probably didn't even remember their names. Press Cruthers was on the A's roster for two seasons and played seven games total. Chick Davies was a rookie in 1914 and played in 19 games with a .239 average. Given more playing time a year later, he could muster only a .178 batting average. He then disappeared from the majors for ten years before briefly resurfacing with the New York Giants. Davies was one of those college fellows whom Mack liked so much, but his signing didn't pay off nearly as well as someone like "Gettysburg Eddie" Plank. Of course, few pitchers in history matched what Plank accomplished. Davies, meanwhile, from Peabody, Massachusetts, was appreciated by his alma mater, the University of Massachusetts, which took note that Lloyd Garrison Davies was the school's first big leaguer.

Ben Rochefort had a day in the sun, one game in 1914. He went one-for-two, and his lifetime batting average was .500. Rochefort was retired before he turned 19. Another one-game wonder was Marvin "Toots" Coyne, oh-for-two. Not even Baseball Reference is positive about his first name. Ferdinand De Paige Moore played in two games in early October, near the end of the regular season, and batted .500 in four official at-bats. And he never played in another big-league game.

Four games in 1914 was the sum total of Dean Sturgis' big league career. He was one-for-four lifetime. Catcher Wickey McAvoy played a bit more in future seasons after the club went bad, but not a huge amount. Likewise, Sam Crane lasted a bit longer, parts of seven seasons with a .208 average.

Mack believed in tryouts at the big league level, throwing his recruits into games, often at the very end of pennant-winning seasons when the standings were cemented. By Labor Day, the A's had little to prove. However, what should have been a pleasant gallop to the pennant was somewhat spoiled in Mack's mind because of the increasing shadow of the Federal League. Mack never imagined that any of his players would turn on him. Of course, he deluded himself by thinking he was actually paying them satisfactorily.

The A's were not a wealthy organization, and many top Athletics were underpaid. Mack took it for granted that they cared more about winning than profiting, and he underestimated the lure of lucre. Even as the 1914 regular season played out and the A's were on their way to 99 wins and an 8½-game spread over the second-place Red Sox, discontent was roiling the franchise.

Mack felt it, saw it and heard it. His loyal A's were after bigger bucks, and the atmosphere was being poisoned even as the squad still marched to the pennant. The A's continued to play well enough to deflect any other American League team's aspirations in 1914, but Mack became increasingly perturbed by Federal League ripple effects and reports that players under contract were being pursued for the next season.

He described the rise of the Federal League as "a sinister menace to Major League Baseball." He recalled how the new league was at first greeted indifferently by the established circuits.

> During the previous winter, the Federal League, an outlaw circuit had been quietly organized. At first it gained little headway and not much attention was paid to it. Later they interested some multi-millionaires in their venture and soon had the financial backing to go ahead and expand.
>
> Federal League scouts popped on Major League teams from all sides. These agents were all former major leaguers and often personal friends of the men they sought. By the middle of July all of our players had been approached and astonishing salary lures were thrown out to them. They had an immediate effect on the players and caused decided unrest in baseball. Instead of playing their normal game and hustling to get their team ahead the men of baseball spent more time on and off the field haranguing about the salaries offered to them.[8]

That about summed up the situation.

Alarmed, Mack sensed dissension. One group of players was intrigued enough by such big-money offers to entertain jumping the team after the season, and the others wished to remain loyal Athletics. His immediate task was to calm things down, and he lectured the players on staying focused on the task at hand, winning the pennant, and then capturing a World Series title. He didn't want them to be thinking farther ahead than October.

There was turmoil, though, and for Mack some uncomfortable dealing with reality. Even before the season, he realized that the Federal League could be disruptive, so he offered a three-year contract to Frank Baker. Baker turned it down because he didn't know what the future would bring, but he told Mack he would play for the A's for less money than any other offer. Mack pressed him, and Baker grudgingly signed the long-term deal.

Mack still held sway over many players. Eddie Collins publicly stated, "There is only one reason the Athletics don't jump to the Feds. Connie Mack."[9]

However, the Federal League did come hard after Collins, offering a three-year, $45,000 contract. Collins, it should be recalled, had written a newspaper column welcoming the Federal League into existence, saying it would only be good for the players. The Brooklyn team, the Tip-Tops, did approach Collins, and he played coy with the sportswriters. Although he did not want to leave the A's, he hoped to use the other league's pursuit as leverage with Mack for a large raise. Such strategy had worked for Walter Johnson, Ty Cobb and Christy Mathewson, all offered Federal League big bucks, but all of them stayed put with their teams, albeit for more money. It was later calculated that during its brief actual major league level of competition, 172 players who had previously competed in the American League or National League suited up for Federal League clubs. The vast majority were fringe players, not to be confused with the Johnsons, Cobbs and Mathewsons.

Meanwhile, the Federal League was playing ball, its second season of doing business, but its first as a major league. The Indianapolis Hoosiers won the season title with an 88–65 record, just ahead of the Chicago Whales. Indianapolis' Benny Kauff was the big hitting star, batting .370 with a .447 on-base percentage, 75 steals and 211 hits. Kauff did have some success with the New York Giants for a handful of years, but nothing so dramatic as this brilliant performance. Steve Evans of Brooklyn was next with a .348 average. He too had his moments with the St. Louis Cardinals, but never otherwise approached this type of hitting in the National League. Likewise, the third-best hitter in the Federal League was Ted Easterly, with a .335 mark. He did his share of work in the majors over seven years, but once again never played as well as he did with the Kansas City Packers.

When it came to pitching, the boss man was Chicago's Claude Hendrix with 29 victories. Hendrix had won 24 games for the Pirates and later won 20 games for the Cubs, though his career wins totaled 144. Jack Quinn won 26 games for the Baltimore Terrapins in his peripatetic and lengthy career that saw him pitch until he was 50 in 1933, if only briefly then out of the bullpen for the Reds. Of note, Doc Crandall, recently of the Giants, showed up on the St. Louis team and won 13 games that summer. George Mullin, who five times won 20 or more games for the Detroit Tigers, won 14 games for Indianapolis in 1914.

The Federal League had declared war on the American League and National League, and past experience showed that as long as the money held out and owners didn't become impatient, the new league could hold out, as well.

While the Federal League assault was causing unrest in the baseball world, the world at large was coming apart. World War I officially broke out on July 28, 1914. Essentially a European war at first, many Americans hoped the United States, standing on isolationist policies, would be able to resist being drawn into the fray.

Exactly a month earlier, Archduke Franz Ferdinand of Austria was assassinated by a Yugoslavian nationalist. This was considered the precipitating event that sparked the war.

The war that raged on till November 11, 1918, eventually killed more than 16 million people and redrew the map of Europe. In 1914, the distant fighting was the stuff of newspaper columns and offered no interruption of sport in daily American life. That would change, and before the war's decisive battles were fought, the United States would be fully involved. Baseball, like all other aspects of society, would feel the ripple effects.

It is likely that only the students of foreign affairs amongst baseball players of the time paid more than cursory attention to the overseas doings when the first shots were fired. But the war went on and on and kept spreading until the U.S. and the game were embroiled in the conflict.

Eddie Grant, who had played in the 1913 World Series with the Giants against the A's, was killed in action in France. Among other prominent ball players who served the country in various capacities were Grover Cleveland Alexander, Jack Barry, Rube Bressler, future umpire Jocko Conlan, Kiki Cuyler, Red Faber, Burleigh Grimes, Christy Mathewson, Stuffy McInnis, Ty Cobb, Tris Speaker and Jeff Tesreau.

But that lay a few years in the future. For now, the war being discussed was the one on the diamond, major league baseball versus the Federal League.

Despite the player recruiting, the whiff of big money in the atmosphere, and the strains on relationships, the Athletics played much as they had in recent years, bulldozing the American League. Philadelphia finished 99–53, the Red Sox 91–62. Except for the disappointing 1912 season, the A's had won pennants in four of the past five years. They had claimed three World Series titles and seemed on the cusp of winning a fourth.

In 1914, the National League pennant winner was not one of the usual suspects, neither the New York Giants nor the Chicago Cubs. Out of nowhere came the Boston Braves. Called "The Miracle Braves," the club that was on no one's radar screen well into the summer swooped in like a dive-bombing eagle to steal the NL pennant. The Braves' run to the National League crown remains one of the most startling and dramatic championships of them all. For the Braves, it was a season to be cherished.

Boston swept to a 94–59 record and finished a surprising 10½ games ahead of the Giants. The Braves had never before exhibited such strength, and they began the season slowly, slipping into last place. Boston won just four of its first 22 games. By the end of the first week in May, the Braves were ten games out of first place. Except for one day between then and July 30, the Braves never got closer than double-digit games behind. After losing a doubleheader to Brooklyn on July 4, the Braves' record was 26–40 and they were 15 games out of first place. At that moment, if any bookmaker had solicited bets on the Braves rallying to win the pennant, he probably would have had to offer 1,000-to-1 odds.

The manager of this sad bunch was George Stallings, who was a native of the Atlanta area and had played big league ball in the 1890s. In 1912, Boston was the worst team in the National League with a 52–101 record. The Braves finished 52 games out of first place. Between 1897 and 1910, Stallings managed the Philadelphia Phillies, Detroit Tigers and New York Highlanders. He inherited the horrible Braves for the 1913 season, and they moved out of the basement with a 69–82 record good for fifth place.

Although the Braves demonstrated signs of improvement under Stallings, there was insufficient evidence that overnight they would become pennant contenders. Stallings was a savvy manager. He moved players around like chess pieces and was futuristic in his planning in the sense of platooning players based on their strengths against certain pitchers.

But even a century later, a baseball fan can pore over the Braves' statistics from the 1914 season and wonder how they did it, how they raised themselves, quite suddenly, from a shaky, muddle-along outfit into a pennant winner. They left all baseball observers baffled. The Braves were short on sluggers, short on great arms, and short on stars. Although they featured two future Hall of Famers who were the glue of the roster, they were not in the prime portions of their careers.

As a team, Boston batted .251 and hit 35 home runs, no one player with more than nine. On the mound, Dick Rudolph had the greatest year of his life. So did fellow righty Bill James, aka "Seattle Bill," by far in a very short career. Indeed, James' season was such an outlier it was probably the single greatest pitching season ever by someone who never accomplished anything else as an active player. Some 30 or so years later, when the Braves fielded an excellent team short on starting pitchers, the phrase went "Spahn and Sain and pray for rain." That's because it was all Warren Spahn and Johnny Sain in that generation. This Rudolph-James combo was much like that.

Catcher Hank Gowdy was young, just 24, although he had been around the league for a few years. He was on his way to a 17-season career with a .270 batting average, although he hit just .243 in 1914. Gowdy's role with that team in the World Series was long remembered, as well as his status as the first major leaguer to enlist in the service when the U.S. entered World War I. He fought in France with the 166th Infantry of the 42nd Division, also called the Rainbow Division.

Second baseman Johnny Evers, of Tinker-to-Evers-Chance fame with the Cubs, turned 33 years old in July 1914, but was still a fierce player. He hit .279 and was a determined competitor who could fire up younger Braves on the field. Walter James Maranville, destined for the Hall of Fame, played shortstop, although at 22 he was at the beginning of a long career. Evers and "Rabbit" Maranville made for a high-class double-play combination—and Maranville led the team with 78 RBI, too. Also, Maranville had been approached by the Federal League and later said he turned down a three-year, $50,000 deal to stay with the Braves.

"That team," Maranville said of the pennant winners, "made runs out of ideas, built victories on dash and spirit and quick instinct." Maranville said the team was tight and players had each other's backs. "George Stallings, manager of the Braves, had a crowd that was a cross between a loving family and a tough gang. If anyone picked on one of us he had to answer to 26 of us. We took talk from nobody and we handed it out whenever it occurred to us."[10]

18. The Year 1914

Their best hitter that season was outfielder Joe Connolly, with nine homers, 65 runs batted in and a .306 average. Connolly did not reach the majors until he was 29, and this was his second of four seasons, and his best. Maranville was never a big hitter. His worth was evaluated by his fielding contributions, hustle and base running (28 steals), not by batting .246. Regular third baseman Charlie Deal batted just .210, but his backup, Red Smith, hit .314 in 60 games. First baseman Butch Schmidt was another whose career lasted a short four years, but who was at his finest with a .285 batting average for the 1914 Braves. It was a strange conglomerate.

Maranville was nicknamed "Rabbit." Evers was called "The Crab." And another outfield backup, George Whitted, was nicknamed "Possum." Maybe Stallings was a zoologist.

Stallings was the masterful hand that guided the group, somehow squeezing the best from a rag-tag collection that practically no one heard of at the time (excepting a few players) and one that didn't stay together long either.

"We practiced squeeze plays and the hit-and-run," Maranville said. "We spied out the enemy and we had a form of counter-espionage against him, as well. We played for a run at a time and every run was precious. Every member of that team was a decent chap, kind to his mother and all that, but there wasn't one of us who weren't forever trying to steal another team's signals."[11]

The Braves succeeded by doing the small stuff well. Maranville, ten years younger than Evers, credited the veteran for aiding him in the field. "After he arrived with the Braves we became one of the great teams of the game," Maranville said. "His effect on me alone was enough to make a real shortstop out of me. That season, with Johnny at my left, I broke the record for starting double plays and I broke the record for making putouts. Evers participated in almost all of the plays which went to make these records."[12]

This was one time the manager (or coach) of a team received considerable acclaim for its success, though despite thorough analysis, a century later people still can't figure out what the magic formula was. "Stallings has a wonderful system of working his men," said pitcher Russ Ford, who had played for him in New York. "He's a wild man on the bench, after his club every minute. The player who loafs or shirks his work is in for an awful panning. He doesn't care what he says, or how he says it. But with all of that he is always fair. And the minute the game's over he lets you know that he is with his club to the finish and that what he said on the field doesn't go."[13]

For sure, taking over a losing team, Stallings realized it needed an attitude adjustment as much as anything else, although the addition of a star or three wouldn't bother him either.

> Mechanical baseball doesn't win games. Natural ability to play ball counts for much, but if players do not have their hearts in the success of the club you might just as well pass them up instead of wasting valuable time with them. In my experience as manager I have tried to work up a spirit of enthusiasm. Harmony is absolutely necessary in building up a ball team. If the players work harmoniously and enthusiastically, half the fight is won.[14]

There was considerable irony in Stallings' comments, since in 1914 Connie Mack was bemoaning the loss of such characteristics that had been a hallmark of his A's teams.

So the dead-meat Braves came alive because they were all laughing and joking? Maybe, maybe not. But Boston did win 94 games and ran away with the pennant after its lousy start. Between July 27 and August 6, the Braves won nine games in a row. They tossed in four- and five-game winning streaks left and right, and at the end of September won seven straight. Boston's lead grew to 11 games on October 1, a remarkable turnaround from the Braves' losing start.

Stalling had once called the Braves "a baseball horror," but he molded them into a five-star attraction. During the 1914 campaign, Stallings' motto was, "You can win, you must win, you will win!"[15]

The National League pennant belonged to Boston.

19

The 1914 World Series

Going into the World Series, the Philadelphia Athletics seemed to have more of the advantages over the Boston Braves. Philadelphia was a veteran team, loaded with big-name stars. Philadelphia won more games, 99 to 94, during the regular season than Boston. The Athletics' roster had a tremendous amount of championship experience. The A's were defending world champions and had won three World Series and four pennants since 1910. The Athletics also had more depth on the pitching staff.

There was no real reason to favor the Braves unless one believed in fate or hunches, or if somehow momentum could be quantified. None of that was empirical, however. Braves manager George Stallings believed in harmony making the sum of the parts more valuable than the whole. A's manager Connie Mack had overseen what in his mind were high-quality work conditions.

But Mack was worried about the mental state of his club. The talk of Federal League raids swirled around the team like a tornado. Rumors ran as swiftly as a river past the dugout, some perhaps tinged with truth, others fantasy. They were mostly about which Athletics would leave the team for higher pay once the Series ended and contracts for the year expired in October.

There was no doubt whatsoever that the Athletics possessed superior talent. There was doubt about dissension, ill feelings, perhaps jealousy, and much uncertainty. Still, it was difficult to look at the lineups and not be confident if you were a Philadelphia booster.

Stallings was still explaining to sportswriters how he cooked up a gourmet chicken dinner out of chicken salad, how a Braves team that reclined in last place in July was able to run the table and qualify for the World Series in October. Another tidbit of philosophy floated out of Stallings' mouth. "Give me a ball club of only mediocre ability and if I can get the players in the right frame of mind, they'll beat the world champions. But they've got to believe they can do it."¹ That's mind over matter, all right. By then, of course, the Braves probably believed anything Stallings said to motivate them.

Apparently Stallings really did subscribe to the mental commitment being worth more than the outright skills, because even when the Braves were flopping around in last place in early summer, he said that he knew they were better than they had shown and that they would improve. He did not predict a World Series appearance while his team was in the cellar, but he did express a certain level of confidence. "This bunch of mine is the worst looking club I've ever seen," Stallings said when the Braves were 4–18. "They can't do anything right. I've never seen such lousy luck. But I don't think we're a tail-end team. It'll take us a month to get back in shape, but then we're going to be hard to beat."² Now that was boldly prophetic.

Mack was increasingly concerned as the opener of the Series approached. He called his players "remote, unfriended, melancholy, slow. The players were tight-lipped and there didn't seem the slightest desire among them to study the ways of the Braves, their opponents in the classic."³

This was no exaggeration. Over the last week of the regular season, when the Braves were playing in New York just 100 miles away, Mack dispatched Charles Bender to scout them and bring in a report. Bender blew off the assignment. Worse, he and Mack ran into each other in Philadelphia when Bender was supposed to be in New York. "I thought you were in New York to look over the Braves," Mack said. "I didn't bother," Bender said. "What's the use of looking at that bunch of bush leaguers?"⁴

That statement seemed out of character for Bender, but variations of the situation did appear in newspapers at the time, and Shag Thompson, the A's outfielder, supported that version decades later. "Chief Bender had been told that the Braves were just a bunch of misfits," Thompson said in 1988, the year before he died. "He didn't even go to New York to scout them because he didn't think it was necessary."⁵ To some degree, the Braves were a bunch of misfits, though amiable ones who were winning and posed a threat.

Also, supposedly Bender added further insult to the "misfits" description when he said he wouldn't have any trouble pitching to them. Mack said, "I hope you don't."⁶

It would have been easy enough for Bender and other A's stars to look at the Boston pitchers' records as a whole and sneer: Otto Hess, 5–

19. The 1914 World Series

6; Dick Crutcher, 5–7; Gene Cocreham, 3–4; and Hub Perdue, 2–5. Behind the big two of Dick Rudolph and Bill James there was Lefty Tyler, 16–13, and Paul Strand, 6–2.

In a short series, though, in an era when starters sometimes pitched on two days' rest and were liable to show up on the mound in relief at any time, Rudolph and James were the ones to fear. Rudolph started 36 games and won 26. He threw six shutouts and 336⅓ innings with a 2.35 earned run average. James won 26 games in 332⅓ innings with a 1.90 ERA. Yes, the Athletics should have been worried about that duo.

Rudolph did not have a formidable look. He stood 5-foot-9 and weighed 160 pounds. He was born in New York City and attended Fordham University, and his first big-league club was the Giants. He pitched in just four games for the Giants in 1910 and 1911, was out of the majors in 1912, and surfaced with the Braves in 1913, when his record was 14–13 with a 2.92 earned run average. He became a star the next year, if only for a short while.

"He was one of the smartest pitchers who ever toed the rubber," said Braves coach Fred Mitchell, who later managed the club. "He wasn't fast, but had a good curveball, which he mixed with a spitball, and he could almost read the batter's mind. I've often sat on the bench with him and heard him tell whether a batter would take or hit." Mitchell called Rudolph "the bellwether of the pitching staff" and a "cocky kid." Mitchell felt Rudolph brought out the best in James and Tyler, who didn't want to be shown up by him because of his attitude and because he was small.[7]

"Seattle Bill" James played at a time when there was also a "Big Bill" James in the majors and a "Lefty" Bill James, and that's why the Braves' James received his nickname. He is also not to be confused with the modern-day stats ubermeister Bill James. James turned in a stupendous year for Seattle in the minors before signing with the Braves, winning 29 games. "Seattle Bill" had a limited big league career, and when World War I broke out he became a bomb-throwing instructor for the Army. No word on whether he heaved the bombs with a curve.

Although many viewed James' career as one with great promise that was never reached, he didn't seem unhappy about his career change. It turned out that once around the league was pretty much enough for "Seattle Bill" because he didn't like to travel. "I like the game well enough," James said, "but I can't get used to the long jumps from one city to another. It looks nice from the outside to think of traveling around the country, but one sweep of the circuit is enough. After that it becomes hard and disagreeable work."[8] That was before flying commercially and long security lines at airports that so many people hate. Whether it was his innings-heavy 1914 or the bomb pitching, James developed shoulder problems and never could resume pitching after the war.

Tyler was the least spectacular of the trio of top starters. In 1912, in an indication of how terrible the Braves were as much as his own pitching, Tyler led the National League in losses with 22 and earned runs with 119. Still, Tyler pitched much longer than his compatriots, winning 127 games in 12 seasons. Basically, throwing Tyler into the mix, these were the problems the A's had to solve if they wanted to triumph again. The task was to beat Rudolph, James and Tyler with some combination of Eddie Plank, Chief Bender, Joe Bush and Bob Shawkey.

Mack and Stallings were irritated with one another before the Series even began. Stallings contacted Mack and asked for permission for the Braves to work out at Shibe Park on the afternoon before the Series started. Mack said no, the A's were going to be using the field in the afternoon, so the Braves could practice in the morning. Stallings wanted the field at that later time so his men could get used to the shadows and the lay of the land during the same hours they would be playing for keeps. Stallings went around telling sportswriters that Mack had refused to let him use the field. Mack felt this was a lie, called Stallings and told him so. "When I get out there Friday the first thing I'll do is punch you in the nose," Stallings said. "Well, whenever you want to start punching, I'll be here," Mack replied.[9]

If the Athletics did not know much about Rudolph before the World Series opened on October 9 at Shibe Park, they did when Game 1 was over. So did Bender, the A's starter in the Series opener. Connie Mack had counted on Bender to start big games many times over the years. Overall, Bender had a superlative record in World Series games. Mack was clearly unhappy that Bender had blown off the scouting assignment, but he surely would have forgiven his go-to guy if he had blitzed those "misfits" as pledged.

In 1905, Bender won a Series game over the New York Giants. In 1910, he beat the Cubs. In 1911, Bender defeated the Giants twice. In 1913, he beat the Giants twice more. On this day against the Braves, however, Bender was blasted all over Shibe Park. His lifetime World Series earned run average is 2.44—and that's after the Braves clubbed him, making his 1914 Series ERA read like a typographical error at 10.12. Money pitcher Bender was lifted by Mack after 5⅓ innings as he allowed six runs on eight hits. Was it a lack of preparation and overconfidence, or merely the law of averages catching up to Bender? Regardless, the result was harsh.

Until that day, Bender had thrown a complete game in all nine other World Series starts for the A's. But the Braves teed off on him and Bender trudged to the dugout, relieved by Weldon Wyckoff in the sixth inning. "Pretty good hitting for a bush league outfit," Mack said.[10] For all of their closeness and mutual respect over the years, a rift was developing between Mack and Bender.

Oh, the stories that surfaced about the A's behavior at different times. Long after all other members of the team had died, Shag Thompson told one author it was believed that Bender and Rube Oldring had been out drinking the night before the game. Mack said he was aware that Bender and Eddie Plank were flirting with the Federal League, and he was going to let them go and retain his young pitchers.

Bender told a different story about not feeling well before his start and about the team's state of mind. "We went into the Series overconfident," Bender said. "We thought we'd take them in a breeze, just put on our suits and walk out on the field." He said he felt sick from vertigo, stomach problems and a gall bladder issue and told Mack, who Bender said replied that he could beat the Braves. Bender said he knew he didn't have his good stuff when he warmed up and informed Mack again about his health concerns.[11]

Boston scored two runs in the top of the second inning, one run in the top of the fifth, and was working on a three-run rally in the sixth when Mack took Bender out of the game. The key hits for the Braves in the second were a double by Hank Gowdy and a single by Rabbit Maranville.

The A's did reach Rudolph for an unearned run in the bottom of the second on a walk, a single and an error, with Amos Strunk scoring. But Rudolph otherwise pitched shutout ball. Philadelphia did not score off him again as his teammates kept piling up the runs. Gowdy led off the Boston fifth with a triple, and Maranville immediately singled him home. The sixth was Bender's undoing. Johnny Evers singled, Joe Connolly walked, and Possum Whitted ripped a triple on a line to deep right-center, scoring both of them. Butch Schmidt, who really was a butcher in the off-season, singled in Whitted. The Braves waved goodbye to Bender.

Boston added one more run off Weldon Wyckoff in the eighth when Schmidt and Gowdy singled and then, in the midst of a complicated Maranville at-bat, Schmidt stole home. The final score was 7–1, and the A's were really never in it thanks to Rudolph. He went the distance, gave up just five hits, one unearned run and struck out eight.

One game does not a Series decide, and the seasoned Athletics generally would not be shaken by the result of a single game. But they were caught off-guard by the Braves' onslaught. These AAA ball players could clobber them like that? Those ragamuffins could manhandle Bender like that? We'll show them tomorrow.

It literally was tomorrow when Game 2 began. This game also was scheduled for Shibe Park before the teams adjourned to Boston. There was no surprise about which pitchers were chosen to start for each team. Mack went with Eddie Plank, naturally. Stallings countered with Bill James, obviously. There was more pressure on the A's to win this game, especially since it was played at home.

There were slightly more than 20,000 fans on hand to watch a second humbling of the Athletics by a hurler they probably had barely heard of and certainly knew little about if they had. It was the Bill James Show on October 10. War horse Plank was in fine form, giving Philadelphia what it needed and wanted to see. Gettysburg Eddie was terrific, spreading out seven hits, pitching a complete game, and allowing just one run. Rarely had he been better in a game with so much at stake.

But James was even better. The A's batters, from the usual stars to the lower end of the order, were all flummoxed by James' stuff. They could barely put bat on ball, could generate no offensive threat, and many a time walked back to the dugout, heads shaking because James' best stuff was sharper than their batting eye.

Savvy veteran Johnny Evers singled off Plank in the first inning. Evers was not always popular in the clubhouse, but he could uplift his team's performance through his own energy and desire to win. He had a resume that was much to be admired, and as someone mixed in with a crowd of players who had little to boast about in their big-league careers except their presence, he stood out on the Braves' roster.

Evers will always be better remembered for his days with the Cubs and the fame accrued there, but for this one season he may have been more important to the Braves than he ever was in Chicago. Evers was pesky, excelling at the things that could drive an opposing manager mad, from bunting to stealing bases, to executing the hit-and-run, and making the big play in the field. The older Evers' temperament was dramatically different from infield partner Rabbit Maranville's. Baseball people were divided over where his nickname "The Crab" originated. Some said it was because of the unusual way he attacked a ground ball. Others said it was because he was grouchy in the dugout.

At one point, Cleveland manager Joe Birmingham addressed the attitude question of the nickname. "They claim he is a crab, and perhaps they're right," Birmingham said. "But I would like to have 25 such crabs playing for me. If I did, I would have no doubts over the pennant. They would win hands down."¹²

Stallings made do with one.

James walked Eddie Murphy in the first inning for a lone Philadelphia base runner. Plank walked Hank Gowdy in the second. They died on the base paths. Evers got another single in the third, but was thrown out trying to steal to end the inning. Butch Schmidt and Maranville touched Plank for singles in the fourth. Lester Mann singled in the fifth. Wally Schang got the Athletics' first hit off James in the sixth inning, a double down the left-field line. An extra-base hit was a rarity in this pitchers' duel.

In the seventh, Eddie Collins singled, sparking interest in the dugout, but then he was picked off first base. Bottom of the eighth, nothing doing for the A's, all zeroes across on the scoreboard. The pitchers were the bosses this day.

Until the ninth. Charlie Deal doubled with one out for Boston. He stole third base and, after a Plank strikeout, Les Mann singled to center to score Deal and bring in the game's only run. Boston 1, Philadelphia 0. Mann, nicknamed "Major," was an unlikely hero at the time. He was just 21 and batted only .247 that season, and he was gone from the Braves by 1915. However, he did have a 16-year big-league career, all but one in the National League, with a lifetime batting average of .282.

Mann enjoyed an eclectic sports career, coaching college football and college basketball, including a stint at Indiana University in the 1920s. He also led the effort to get baseball into the 1936 Summer Olympics as a demonstration sport. However, it could be argued that his finest moment in sport was driving in the winning run in a World Series game.

Philadelphia did have a chance in the bottom of the ninth. The Athletics were on the edge of a comeback that might have changed history. Jack Barry walked to lead off. After Wally Schang struck out, Jimmy Walsh pinch-hit for Plank and also walked. Two men on, one out, one run to tie, two runs to win. James induced Eddie Murphy to hit a grounder to short, scooped up by Maranville, who tossed to Evers, who fired to Schmidt. The double play ended the game.

If no one realized it before, it was clear now that the A's were in a precarious position. Stars like Eddie Collins or Frank Baker, lesser contributors like Rube Oldring, Eddie Murphy or Jack Barry, it didn't matter because James and the Braves had the hitters handcuffed.

There was gloom in the A's clubhouse after the second loss.

Game 3 was a fight to the death, it seemed, an aggressive, aggrieved Athletics team awakened and fiercely seeking to revive its chances for another world championship. The scene was Boston, at Fenway Park, on October 12, after a rare day off in the middle of the Series. Although attendance was not particularly impressive league-wide in 1914, the Braves had led the AL by attracting 382,913 spectators, split between the South End Grounds and Fenway when available. For this World Series game, 35,520 turned out, nearly one-tenth as many fans as witnessed the Braves play during their entire home regular season.

The mood was jubilant in Boston as Braves supporters sensed that for the first time in their club's existence, it could win it all. Better yet, the victim would be the powerful Philadelphia A's. But that was secondary.

The selection of the starting pitchers was as expected. The No. 3 starter for Philadelphia all season was Bullet Joe Bush. Mack anointed him. The No. 3 starter for Boston all season was Lefty Tyler. Stallings chose him.

Fired up, feeling a bit embarrassed by the way Rudolph and James had handled them by holding the order to just one run in 18 innings, the Athletics felt optimistic about things after scoring a first-inning run off Tyler. Eddie Murphy led off the game with a double down the left-field line. Rube Oldring bunted Murphy to third on a sacrifice. Eddie Collins reached on an error, but that was good enough to score Murphy for a 1-0 A's lead that probably felt disproportionately good. A little more annoying was how the inning ended. Collins stole second, but was picked off for the third out. In the modern media age, that gaffe would be dissected forever and shown indefinitely on film.

If anyone believed this game was going to be a repeat of Game 2 and James' and Plank's marvelously stingy presentations, it was learned early the one run would not hold up for long. The Braves tied the contest in the bottom of the second inning. Maranville walked, stole second base, and scampered home on a double by Hank Gowdy to make it 1–1.

The A's took the lead again in the fourth. A Stuffy McInnis ground-rule double to left field set things up. Jimmy Walsh singled to left, sending McInnis home. 2–1 Philadelphia. The lead lasted only minutes. There was one out in the bottom of the fourth when Butch Schmidt singled to center field. Deal grounded out, but Schmidt moved to second base. Maranville singled to center, sending Schmidt home. Then, with two outs, Maranville tried to steal home plate, but was thrown out.

That inning very much illustrated the offense of the times, the offensive style of the Deadball Era when teams scratched for one run at a time and did not rely on booming bats to produce long-distance home runs. It was situational baseball, featuring incremental movement around the

19. The 1914 World Series

bases. Scoring a run was like scoring a goal in hockey, something to be celebrated, protected and prized because the runs didn't come along so often. So Game 3 was tied once more.

Peace broke out after that for a while. There were no more fireworks, no more runs. Bush and Tyler toiled, putting up zero after zero on the scoreboard. They cancelled one another out through the fifth, sixth, seventh, and eighth innings, yes, even the ninth inning. The hurlers got nastier, the hitters more anemic. After the regulation nine innings, the game was knotted, 2–2.

Just when it seemed no one would ever score again, the Athletics came to life against Tyler in the visitors' half of the tenth. Wally Schang kindled hope for Philadelphia with a leadoff single. Bush struck out attempting to bunt. The Braves went after Eddie Murphy when he hit a grounder, but everyone was safe, Schang moving to second. Oldring hit a grounder. He was out at first, but the runners moved up. So here was opportunity for the Athletics, men on second and third. Collins walked, loading the bases. Boston longed to escape damage with a potential force play at any base. Baker, whose bat was silent for much of the Series, did not pop another home run in championship play, but he did single, driving in both runners to send Philadelphia ahead, 4–2.

Only three more outs. That had to be what Philadelphia was thinking. But Bush couldn't get them. Leading off, Gowdy hit a ball so hard and deep to center field that it probably didn't stop rolling until it hit the Delaware River. After the home run, Herbie Moran walked, Evers singled, and Moran ran to third. He scored the second Boston run of the inning on a Joe Connolly sacrifice fly. The game was tied again, this time 4–4.

At the beginning of the 11th inning, Stallings took out Tyler and put Bill James into the game in relief. He was about to find out if James' mastery of the A's would continue or if they had figured out a way to solve his stuff since Game 2. James brought the goods again, and a walk was all he surrendered.

Although Tyler was showering, Bush was still hurling. He took care of Braves hitters one, two, three. Itching to end it in the 12th inning, hopeful of a happy ending, the Athletics did little beyond advance Murphy to second after he walked. Things went better for Boston. Gowdy, who played a brilliant Series, led off with a ground-rule double. After an intentional walk to Larry Gilbert, Moran came to the plate. If he smacked a home run, or something akin to that, Moran would have become much more famous. However, Bush made an error throwing to third to cut down the lead runner after a bunt attempt, and pinch-runner Les Mann crossed the plate.

That's how the Braves won, 5–4. By the standards of the day, it was an extraordinarily long contest, lasting three hours and six minutes. It probably felt longer for the A's. Falling behind 3–0 in a best-four-out-of-seven Series is a prescription for disaster, and here the Athletics were, in a funk, losing two one-run games in a row. If Boston was labeled "The Miracle Braves" for the way they ambushed the National League over the last couple of months of the season, it would take a similar miracle for Philadelphia to get past the Braves now. The World Series has been around since 1903. Major League Baseball dramatically expanded its post-season playoffs in recent decades. Yet on only one occasion has a team rebounded from trailing 3–0 in games in a post-season series. The Philadelphia A's of 1914 were not the first. The Boston Red Sox trailed the New York Yankees, 3–0, in the American League Championship Series in 2004, abruptly turned things around to eliminate New York, proceeded to the World Series—and won it.

When the Red Sox won that championship, it was their first since 1918, or 84 years. The Red Sox also won in 1915 and 1916, but the Braves' achievement of 1914 was from the same time period, meaning it had been a long time since Boston baseball fans had anything to celebrate. At the time of the Miracle Braves, the two Boston clubs co-existed the way the New York Yankees and New York Giants did, and how the Chicago Cubs and Chicago White Sox, and the A's and the Phillies shared a town. It was common to have more than one big-league team in the nation's largest cities, where baseball heritage ran deep. Certainly, the Braves and Red Sox had their own distinctive cliques of fans, but after the Braves fled Boston for Milwaukee (and then Atlanta) some local fans seemed to appreciate the Braves' World Series title of 1914 retroactively a little bit more.

By Game 4 on October 13 at Fenway Park, it was apparent to everyone, the Athletics included, that the Braves were doing to win the crown. The A's last best chance—that 12-inning epic that ended with a one-run loss—had passed. Dick Rudolph was coming back at them in this game, hopefully, from the Boston standpoint, the decider. Unless the A's bats could come alive as they had so many times in recent years, the trophy was going to the Braves.

From Philadelphia and Connie Mack's perspective, the Braves had already beaten his best and most reliable hurlers, Bender, Plank and Bush. He went with Bob Shawkey, optimistic that the young pitcher could interrupt the smooth Boston cruise.

For three full innings, it was a double shutout, Rudolph and Shawkey entertaining everyone watching except the hitters with their dominance.

The A's actually scratched out a hit per inning, singles by Collins and Oldring and a double by Jimmy Walsh, but Rudolph didn't let anything get out of hand. Shawkey didn't even permit a hit in those three innings.

The A's posed a threat in the top of the fourth inning, offense sorely needed for the psyche and the scoreboard. With one out, Collins and Baker singled, but when the inning ended home plate was still over a distant horizon. Boston finally reached Shawkey in the home half of the fourth inning, though the Braves did not exactly belt him around. A walk, a single and two groundouts sent Evers around the bases for a 1–0 lead.

In contrast to what they so often failed to do in this Series after the Braves took a lead, Philadelphia surged right back to tie the score, 1–1, in the top of the fifth inning. Jack Barry singled and went to second on a groundball out. Shawkey helped himself with a double that scored Barry. However, whether he was tired from running the bases or the Braves were just beginning to figure him out, after collecting two outs in the bottom of the fifth inning, Shawkey lost his focus long enough to give up a single to Rudolph, a double to Moran, and a single to Evers in rapid succession, adding two runs to Boston's total. The Braves were on top, 3–1. It seemed that no matter what poker hand the A's held, the Braves were able to beat it.

After the fifth, by which time Shawkey had surrendered three runs (two earned) on four hits, Mack sat him down and handed the ball to Herb Pennock. Shawkey would go on to have a terrific career with the New York Yankees and appear in four more World Series, but this was his debut on the biggest stage in the sport. Similarly, Pennock, who was successful both with the Red Sox and as a New York teammate of Shawkey's, would pitch in four more World Series. This was also his first time in the championship series.

After the fifth inning, the Athletics never threatened to score again. Rudolph overpowered the Philadelphia bats. The final score was 3–1 Boston, the A's vanquished. Rudolph sprinkled around seven hits and one run to capture his second victory in the World Series, the capper to his splendid season.

Given the single day of travel and the shortest number of games possible, the entire World Series was over by October 13, within just five days. Boston took the Series, 4–0, over the shell-shocked A's. Philadelphia scored only six runs, four of them in one game and the other two in three games combined. As a team, the A's batted .172. Except for Bender's off-day, the Philadelphia pitching was pretty good. As a team, Boston batted .244. Almost all the Athletics' individual averages were sub-par. Boston was uplifted by Maranville, .308, Evers, .438, and Gowdy, .545. Presumably, Evers was not crabby when the Braves were proclaimed champions.

Although Stallings did not punch him the nose, this was a loss that stung Connie Mack for a long while, probably forever. His team did not play like his team. He was disturbed by the fractionalization and the result, as well as the seemingly lethargic manner in which it occurred. This all contributed to his immediate plans for the Athletics.

Perfectionist Stallings, whose pitchers controlled the action, could have nitpicked if he chose. Often driven mad by walks, otherwise known as free passes, when he was an older man in retirement and a doctor informed him he had a bad heart, asking why he thought that was, Stallings growled back at him. "Bases on balls, all those bases on balls, you son of a bitch," Stallings said. He was probably thinking back to an occasion when he yanked a pitcher for giving up too many walks. "You bases-on-balls bonehead," Stallings said. "G'wan to the clubhouse and burn up your uniform."[13]

It would surprise many (though probably not Stallings, and this time around he might not have let it bother him much), but the Braves' trio of top pitchers actually issued 13 walks to A's batters during the four-game Series. For once, it did not matter.

Mack very much blamed the distraction of Federal League recruiting for his team's demise.

> During the World Series our team fell apart. The Boston Braves slaughtered us. I felt this keenly, as I knew we could walk away with the Series if only we had been united. It was the proof of the slogan, "United we stand, divided we fall." And we fell. They [sportswriters] said the wonder team was taking it lying down. I knew that the "wonder team" was engaged in a civil war, fighting one another.[14]

Athletics players headed out onto the field to congratulate the Braves on their victory, but neither Mack nor Stallings, still angry at each other, ever budged. "I am more than pleased we beat the Athletics four straight games for, of all the poor sports in the world, Connie Mack is the worst," Stallings said.[15]

The Series result hurt Mack like a very bad toothache. He was not pleased with much that was said, by him or the opponents, though he spoke graciously about the Braves later. That was not within Stallings' hearing, but likely within his reading capability in some publication.

> I haven't enough vanity to think that I'm going through my baseball career without ever losing. [John] McGraw, [Frank] Chance, [Fred] Clarke and other great managers have their years of adversity. I am no exception. I'm thankful for the fact that we won the pennant and played in the Series, so the season was not exactly mis-

spent. Don't misunderstand me. The Braves were entitled to their laurels. They won every game on sheer merit.[16]

Still, the Philadelphia Athletics did not merely lose a ball game, or four of them. They did not just lose a World Series. They seemed to have lost their identity and, as swift-moving events would show, the A's dynasty died on the field when the last pitch was thrown by Dick Rudolph on October 13, 1914.

20

The Breakup

The 1914 season may have produced another American League pennant for the Philadelphia Athletics, but it gave Connie Mack so much aggravation watching his favorite players seemingly self-destruct as the people he thought he knew that it almost wasn't worth it. And then the World Series was a total disaster.

The Federal League was the enemy, and it had infiltrated his clubhouse. As the 1914 season came to an end, no member of the Athletics had jumped to a Federal League team, but it seemed to be an inevitability that some players would leave for more money.

With some minor tweaking, the Athletics were not an over-the-hill team. Eddie Plank was the old man of the team at 38. He had performed yeoman service for Philadelphia since the team was founded in 1901. Maybe he still had enough left to keep on pitching—Gettysburg Eddie thought so—but maybe it was time to part ways. Charles Bender, who had been a mainstay with the A's since 1903, wasn't even old. But he and Mack had had a falling out after being so close for so long.

Arguably, Mack could have let Plank and Bender go, as terrific as they had been, and made a stand with the rest of the existing pitching staff. The younger guys like Joe Bush, Bob Shawkey and Herb Pennock were coming into their own, and there seemed to be ample arm support amongst the others.

The $100,000 infield was still in its prime. The best quartet in the game didn't have a man over 28, Frank Baker's age. No reason to mess with that success. Heck, Stuffy McInnis was only 23. Collins and Barry were just 27, and catcher Wally Schang was only 24. The outfield always had been more in flux anyway. Amos Strunk always seemed to come through in the clutch, but since 1910 there had been varying combinations patrolling the grass at Shibe Park. The outfield had never been the Athletics' strongest point.

20. The Breakup

So there was no clear-cut reason to take extreme measures. At least not on paper, it seemed. But something in the atmospheric conditions had changed. Mack sensed a loss of trust, something that was a prized commodity for him. It does not seem to be much of an exaggeration to say he was tormented about what to do with his ball club.

He did reach one absolute conclusion. Mack did not want to fight the Federal League on the basis of who had the deepest pockets or fattest bank account. Head-to-head with rich owners of the Federal League, Mack knew he couldn't compete, and he didn't want to pay out too much to one player so that he had a salary imbalance and could not afford enough good men.

> After giving the crisis much careful thought, I had decided the war had gone too far to stop it by trying to outbid the Federal moneybags. Nothing could be more disastrous at this time than a salary war. There was but one thing to do: To refuse to be drawn into this bitter conflict, and to let those know who wanted to risk their fate with the Federals go with the Federals.[1]

Oh, there were major league players with a sweet tooth who couldn't resist biting into the candy the Federal League offered. Many of them were fringe players who did not get much playing time, but some were big names. Ed Reulbach once put together five straight excellent pitching seasons for the Chicago Cubs, three years in a row leading the National League in winning percentage. He was also the last living player who competed for the Cubs in the 1908 World Series when he died in 1961. But Reulbach was fading as he turned 30, and he jumped to the Brooklyn Tip-Tops.

Outfielder Edd Roush was a young player with almost no big-league experience when he shifted to the Federal League for two years. He returned to the majors, mostly with Cincinnati, and became a Hall of Famer.

Hall of Famer Mordecai "Three Finger" Brown was approaching the end of his career when he joined the Federal League. Pitcher Cy Falkenberg was a solid player, but also a long-time veteran ready for change. Hooks Wiltse also fit that description.

Truly, though, perusal of all the names of players who signed with the Federal League who had big-league ties produces a list of mostly anonymous ball players with no claim to fame and for the most part only remembered within the confines of their own families. Yes, overtures were made to many stars of the majors, but most chose to stay put with their teams, though they did receive raises. They did take the upstart league's offers to their bosses and gained better contracts. Mack did not want to play ball with members of his team who wanted to hold him up for better pay when he felt he had been paying them sufficiently. Mack may have been blind to a fault on this topic, and if he had shown signs of compromise he may well have retained most of his key men. For the most part, they liked him and liked being Athletics and winners.

Instead, seemingly out of pure spite more than economics, Mack chose to dynamite his team, blow up the Athletics. He imploded his own dynasty. Rarely, if ever, has such a successful ball club been purposely destroyed by its owner to the extent that Mack reshuffled his roster. It was almost as if overnight he went from trying to win every American League pennant and every World Series to trying to lose.

This was such an act of stubbornness that more than a century later it remains somewhat inexplicable, even if Mack explained his deeds. Mack indeed did quite a bit of thinking about how to remedy his team's second-half, so-so showing and awful performance in the World Series. Getting to the World Series is the prime goal of every team. Just getting there, after winning three championship trophies in a few years, was not good enough for Mack. He wanted to do it his way, as if he had a point to prove. What he was doing was abdicating, washing his hands of what the Federal League represented rather than combating it.

> At the end of the debacle, when I reviewed the season and saw how easy it was for us to win in the first half when the players were a happy family and with an unconquerable ambition to win, it made me sick to feel that Federal League scouts with theatrical salary offers could change all of this. It was a shock to me that so many of our players were in a receptive mood to talk business and at once neglect their playing to deal to the best advantage with outlaws. I became absolutely disgusted with conditions.[2]

Mack made those comments in 1930, long after the events transpired that destroyed the A's dynasty. It did not take much more reading of his feelings to recognize that he felt betrayed by the players he had scouted, hired, and in his mind paid fairly.

"Then to see them turn against the club and willingly negotiate with a new organization caused me for a time to lose all confidence in players," he said. Left unsaid is that he couldn't field a team without players, and better for all concerned if they had been good players rather than players who didn't really belong in the majors. "This may have been a mistake on my part. Perhaps I should have used more temperate methods, but remember, I had discovered, coached and developed the majority of our players and regarded them as sons."[3]

Mack was a father disappointed by his boys. When it came to running

20. The Breakup

his team with the goal of being the best it could be, Mack pretty much lost his mind over this episode, almost becoming an arsonist in his own house. Through his own actions, more than any devious plot by the Federal League, Mack was left with the wreckage.

Once Mack made up his mind to let players walk and to trade away others, things got crazy. Mack was seized by a frenzy to clean house overnight. Rather than fine-tune the A's for the 1915 season, chasing a fifth pennant in six years, he surrendered all pretense of seeking another championship in the immediate future. He took out his pique over the Federal League doings on himself, even though the Federal League was barely self-sustaining. Mack could not know that the Federal League had just one more year to live, but even so, with a little patience he could have outlasted the threat and still controlled a powerful American League club. And he wasn't fooling himself, either, about what he was about to do.

> I could build and now for the first time in my life I was to tear down. It was impossible for us to increase salaries to a war basis for many reasons while we had been championship contenders or winners ever since Shibe Park was opened to the public in 1909. We found that Philadelphia was being cloyed a bit with pennant baseball. Capturing a pennant seemed to have lost its novelty of long repetition.[4]

Accurate or not, with the capacity of Shibe Park at just 23,000, there were limits to how much fans could contribute to Mack's budget through ticket sales. The Braves drew more than 36,000 fans to the two 1914 World Series games at Fenway Park. Mack was right that something was affecting attendance, since the A's drew just 346,461 for the regular season, only fifth-best in the AL.

Whether Mack told everyone what he was going to do or not, the newspapers began to play a role in informing fans of the future of some of their favorite players. A headline in a New York newspaper read, "Plank And Bender Put On Market," Then two sub-headlines followed: "Mack Asks Waivers On Two Best Pitchers To Thwart Feds." The other read, "Jack Coombs Slated For Sale."[5]

The report continued, pointing out that Mack's motive was to have these players remain with the established leagues. American League teams would have first crack at the pitchers for the $2,500 waiver price. If no AL team wanted them, a National League team could step in. The article noted that such a path had been followed by other, older stars in the past, but these pitchers could be on "the road that may possibly lead to oblivion."[6]

Mack preferred that the players stay with the official majors and was of the same strong opinion as AL president Ban Johnson, his long-time ally. Johnson and Mack had once played the same role as the Federal League was now doing, taking on the National League in 1901. But now they were the establishment, and they were not sympathetic to new challengers. "The Federal League must be exterminated," Johnson said. "Personally, I think the Federal League movement is a joke. We are determined to put the Feds out of business."[7]

Actually, newspapers obtaining information about Mack's intentions made a big splash. Placing a player on the waiver wire was supposed to be confidential. The player could be withdrawn with no one the wiser. Not this time. The likelihood of the trio of pitchers departing was leaked. Once the word was in the public domain, Mack was besieged by sportswriters. Philadelphia fans who retained a strong allegiance to the trio of hurlers were upset, and they were looking for explanations, too.

Pushed into a corner when asked if it was unusual for such star pitchers to be subject to waiver scrutiny, Mack said, "It is." He said he expected Coombs to make a comeback, and he gave no reason for parting with Bender, but did say he knew Plank was negotiating with the Federal League. Mack was ready to dispose of two of his old mainstays. "I am through with them and that's all there is to it. I don't mind saying now there are more surprises for the fans. I know that I may be criticized, but I am going to shake up the team."[8]

Mack even admitted that the steps he was taking were rare for a team that was still at the top of the American League and had just put together a tremendous run of success. "I'm willing to start all over again and develop a new team," he said. "I did it once and I can do it again."[9]

Then the exodus actually began of some of the Athletics' most beloved, triumphant and accomplished players. At 39, Eddie Plank jumped to the St. Louis Terriers of the Federal League, signing a two-year contract. Charles Bender jumped to the Federal League, too, and ended up with the Baltimore Terrapins. Coombs was still trying to battle back from his serious illness, and at first no major league team wanted to take a chance on him. Mack released him. Coombs did not go with the Federal League. He joined Brooklyn in the National League and made a fine comeback. Call that another hasty decision by Mack.

Outfielder Danny Murphy, whose playing days were nearly at an end and who had never truly recuperated from a knee injury, thought he might be able to make some dough and obtain a last chance to play with a Federal League team. He went to Mack and asked permission for his departure. Mack gave him his blessing.

Then came a real bombshell. Ira Thomas was still around, if basically

20. The Breakup

as a coach and as someone who might be dropped into a game as an emergency catcher. Whether as a gesture of loyalty to Mack or not, Thomas penned a strongly worded, sound-off diatribe against Eddie Collins. Collins was opinionated and had said that the Federal League was good for the players. He even rashly admitted having dinner with the president of the Brooklyn franchise but said he would give the Athletics any chance to match an offer. But Thomas suddenly popped off with an attack on Collins, saying, "The players blame Collins for the loss of the world's series to the Boston Braves because of the series of articles he wrote before and during those games."[10]

Apparently, Thomas was indicating the pen was mightier than the bat. But soon Collins, the reigning American League Most Valuable Player, was also out in Philadelphia. On December 8, Mack sold Collins to the Chicago White Sox for $50,000. That was an enormous sum of money for a transaction in those days. Collins was only 28 and had many good years left. White Sox owner Charles Comiskey paid him $15,000 for 1915. Collins made $7,000 with the A's in 1913.

Third baseman Frank "Home Run" Baker wasn't going to the Federal League. He still had two years left on a three-year contract. But Baker approached Mack to re-negotiate the deal. As was predictable, Mack refused. Disgruntled with his situation, Baker never reported to the A's, sitting out the entire 1915 season. He couched his absence as retirement. Mack told him he was welcome back with the A's, but only under the terms of his already-signed contract. Mack even gave Baker permission to play semi-pro ball, as long as it was not in the immediate Philadelphia area. Yet Baker joined up with Upland, a small town in a county near Philadelphia, and began making noise about a comeback—for more money.

That's when Mack got mad. He said, "I would not sell him for $1 million in cash." He then called Baker a "contract jumper" and added, "I hope I never see him again. He has treated the club unfairly and I have no time for a man who is not fair in his dealings."[11] Mack let Baker rot in the boonies for the entire season and then in February of 1916 sold Baker to the New York Yankees for $37,500, a little shy of a million. But that was hyperbole, anyway.

To make up for these key departures, Mack went to work on the personnel trail. He signed Larry Lajoie to play second base instead of Collins. Lajoie, one of the few men in history who was Collins' equal at the position, was 41 at the time, however. He batted .280 for Philadelphia, but for all his greatness was clearly no longer in his prime. Mack moved catcher Wally Schang to third base and inserted Jack Lapp as his catcher. Lapp had one of his better years, hitting .272, but ended up with the White Sox. Jack Barry appeared in just 54 games and was replaced by weak-hitting Larry Kopf (.225) at short when he was sold to the Red Sox in July for $8,000. There were still familiar names in the outfield, but the outfield had been the soft point of the club. Rube Oldring, Amos Strunk, Jimmy Walsh and Eddie Murphy were around, but only Strunk (.297) hit well. In July, Mack sold Murphy to the White Sox.

Mack gave things a whirl with pitchers he had nurtured. For one reason or another, the next generation of pitchers, those hurlers who had seemed so promising, pretty much all had off-years. That included Joe Bush, Bob Shawkey and Herb Pennock. There was no ace that year. Weldon Wyckoff, with ten victories, was the only pitcher to reach double figures. He also lost a league-worst 22 games. Rube Bressler finished 4-17, Bush 5-15. When it was clear to him how lousy his team was going to be, Mack became even more reckless in his dealings. Shawkey, 6-6, was sold to the Yankees. Pennock 3-6, was put on waivers. Mack sent 27 different pitchers to the mound that season, five of them only once, all of them 25 or younger. Four other pitchers were used just twice. He also sent 57 different players to the plate, trying to unearth fresh talent. This was all a quiet plea of desperation.

Only Stuffy McInnis, the one incumbent from the $100,000 infield, batted .300 that year, hitting .314.

The Athletics were a sad mess of a team, so horrible that most of the rest of their fans deserted them, and they went from first to worst in the American League in 1915. The record was 43-109, and a mere 146,223 fans, turning their noses up at the situation, showed up at Shibe Park. The A's scored 545 runs and gave up 889.

This was better than winning a pennant and being swept in a World Series? Not hardly.

Before the 1915 season even began, the Federal League decided to attack major league baseball on another front. The Feds filed an anti-trust lawsuit. The case ended up being sent to Judge Kenesaw Mountain Landis, who only a few years later would become the first commissioner of baseball.

As this was all playing out, the Federal League was playing out the 1915 season. There was a suspenseful battle for the best record, with the Chicago Whales prevailing with an 86-66 record. St. Louis finished 87-67 and the Pittsburgh Rebels 86-67. The 1914 champion Indianapolis Hoosiers relocated and became the Newark Peppers.

Landis halted the progress of the lawsuit by taking an inordinate time

20. The Breakup

to deliberate. This gave both sides time to reach a settlement, which is what he wanted. By December of 1916, with no end to the court case in sight and the United States poised to enter World War I, for all its big talk the Federal League essentially folded its tents. The money men capitulated. The league was not strong enough to continue the baseball war indefinitely. The American League and the National League wanted the Federal League out of the way. As the court case fizzled, agreements were made. Charles Weeghman, the man who built the stadium for his Chicago Whales which would become iconic Wrigley Field, was allowed to buy the Chicago Cubs. Phil Ball of the St. Louis Terriers was allowed to buy the St. Louis Browns. There was a dispersal sale of the players from the other six teams.

Harry Sinclair, the oil man, ended up with the dead Newark franchise. It wasn't as if, with his bank account, he folded first in this fight, though. At one point he issued a challenge to the major league owners: "I'll tell you what I'll do," Sinclair said. "I'll meet you people on the waterfront and we'll toss dollar for dollar into the Hudson River. Then we'll see who runs out of money first."[12] Others might have said he was already throwing his money down the toilet, so the action would have been redundant.

After all of the unrest and tumult, many, many of the major league players who sought more opportunity and bigger salaries never played in the majors again, and some lasted only briefly. Their belief in the long-term success of the Federal League was misguided.

Joe Tinker, the former Chicago Cubs second baseman, was the most outspoken agent, scout and salesman for the Federal League. When the new league was starting, he was a front man seeking to round up players, one of its key salesmen.

"It is not a little tank-town circuit," Tinker said early in the 1914 season, "but a powerful combination that has taken rank right up with the National and American Leagues. I have found myself almost in the position of intermediary between the businessmen and who are backing our league and the suspicious mass of ball players who wonder what it was all about."[13] He cited the multi-million-dollar riches of the owners, but in the end Tinker was snowed by the same snow job he passed off on the players he recruited. When it was all over, and there was no more Federal League, Tinker, too, was without a job.

Tinker had been a Cubs mainstay and was managing the Federal League's Whales. When Weeghman bought the Cubs, that positioned Tinker to return to the National League. However, he suited up for just seven games in 1916 and played no more.

During the 1915 season, Plank, competing for St. Louis, compiled a 21–11 record with a 2.08 earned run average. Plank seemed ageless. Bender (who signed for a $5,500 bonus and an $8,500 salary after making $5,000 with the A's) was with an awful team, 47–107 Baltimore, and he was awful himself that year, going 4–16. Bender said he was a nervous wreck after departing Philadelphia and, as someone known for being stoic, he internalized his stress. "After the 1914 season, my nerves reached such a pitch that I broke out in hives," he said. "My stomach still bothered me. I was weak and my pitching showed it. I spent hundreds of dollars on doctors and lost two big years."[14]

Coombs did make a successful return with Brooklyn, at last overcoming his illness. He was 15–10 with a 2.58 ERA for the NL team that year.

In 1915 and 1916, sportswriters chose a wide variety of figures to suggest how much money the Federal League principals lost on the venture. After holding his silence for quite some time, league president James Gilmore said the debits were not as big as most people thought. He claimed the net loss by all of the teams was just $500,000 because the settlement with the other leagues returned some cash, and the sale of players brought more money. Before being reimbursed for some of its deficit, he said, Brooklyn was the biggest loser because of a $350,000 investment. Pittsburgh's gross deficit was $150,000. He did not say how much the net loss was, but insisted that those teams gained back much of their deficits. That's because the remaining big leagues anted up $600,000 in payments to soothe the egos of the Federal League moguls. "Those who have been making wild estimates of our losses forget two or three very important things in our favor," Gilmore said, pointing to the player sales and some money received from the American and National leagues.[15]

Landis never handed down a ruling on the court case, and many speculated for years what turn things might have taken. The Baltimore Terrapins did not want a settlement. As descendants of the Baltimore Orioles, they wished to return big league ball to their city—and keep it. The Terrapins filed their own anti-trust suit against major league baseball, claiming it was a monopoly. In the early stages of the case, Baltimore won approval. The suit passed through the levels of jurisprudence, taking years as justice was sought. The Court of Appeals ruled against Baltimore, so the Terrapins pursued the matter to the United States Supreme Court.

"Federal League Baseball Club vs. National League," as the case was officially known, was decided by the Supreme Court in 1922 after being heard in the term which began in October of 1921. The Terrapins were

20. The Breakup

seeking triple damages from the claim, charging baseball had violated the Sherman Anti-Trust Act of 1890. In the end, the nation's highest court concluded on May 29, 1922, that major league baseball was not guilty of violating interstate commerce laws.

The opinion was written by Justice Oliver Wendell Holmes, Jr., and his statement compared baseball to a firm of lawyers sending an employee out of state, or a speaker's bureau hiring out a client to another state. "A firm of lawyers ... [or a] lecture bureau sending out lecturers does not engage in such commerce because a lawyer or a lecturer goes to another state. If we are right, the plaintiff's business is to be described in the same way."[16]

The Baltimore Terrapins lost their noble case and were out of business with no recompense. Baseball has forevermore relied on that court decision that the sport is not engaged in interstate commerce.

By the time the Federal League went out of business, it was too late for Connie Mack to resurrect the Philadelphia Athletics. It was like Humpty Dumpty taking his great fall off the wall, where the nursery rhyme refers to all of the king's horses and all of the king's men being unable to put him back together again. Whether it was arrogance, misjudgment, or feeding off spite, Mack had done so much damage to his team that it was not readily repaired.

At 36–117, the Athletics were even worse in 1916 than they had been in 1915, with a post–1900 low winning percentage record of .235. In June of 2016, 100 years later, *Sports Illustrated* examined that club and raised the question of whether this was the worst modern single-season team. Part of the opening headline read, "The 1916 Philadelphia Athletics May Have Been The Most God-Awful Team In Modern Baseball History."[17]

For starters, the 1916 A's scored 447 runs and gave up 776, an incredible differential. And then there was the fate of the starting pitchers. Joe Bush was 15–24 with a 2.57 earned run average, almost a stupendous achievement. Young Elmer Myers went 14–23. Those were the best guys. Jack Nabors, from Montevallo, Alabama, finished 1–20. Wrapping a couple of years of minimal appearances around both sides of that depressing season, Nabors retired with a 1–25 lifetime record. Tom Sheehan, who was 4–9 in 1915, went 1–16 the next year. Sheehan, who was from Illinois, escaped Philadelphia after that, but was never better in a season than 9–11 the rest of his career.

That meant two guys in the rotation for Mack in 1916 were a combined 2–36. Even with Lajoie, McInnis and Strunk (.316) around, the hitters weren't much better either. As a team, the A's hit .242.

Poor season after disastrous season after lousy season followed for the Athletics. The 1919 season, when the A's finished 36–104, was in the same category as the 1916 club. There wasn't much to choose from between those two pathetic years (although *Sports Illustrated* did). In 1919, the A's scored 457 runs and gave up 742, a similar, mind-boggling deficit. Some 49 players came to the plate for Philadelphia that year. The pitching was likely worse than in 1916. The high-game winners were Jing Johnson and Walt Kinney, each 9–15. Neither won as many games in another big league season.

The Athletics kept losing. The franchise's first winning season after 1914 did not occur until 1925. Mack learned that it was not so easy to rebuild after all.

21

Where They Went

Connie Mack didn't just break up the old gang, he blew it to smithereens. The once-harmonious Athletics fragmented, spread out, and settled with different teams in different states in different leagues.

There were several Hall of Famers of great note who made the Philadelphia Athletics of 1910 to 1914 great. There were players just coming into their own who became great. There were players who did their jobs and experienced the highlight of their lives playing for the A's dynasty that Connie Mack soldered together and by his own hand demolished.

Once they were Connie's boys, the lads he loved and trusted. Then they became pariahs to him. Still later, there were renewed acquaintances and some social time spent together, grudges buried in the sand. After 1914, though, they never made baseball magic together again.

Some did well elsewhere. Except for the few who were still on their way up during the dynasty, none did as well individually as they did collectively under Mack in Philadelphia.

Even the best teams do not remain together forever. The finest teams of all, in all professional sports, had core players who led them for a decade or more, but they kept replenishing the talent as some players aged and lost their skills. The Boston Celtics in basketball followed that model for 13 years. The Montreal Canadians in hockey seemed capable of going on and on. The Chicago Bears owned the 1940s, but World War II cut their rule short. For that matter, World War I, when the United States fully engaged, resulted in several of the Athletics players wearing different uniforms in 1917 and 1918. Mack could have filled in with skilled players at selected positions, dealing with the course of business and changing personnel in a normal fashion. But he could not rebuild an entire team in one swoop.

The A's coulda, woulda, shoulda been great for longer, but they were not. There are no maybes, only facts.

Major League Baseball was fortunate that the Federal League evaporated quickly. Americans were fortunate that their involvement in World War I was shorter than it was for European allies. Many ex-Athletics played on with other teams, only a select number of them winning World Series titles elsewhere. A couple of the pitchers were notable exceptions. Rather than hurling for the A's as aces the way Eddie Plank and Charles Bender had supplemented each other for years (with some help), the exiles actually helped make big winners out of other teams. Others just kept doing what they had been doing so well for a little bit longer at other home stadiums.

Eddie Plank

In some ways, Gettysburg Eddie was the Original Athletic. He was a member of the starting rotation in 1901 when Philadelphia was one of the original eight cities in the American League. Already 25, Plank finished 17–13 that year. He remained in a Philadelphia uniform through the 1914 season, and he seven times won at least 20 games for the A's.

For years, baseball observers suggested that the southpaw was getting too old. As each season dawned as Plank passed his 36th, 37th and 38th birthdays, the chorus became louder. He ignored the noise and just kept winning. Although his sojourn to St. Louis of the Federal League was brief, just one season, Plank won 21 games there, too. Plank pitched big league ball until he was 41 and won 326 games. He was elected to the Baseball Hall of Fame in 1946.

Plank was known as one of the pitchers who delayed the longest in making his delivery to the plate. Once he received the ball from a catcher, he did not immediately look to the plate, did not immediately check the sign, did not appear even to be thinking about the fact that a batter was in the box waiting for a pitch and thousands of fans in the grandstands had their eyes on him, wondering what the heck he was doing for so long.

Delay was a characteristic, but also a strategy, depending on which player from the enemy lineup was waving a club at him.

"To some he would pitch without fussing," said long-time teammate Eddie Collins. "To others he would throw a ball only after the umpire warned him against delay." Some umpires practically broke out in a rash, Plank made them so edgy. "Plank would fuss and fiddle with the ball, with his shoes, and then try to talk with the umpire. His motion was good enough to give the batter nervous indigestion."[1]

Plank was only 50 years old when he died in 1926. He had gone home

Southpaw Eddie Plank was the mainstay of the Athletics' staff during the early years of the 20th century, won 326 games and was elected to the Hall of Fame (Library of Congress).

to Gettysburg, and after a restful night's sleep he woke up and suffered the stroke that killed him.

A year later, in 1927, Gettysburg College opened a new gym and named it after Plank.

Jack Coombs

It was a slow recovery from typhoid fever for Jack Coombs, but he definitely surprised naysayers who thought he would never again be able to pitch in the majors. The seasons of 1913 and 1914 were lost years for him, but the Athletics certainly could have used his right-handed pitching in 1915. At 32, he won 15 games for the Brooklyn Dodgers, and a year later he won 13. Coombs stuck with Brooklyn through 1918 and made a brief comeback with the Detroit Tigers in 1920 before retiring. He pretty much went out on his own terms with 158 career victories thanks to recovering from his disease.

For the next stage of his life, Coombs became the baseball coach at Duke University in North Carolina, staying for 24 years until 1952. It is probable that most people stopped calling him "Colby Jack" once he made that move, except for guys from the old days. Coombs also taught a baseball course at the school, and years into his tenure he supplied the test to a sportswriter that he administered to students. The questions were printed in a newspaper. They included such quiz items as: "State the infield fly rule"; "What defensive plays should bring a pitcher back of third base? Back of the catcher?"[2]

Since Coombs did do some teaching, whenever the sportswriters looked him up for a chat, they referred to him as "Professor." He became a sports historian and wrote one book about baseball, and it was called a textbook. Long forgotten was his college-aged ambition to become a chemist.

Unlike many coaches in earlier decades who did not specialize, but were paid by their schools to lead more than one sports team, Coombs did not believe in that approach. He felt a coach could master only one sport or otherwise would short-change some of his pupils. So he was solely a baseball man.

> A coach must know the game from all angles if he expects to gain the confidence of his squad members. It is the task of each coach and the definite aim in his life to shape the character and ambition of each young man with whom he associates so that lad will face the competition of life with a firm determination to succeed with a high standard of character and sportsmanship, which can be, and is taught upon our athletic fields.[3]

When Coombs finally decided to retire from Duke, he said his next plan was to "catch all the damned catfish in Texas."[4] Coombs died on April 15, 1957, at age 74 of a heart attack in Palestine, Texas, though no one took note of just how close he came to obliterating the local catfish population. Obituaries focused on his tenure with the Athletics (as well as his time at Duke) and stressed his 31-victory season and his completion of the 24-inning marathon game.

"No pitcher ever gave me more than Coombs gave me in 1910," Mack said of Coombs' spectacular winning year when he also recorded 13 shutouts.[5]

Charles Albert "Chief" Bender

The move to the Federal League was disastrous for Charles Bender. He had the worst season of his career in 1915, going 4–16. He attributed it to poor health, but Bender's stay with Baltimore was a big flop. As soon as the Federal League went out of business, though, Bender was able to find a job back in the majors, and in Philadelphia. Just not with the Athletics. He joined the National League Phillies. He still wasn't his old self, but was much better than he was the year before, going 7–7. Proving he still had some of his good stuff at 33, the next year Bender finished 8–2 for the Phillies with a 1.67 earned run average. He retired, but made a fitful comeback at 41 with the Chicago White Sox in 1925 after a layoff of eight years. Bender pitched in just one game that season.

Bender's lifetime mark was 212–127, a winning percentage of .625, and he had an excellent ERA of 2.46. Ultimately, he was elected to the Hall of Fame in 1953.

There was a reason why Bender was intrigued enough to give it one more try with Chicago so long after his last major league showing. He spent several years pitching in the minors while also managing teams. He became very popular in the Virginia League. He actually turned down offers to pitch in the majors again during those years because he so much enjoyed managing. "I didn't have more stuff in 1919 than I did in 1905," he said. "I knew how to pitch and those minor leaguers didn't get one where they could bust it. I used to chuckle when I heard them say, 'Why that fellow Bender never gives you a good ball to hit at.'"[6]

Long after Bender stopped stressing his right arm with full-blast throws from the mound, he continued in the game as a prominent pitching coach. Bender made good investments in businesses, using money earned in baseball, and so could stay in the sport as a coach or a scout into his later years as much for the pleasure of it as for the income.

Bender even reconnected with the Athletics and Mack in the 1930s and worked with the team well into the 1940s. In 1951, Bender, then 68 years old, became the Athletics' major league pitching coach. He was still doing what he loved to do, was still enamored with baseball and working with young people. "I love baseball," Bender said in 1942. "I love working with the youngsters. The game was good to me. It had its heartaches, but they were a drop in the bucket compared to the fun I had and the friends I made."[7]

Throughout his career, Bender had been subjected to racist taunts because of his Native American heritage and was the object of so-called clever observations also based on being an Ojibwe Indian. He never showed his distaste or irritation about these slurs. In 1954, a year after being elected to the Hall of Fame, Bender died at 70. At least one headline on a story reporting his death read, "Chief Bender Answers Call To Happy Hunting Grounds."[8]

Even in death, Charles Albert Bender could not outrun his times and narrow attitudes.

Herb Pennock

While it seemed that Connie Mack was grooming Herb Pennock for stardom in the rotation, he lost patience with him—too quickly—after his first few seasons with the Athletics. Pennock should have been one of the guys that Mack kept around as he was ridding himself of older pitchers. Pennock's 1914 season, when he finished 11–4, was all he needed as a calling card to demonstrate that he was ready for more responsibility.

Things went awry in 1915 and Pennock finished just 3–6, but the A's were beginning their horrible stretch. Still, in June Mack put Pennock on waivers, and he was claimed by the Red Sox. He went into the service, and when he returned to baseball in 1919, he blossomed, going 16–8. A couple of years later, Boston traded Pennock to the Yankees, and New York agreed with him. His best seasons came with the Yankees, and when Pennock retired he had 241 victories. He pitched until 1934, retiring at 40.

Pennock was only 53 when he died in 1948 of a cerebral hemorrhage. In the same year, he was inducted into the Baseball Hall of Fame.

When he wasn't throwing a baseball, Pennock raised silver foxes for their pelts and hounds for hunting, and he grew vegetables. Also, Pennock's daughter married Eddie Collins, Jr., son of Pennock's second base teammate with the A's.

Bob Shawkey

Right-hander Bob Shawkey, like Herb Pennock, is best remembered as a New York Yankee. Shawkey won 207 games in his career and also was the starting pitcher for the home side on April 18, 1923, the day Yankee Stadium opened for business.

He called that game in front of 74,200 fans "the greatest thrill of my life."[9]

During World War I, Shawkey served in the Navy. Over the course of his career, Shawkey won at least 20 games in a season four times and played for seven American League pennant winners. He struck out 15 batters in one game, which remained a Yankees record for years. A personal trademark was wearing a red, long-sleeved shirt under his short-sleeved uniform top.

Pitcher Bob Shawkey broke into the majors with the Athletics in 1913, but reached stardom after joining the New York Yankees in 1915 (Library of Congress).

As he aged, Shawkey worked as pitching coach for New York and helped younger Yankees hurlers. George Pipgras raved about him after winning 24 games in 1928, he said by applying Shawkey's advice. "Bob taught me everything but how to wear a red undershirt," Pipgras said. "He taught me control, how to put a hop on the fast one, and added another wrinkle to the curve. Bob changed my pitching movement, too, and that improved my effectiveness a lot."[10]

In 1930, after Miller Huggins died, Shawkey briefly managed the Yankees. When he was much younger, Shawkey pitched for Slippery Rock State in Pennsylvania. When he stepped away from the majors, he coached Dartmouth College baseball. Shawkey lived to be 90, passing away in 1980.

Bullet Joe Bush

While Leslie Ambrose "Bullet Joe" Bush probably should have been a member of the Philadelphia Athletics for life, he came along too late in the dynasty to have that distinction. Bush played big league ball from 1912 to 1928, coming up with the A's but also playing for the Red Sox, Yankees, Browns, Senators, Pirates, Giants, and for a last hurrah in 1928, one last season back with the Athletics.

Bush, who pitched a no-hitter in 1916, won 195 games in his career and during his travels played for three World Series champions. That no-hitter was recorded during one of the Athletics' horror-show seasons after Connie Mack dismantled the roster. In 1922, Bush went 26–7 with an American League-leading .788 win percentage.

Bush is credited with the invention of the forkball, held deep between the first two fingers of the throwing hand. It was little-used for decades, however. "Probably one of the most bewildering balls ever pitched was of my own invention, the forkball," Bush said, "which I discovered in 1920 when I was essaying a comeback with the Boston Red Sox after I had hurt my arm several years before and was forced to stop throwing curveballs."[11]

Wally Schang

While Connie Mack expressed great admiration for Wally Schang's catching ability, that did not prevent him from shifting him to third base to replace Frank "Home Run" Baker when he needed to, or from dumping him along with so many of his prominent players a little later when he felt like it.

Schang played 19 years in the majors, but after his first five seasons for the Athletics between 1913 and 1917, he was traded to the Boston Red Sox, where he also flourished and competed in an additional World Series. After another lengthy stay with the New York Yankees, Schang did make his way back to the A's for a year near the end of his career. Schang was actually a key player for two teams—Philadelphia and Boston—broken up by their owners for financial reasons.

In all, Schang played in six World Series, representing Philadelphia, Boston and New York of the American League and hitting .284 lifetime. He was a switch-hitter whose career on-base percentage was a solid .393. Schang, who did not retire until he was 41, batted .300 six times and appeared in 1,842 games. In an interesting switch, Schang caught for the Red Sox when Babe Ruth pitched and played for the Yankees after Ruth moved to the outfield.

Despite Mack's belief that Schang was a talented receiver and had a general appreciation for his athleticism and his longevity at the position, Schang committed 223 errors as a catcher, the AL record.

Schang was 75 when he died in St. Louis in 1965 after playing and managing for years in the minor leagues and then running a farm.

Amos Strunk

The left-handed hitting and throwing outfielder nicknamed "Lightning" was often an overlooked member of the championship A's ball clubs because Amos Strunk played in the shadow of the $100,000 infield. Strunk broke into the majors in 1908 at 19 and had a 17-year big league career.

During his first ten seasons, all with Philadelphia, Strunk was not a star, but was a major contributor to pennant-winners, hitting as high as .316 and seven times stealing in double figures for the A's. He was also most appreciated for his excellent play in center field. After leaving Philadelphia when Mack was in a player-exiling frenzy, Strunk did return to play for the Athletics again during parts of the 1919 and 1920 seasons. Strunk also played his final games with the A's in 1924.

Mack once called Strunk "the most underrated outfielder in baseball."[12] Strunk, who was born in Philadelphia in 1889, was 90 when he died in Llanerch, Pennsylvania, in 1979.

Stuffy McInnis

The first baseman in the $100,000 infield should probably be in the Hall of Fame, but is not. Given McInnis' statistics, it is an easy case to make, and fans and supporters of his just hope that some day the Veterans Committee recognizes the Hall's oversight in not including him.

Supremely skilled around the bag, McInnis suffered from playing his 19-year, major league career before Gold Glove Awards were handed out to the top fielders at each position. He also played essentially in the Deadball Era, long before first base became a power hitter's position. McInnis practically never hit home runs, but his lifetime batting average was .307. The right-handed hitting McInnis recorded ten full seasons over .300 and also did so in parts of two others. He played in 2,128 games and knocked in 1,063 runs while stealing 172 bases. McInnis made ten or more thefts in a season six times, with a high of 27. McInnis starred for the Athletics through the 1917 season before Connie Mack traded him to the Boston Red Sox. Eventually, McInnis suited up for the Cleveland Indians, Brooklyn Dodgers, and the Pittsburgh Pirates before playing his last game in 1927 for the Philadelphia Phillies.

McInnis was likely one of the best fielding first basemen ever, topping a .990 fielding percentage 12 times. His lifetime fielding record at first base was .993. In all, while playing first base McInnis committed 160 errors in 17,487 chances.

McInnis was from Gloucester, Massachusetts, the fishing community about 40 miles north of Boston, and when he died in 1960 at age 69 his hometown newspaper, the *Gloucester Daily Times*, did not equivocate, flat-out calling him "the greatest first baseman in Major League history." It was also noted when McInnis broke into the bigs in 1909 at 18, he was called "the boy wonder of the American League."[13]

McInnis appeared in three World Series for the Athletics, one for the Red Sox, and in a final one in 1925 for Pittsburgh when the Pirates outlasted the Washington Senators and had to best Walter Johnson to do so. "That last game of the Series was one of the happiest and yet one of the saddest days of my life," McInnis said. "Happy because my team had two out after an uphill fight, but sad because were defeating one of the gamest and squarest players I have ever met—Walter Johnson."[14]

McInnis coached the Harvard University baseball team after he retired from the majors as a player. Forty years after he passed away, that same hometown newspaper began a campaign to get McInnis elected to the Hall of Fame. During that era, 2000, Bob Ryan, the prominent *Boston Globe* columnist, had written that McInnis seemed as qualified as any other player not in the Hall. Much earlier, one of McInnis' contemporaries, Grantland Rice, said of McInnis, he "was a war god of the diamond."[15]

Eddie Collins

There are few second basemen in the history of baseball that accomplished as much as Eddie Collins did at the position, or for as long. The left-handed hitting Collins broke into the majors in 1906 at 19, and his longevity and tremendous list of achievements, not only with the Athletics but after he was sent elsewhere, made him a remarkable Hall of Famer. In addition, long after his playing days ended, Collins remained in the sport in a prominent manner.

For starters, Collins spent 25 years in the big leagues. He batted .333 in 2,826 games, and his 3,315 base hits remain 11th on the all-time list 86 years after he retired. Collins also stole 741 bases, four times leading the American League in that category. He once stole 81 bases in a single season. Collins three times led the AL in runs scored, and he owns a less appreciated, but significant record of 512 sacrifice bunts. In 1914, Collins earned the Chalmers Award as the American League's Most Valuable Player.

Collins was as much a star with the Chicago White Sox as he had been with the A's, and after participating in four World Series with Philadelphia, he played in two more with the Sox, winning the title in 1917, but being a "clean Sox" player in 1919 while Black Sox teammates were fixing the Series in Cincinnati's favor.

At the tail end of Collins' playing career, he returned to the Athletics, more as a coach than player, but did suit up for some games even past his 43rd birthday. Then he became a full-time coach for the A's before moving on to become general manager of the Boston Red Sox for 15 years. Collins was a close friend of Tom Yawkey, who bought the Boston club in 1934 and installed his pal as the chief personnel man.

In 1939, Collins became an early Hall of Fame choice. It was no accident that Collins was nicknamed "Cocky." He was very confident and an Ivy League graduate from Columbia at a time when many ball players came to the majors right off the farm and had limited educations.

Recalling that dissension was a major reason why Mack broke up his championship club after so much success, it was no small irony that Collins, who was not well-liked by many of his greedy and cheating teammates, ended up on that infamous 1919 Chicago team. He was on the outs with the planners and he was in the dark about the conspiracy, but he recognized early that this was not the friendliest bunch of guys he ever shared a locker room with. First baseman Chick Gandil, one of the organizers of the fix, and Collins may have played next to one another in the infield, but Collins said they went months without speaking because of their disdain for one another.

> From the moment I arrived in training camp from service, I could see that something was amiss. The club was torn by discord and hatred during much of the '19 season ... in '19 we were a club that pulled apart rather than together. There were frequent arguments and open hostility ... and yet it was the greatest collection of players ever assembled, I would say.[16]

Collins, who died at 63 in 1951, long after other generations of great players came along, said he would probably have been better remembered by history if he hadn't played at the same time as Ty Cobb, who in many minds is the greatest player of all time. "There was never a more dynamic player than Cobb," Collins said, "and as long as it had to be a player of Ty's stature that dimmed my own shining star, I can't say I have any regrets."[17] He also said, "I chased him right to the wall for 15 seasons trying to nose him out for the record in either base running or batting, but he was always ahead. Looking back, I feel more pleasure and pride at having been second to Cobb than I do at having been ahead of anybody else."[18]

Collins was not bragging about where he stood in the pantheon of baseball stars. John J. McGraw, the three-decades-long manager of the New York Giants, in 1913 called him the best player he ever saw.

Jack Barry

Given that today the shortstop is often the weakest-hitting position player, it should probably be no surprise that Jack Barry was no Hall of Fame swinger as a member of the $100,000 infield.

Most of Barry's distinguished seasons during his 11-year career occurred in the uniform of the Philadelphia Athletics when the A's were the best team in baseball. A graduate of Holy Cross College in Worcester, Massachusetts, Barry was 21 when he made his big league debut for Philadelphia in 1908 and 28 when he moved to the Boston Red Sox. He missed one season, 1918, because he was in the service during World War I, and then retired with Boston in 1919 at age 32.

Barry was a lifetime .243 hitter and never batted higher than .275 in a season. He played in 1,223 games, and his primary asset was his glove. Barry appeared in four World Series with the A's and one with Boston. Connie Mack understood that Barry's greatest contributions were made in the field. "The Athletics have never had a shortstop who could fill his shoes," Mack said.[19]

After retiring, Barry became the baseball coach at his alma mater in 1921. Once Barry took over that job he never left it, leading the Crusaders for 40 years until he died in 1961 of cancer. Not being the hitter the other three members of the A's famed infield were, Barry was never seriously mentioned as a Baseball Hall of Fame candidate. However, his .806 winning percentage leading Holy Cross opened the door to the American Baseball Coaches Hall of Fame, and he was also inducted into the College Baseball Hall of Fame. Barry's 1952 Holy Cross team won the College World Series.

Frank "Home Run" Baker

The man with one of the niftiest baseball nicknames of them all made his reputation with the Philadelphia Athletics, but also thrived with the New York Yankees—just a little bit too soon to become an integral part of another dynasty.

Following Baker's unhappy split from the A's after sitting out the 1915 season, he played for New York from 1916 until he retired in 1922, except for sitting out the 1920 season. He was a teammate of Babe Ruth's, but retired at 36 just before the Yankees became golden. Baker's lifetime average was .307. He led the American League in home runs four straight years in the Deadball Era and three times knocked in more than 100 runs in a season. Baker also stole 235 bases. He swatted 96 regular-season homers with his 52-ounce bat.

That catchy nickname carried Baker a long way. He was elected to the Hall of Fame in 1955 and lived to experience his induction, not passing away until 1963 at age 77. Born in Trappe, Maryland, where he made his home after leaving baseball, Baker was honored by the creation of a Home Run Baker Park there.

Baker was as proud of his fielding as he was of his acclaimed slugging. "It was not because I was fast," he said. "I was the slowest runner. But very few ever could get a quicker start." He also turned stealing third base into a particular preference rather than mostly going from first to second. "I could get a longer lead off second, plus a better study of the pitcher."[20]

Baker realized he was a different kind of home-run hitter in his day from the modern players he saw in the early 1960s, when the ball sailed beyond the fences much more frequently.

> Baseball is just a different game than when I played it. Our game was good and fun to play. Home runs were much rarer, but I used to get a big bang out of hitting one and so did the Philadelphia fans. Now they hit as many home runs in a day as we sometimes hit in a month, but the present game is a good spectacle and the crowds certainly do enjoy it.[21]

Earle Mack

Connie's son, Earle Mack, spent decades at his dad's side with the Philadelphia Athletics in several capacities, playing a little bit (very little), coaching, advising and scouting. Earle was assistant manager for much of his adulthood, and although it was said to be his dream to some day succeed his father as full-time manager, he sometimes denied that.

Although it never came to pass that Earle became the field boss of the A's as a permanent holder of the job, twice, in 1937 and 1939, he filled in for substantial amounts of time. The club went 15–17 in the first stretch and went 30–60 over the second stretch.

The younger Mack appeared in just five games over three seasons in 1910, 1911 and 1914, with just two hits in 16 at-bats. He tried three different positions, catcher, third base and first base. Earle played 14 seasons in the minors, however. Some of those years on the field were quite solid. He batted .294 at Moline in 1921 in 132 games, .321 in 95 games at Martinsburg, West Virginia, for the Blue Ridge Blue Sox in 1923, and .287 in 114 games at Raleigh in 1913. For a time, Earle also coached the University of North Carolina baseball team.

In 1954, 13 years before Mack died at 77, the Athletics were sold out of the family. Connie, Earle and his brother Roy were bought out.

Rube Oldring

Oldring was an outfielder and third baseman during his Major League career, which spanned 1905 to 1918. Interestingly, he broke in with the New York American League team when it was called the Highlanders and returned to New York for one year, 1916, after the team had changed its name to the Yankees.

Earle Mack was Connie's son, and for decades he was anointed to succeed his father as manager. That never happened, but Earle caught, coached and scouted for the A's (National Baseball Hall of Fame Library, Cooperstown, New York).

In 1918, Oldring, who had departed Philadelphia when the A's were breaking up, returned to the team for 49 games at the end of his big-league career.

Oldring was a lifetime .270 hitter in the majors, but kept playing ball for several more years in the minors in Seattle, New Haven and Virginia. He died in 1961 at age 77 in Bridgeton, New Jersey.

Daniel Murphy

A major league second-baseman and an outfielder after Eddie Collins took over his old job, Daniel Murphy compiled a .289 Major League average between 1900 and 1915, including his stay with the Federal League's Brooklyn Tip-Tops at the end of his career.

He four times hit over .300 in full seasons for the A's and topped that mark in two other part-time seasons.

Murphy was part of three World Series champs with Philadelphia. He died at 79 in 1955 in Jersey City, New Jersey.

Bris Lord

The outfielder whose career covered part of eight seasons between 1905 and 1913, was best known as "the other guy" in the trade where the Philadelphia A's divested themselves of "Shoeless" Joe Jackson. Bris Lord batted .256 during his major-league career.

After his playing days ended, Lord managed in the minor leagues.

Lord passed away at 81 in 1964 in Prince Frederick, Maryland.

22

Connie Mack

He was the constant. Connie Mack was the long-term link, the river winding through Philadelphia Athletics history, staying in his job of manager, through his full- or part-time ownership of the franchise, for a half-century. It will never happen again that one man will for so long coach or manage any professional sports franchise. It was improbable as the longevity unfolded and became impossible to equal as times and circumstances changed.

Mack managed the Athletics from 1901 to 1950, transforming from a recently retired player to a super-senior citizen in the dugout across two world wars and for a record 7,755 regular-season games. By sheer dint of stamina, he presided over 3,731 victories, also a record, and 3,948 defeats, still another record. If there is a number in managing associated with the word "most," Connie Mack's name is usually attached to it. Remarkably, Mack managed until he was 87 years old.

Under his personnel and handling, the Athletics won nine pennants and five World Series crowns. Never a deep-pockets owner, Mack relied on his own scouting acumen, the advice of friends, and the wisdom of his aides to recruit and develop talent. At times, after years of effort, he built his club into the best in the world.

The A's were the best team in baseball during this first dynasty period and again, accomplishing the difficult task of dethroning the American League rival New York Yankees when the Yankees were at the height of their power with Babe Ruth and Lou Gehrig hugging the middle-of-the-lineup batting slots, they superseded them again for a time.

From 1929 through 1931, the updated Athletics were the best team in the American League, not the Yankees. Philadelphia won three straight pennants and two World Series during that span after Mack cobbled together another phenomenal group of players. Of course, after Mack's demolition job on the 1910–1914 bunch, it took that long to re-achieve greatness. By Chicago Cubs and Boston Red Sox standards, that was not so long at all, but tell that to the waiting Philadelphia fans.

In 1929, the A's finished 104–46. Among the players on that club were such future Hall of Famers as catcher Mickey Cochrane, first baseman Jimmie Foxx, outfielder Al Simmons, and pitcher Lefty Grove. That was the core of those three-year wonders.

Years later, in 1939, on the occasion of what was believed at the time to be the 100th anniversary of the invention of baseball by Abner Doubleday (since discredited), Mack wrote a story about the sport for the American Legion's magazine.

"Those half million boys who take part in the Legion's program each year will, in most cases, play very little baseball after they get to be 21," Mack said. "But the memories of their experiences in fitting themselves into a group in team play will help them no matter what field of work they may enter in adult life."[1]

That was the idealistic Connie, the true lover of the game, speaking, shedding all of the trappings of the business side. One thing Mack admitted was that it wasn't always easy running teams that finished eighth in the AL standings. "Yes, I've had my downs as well as my ups," he said. "For seven straight years we were in the American League cellar and it was a long, hard pull from 1921, the last year we finished eighth in that particular series of years, to 1929, when we came back to win the World Championship."[2]

There were certainly times when Mack had disagreements with his players, and even those he much admired and long appreciated were traded away when that occurred. However, for someone who spent so many years in the game spanning generations as a player, manager and owner, Mack did have a diverse fan club. Those in the sport considered him a gentleman, and those who played for him generally admired him.

"He is a leader of men and a wonderful baseball tactician," said Eddie Collins, one of the Hall of Famers Mack tutored. "From the very first I was favorably impressed. He seemed to have a fatherly air about him. He was so affable without being artificial and he seemed to convey that he was very much interested in me."[3]

As a rule, Mack very much took an interest in the men he managed, not simply because of what they could do for him on the field, but in the broader picture of life. Mack recognized the superstition in many men's souls and allowed it to flourish if it fed their minds. He also played psychiatrist in the way he handled his players. "It's the psychology of it," said Mack, linking superstition and mind analysis together. "If a man goes to the bat, for instance, believing that he is carrying some potent charm, it gives him confidence. That is why I indulge the men."[4]

Although over the years Mack said many times that he thought his son Earle would eventually succeed him as manager, towards the end of his tenure, when sportswriters asked when he was going to retire, Mack implied that the operative word was never. In spring training of 1950, as the season approached, Mack refused to commit to retiring even after that year was over. "Retire?" he said. "I couldn't do that. It wouldn't be like me." Mack added through facial and hand gestures that he wouldn't be retiring until he passed away.[5]

For anyone who suggested a man of 87 could not manage a big-league ball club, Mack kept a daily schedule that pretty much followed the pattern of 7:30 a.m. to midnight. He even woke up without the aid of an alarm clock. Mack's vigor embraced signing autographs by the bushel and watching every minute of Athletics team practice. Mack was indeed an old-timer who had seen it all, but he didn't act old.

For decades following the earliest days of the franchise, Mack was the manager and personnel director of the Philadelphia Athletics, a co-owner with Ben Shibe and then Tom Shibe. After the younger Shibe died in 1937, Mack and his family became the principal owners. Shibe Park's name also changed to Connie Mack Stadium.

The A's were never amongst the wealthiest clubs in baseball, and that was one reason why the fortunes of the team took such dramatic swings. The Athletics were great when Mack could build them from nothing, when savvy and an eye for talent meant more than big spending. But he could not afford to replenish through splashy player deals and instead was almost always the seller, not the buyer, when it came to dispersing talent. A shortage of cash contributed significantly to the end of Mack's and his family's official connection with the Athletics, too.

In the end, there was a family feud with Mack and his sons in the main event and, as the team's budget shortfall proved fatal, the club was sold in 1954 to a Chicago businessman named Arnold Johnson for $3.3 million. Though there were debts taken out of the hide of the payoff, the team was definitely no white elephant.

Mack's 6-foot-2 erect demeanor, straw boater on his head, a full suit on his body instead of a baseball uniform, always cut a dashing figure in the sport. He was imposing and distinguished in look, but he was not nearly such an authoritarian figure at the end. Mack died on February 8, 1956, not so terribly long after parting ways with his beloved Athletics.

Some 70 years had passed since Mack was a rookie ball player. He outlasted all of his teammates in the sport and outlived his contemporaries. He was present at the birth of the American League and was still in the dugout when old-timer Casey Stengel began running the New York Yankees in an opposing dugout.

Probably much worse when it came time to coping with emotions, Mack was still alive when the Philadelphia Athletics became the Kansas City Athletics, when the moving trucks rolled down the highway containing so much of the hardware representing his team. One sportswriter observing the departure of two king-sized vans referred to the action as "like any funeral [a] sad occasion." "They asked for everything and there it goes," added Roy Mack, one of Connie's sons, who performed the role of funeral director. "I still can't believe it and apparently a lot other people can't believe it, either."[6]

Connie Mack's own funeral in Philadelphia was conducted in the rain. Among those from the 1910 era who paid respects were Frank Baker and Ira Thomas. The mourners cried softly as they said goodbye. The night before the service, 3,000 mourners walked past his open bronze casket in tribute. Mack wore a dark suit, as he had for many years at the ball park. Ford Frick, who had ascended from baseball writer to commissioner of the whole sport, said he remembered one hot and humid ball game from way back when the temperature felt like 120 degrees. "Mr. Mack," he said, "wore as he always did, a starched collar. I remember seeing him after the game. The collar wasn't wilted at all. It was never wilted."[7]

In East Brookfield, Massachusetts, in 1970, a monument to honor Mack was installed in front of his childhood home with a plaque reading, "Cornelius (Connie Mack) McGillicuddy, 'Grand Old Man of Baseball,' Born, Dec. 22, 1862, Died Feb. 8. 1956."

In 2012, the community celebrated the 150th anniversary of his birth with a Connie Mack Day celebration.

That 1970 plaque did more than recite simple facts. It was complemented by a comment reading, "He became a baseball legend in his own time."[8]

That was no hyperbole, but mere truth. Connie Mack was indeed a baseball legend during his lifetime—and beyond it.

Chapter Notes

Introduction

1. John Odell, "The Elephant in the Room: Pachyderm Images Made Famous by the Athletics Have Home at the Hall of Fame," *Memories and Dreams* 34, no. 6 (Winter 2012): 20–23.

Chapter 1

1. Connie Mack, "My Fifty Years in Baseball," Part 1, *Philadelphia Inquirer*, September 8, 1930.
2. Ibid.
3. Norman L. Macht, *Connie Mack and the Early Years of Baseball* (Lincoln: University of Nebraska Press, 2007), 118.
4. Ibid.
5. Connie Mack, *My 66 Years in the Big Leagues* (Philadelphia: The John C. Winston Company, 1950), 27.
6. Frederick G. Lieb, *Connie Mack: Grand Old Man of Baseball* (Kent, OH: Kent State University Press, 2012; first published New York: G.P. Putnam, 1945), 72.
7. Mack, *My 66 Years in the Big Leagues*, 29.
8. Henry Beach Needham and Connie Mack, "Clean Living and Quick Thinking," *McClure's Magazine*, May 1914, 53–62.
9. Ibid.
10. 1948 Schedule Card for the Connie Mack Sportsmen's Club of the Brookfields, June 1948.
11. Ibid.

Chapter 2

1. Macht, *Connie Mack and the Early Years of Baseball*, 179.
2. Alan H. Levy, *Rube Waddell: The Zany Brilliant Life of a Strikeout Artist* (Jefferson, NC: McFarland, 2000), 104.
3. Ibid., 115.
4. Tim Hornbaker, *Fall from Grace: The Truth and Tragedy of Shoeless Joe Jackson* (New York: Sports Publishing, 2016), 7.
5. Mack, *My 66 Years in the Big Leagues*, 43.
6. Hornbaker, *Fall from Grace*, 26.
7. Levy, *Rube Waddell*, 264.
8. Mack, *My 66 Years in the Big Leagues*, 96.

Chapter 3

1. Lieb, *Connie Mack*, 129.
2. Mack, "My Fifty Years in Baseball," Part 30, *Philadelphia Inquirer*, October (no date), 1930.
3. Lieb, *Connie Mack*, 131.
4. Ibid., 81.
5. Macht, *Connie Mack and the Early Years of Baseball*, 361.
6. Edgar Williams, "Amos Strunk, 89, Outfielder for Pennant-Winning Athletics," *Philadelphia Inquirer*, July 25, 1979.
7. Ibid.
8. Frank Yeuter, "Amos Strunk Won Baseball Fame After 'Jumping' S. Carolina Team," *Philadelphia Bulletin*, March 3, 1958.
9. "Ira Thomas Succumbs at 77; Caught 1909–10 Champ A's," *Sporting News*, October 22, 1958.
10. Hal Lebovitz, "Paddy Livingston, 83, Urges Spitball Return," *Cleveland Plain Dealer*, June 2, 1963.
11. Ibid.
12. Regis McAuley, "A Grand Old Man," *Cleveland Press*, January 16, 1968.
13. Dan Coughlin, "Livingston, 94, Recalls Early Days," *Cleveland Plain Dealer*, March 24, 1974.

14. *Ibid.*
15. Associated Press, "Earle Mack to Manage Athletics When 'If Ever,' Connie Retires," *New York Times*, May 12, 1943.

Chapter 4

1. Macht, *Connie Mack and the Early Years of Baseball*, 367.
2. "Coombs Disclaims Credit for Pitching 24-Inning Victory," *New York World*, April 27, 1929.
3. John P. Tierney, *Jack Coombs: A Life in Baseball* (Jefferson, NC: McFarland, 2008), 52.

Chapter 5

1. Mack, *My 66 Years in the Big Leagues*, 30.
2. William C. Kashatus, *Money Pitcher: Chief Bender and the Tragedy of Indian Assimilation* (University Park: Pennsylvania State University Press, 2006), 57.
3. Harry Grayson, "Bender Greatest of Money Pitchers," paper not available, Newspaper Enterprise Association, n.d., Baseball Hall of Fame Archives.
4. *Ibid.*
5. Robert Peyton Wiggins, *Chief Bender: A Baseball Biography* (Jefferson, NC: McFarland, 2010), 120.
6. *Ibid.*
7. Kashatus, *Money Pitcher*, 85.
8. Tom Swift, "Chief Bender," Society for American Baseball Research Biography Project/*Baseball Magazine*, 1911.
9. Kashatus, 85.
10. Grantland Rice, "Setting the Pace," syndicated column, February 11, 1944.
11. *Ibid.*
12. *Ibid.*

Chapter 6

1. Philadelphia Athletics World Series program 1910.
2. *Ibid.*
3. *Ibid.*
4. *Ibid.*
5. Gene Schoor, *The History of the World Series* (New York: William Morrow, 1990).
6. Macht, *Connie Mack and the Early Years of Baseball*, 483.
7. Frederick G. Lieb, "Heart Attack Proves Fatal for Overall, Old Cub Ace," *The Sporting News*, July 23, 1947.
8. "Mordecai Brown Chicago," *Deadball Stars of the National League*, Society for American Baseball Research, 2004.
9. Macht, *Connie Mack and the Early Years of Baseball*, 483.
10. Yeuter, "Amos Strunk Won Baseball Fame After 'Jumping' S. Carolina Team."
11. Tierney, *Jack Coombs*, 64.
12. Macht, *Connie Mack and the Early Years of Baseball*, 489.

Chapter 7

1. Lieb, *Connie Mack*, 48.
2. Macht, *Connie Mack and the Early Years of Baseball*, 243.
3. *Ibid.*, 490.
4. *Ibid.*, 502.
5. *Ibid.*
6. *Ibid.*, 412.
7. "Jack Barry, Famed Member of $100,000 Infield, Dead," *The Sporting News*, May 3, 1961.
8. Mack, *My 66 Years In The Big Leagues*, 50.

Chapter 8

1. Stan Baumgartner, "Collins Went from Campus to A's," *The Sporting News*, August 16, 1950.
2. Macht, *Connie Mack and the Early Years of Baseball*, 411.
3. Eddie Collins and Jim Leonard, "From Sullivan to Collins: Colorful Life Story of Game's Greatest Second Baseman," Chapter II, *The Sporting News*, October 18, 1950.
4. Baumgartner, "Collins Went from Campus to A's."
5. Collins and Leonard, "From Sullivan to Collins."
6. Mack, *My 66 Years in the Big Leagues*, 196.
7. Collins and Leonard, "From Sullivan to Collins."
8. Collins and Leonard, "From Sullivan to Collins."

Chapter 9

1. Macht, *Connie Mack and the Early Years of Baseball*, 501.
2. Mack, "My Fifty Years in Baseball."

3. Steve Steinberg, "Dave Danforth," Society for American Baseball Research, *The Louisville Courier*, August 7, 1915.
4. Bob Broeg, "Dentist Dave Still Under Doctoring Suspicion," *The Sporting News*, September 23, 1978.
5. Lieb, *Connie Mack*, 149.

Chapter 10

1. Mack, "My Fifty Years in Baseball," Part 32.
2. *Ibid.*
3. Baseball Almanac, Christy Mathewson Quotes, www.baseballalmanac.com.
4. Alan Goldstein, "Yesterday's Heroes Today: Marquard Could Pitch Today—If Legs Were in Shape," *Baltimore Sun*, December 2, 1979.
5. *Ibid.*
6. "Extra Innings: Faust," *Freeman's Journal*, September 4, 1985.
7. Bob Broeg, "They Still Remember Larry Doyle," *The Sporting News*, December 30, 1972.
8. *Ibid.*
9. "My First Ball Game," no newspaper identification. Baseball Hall of Fame Library Archives.
10. "Larry Doyle, Captain of Giants Under John McGraw, Is Dead," *New York Times*, March 2, 1974.
11. *Ibid.*
12. R.J. Lesch, "Larry Doyle," Society for American Baseball Research Biography Project.
13. Arthur Daley, "Captain of the Giants," *New York Times*, May 12, 1958.
14. Kashatus, *Money Pitcher*, 97.
15. Joe Williams, "Fletcher Wasn't the Type to Run Club," *New York World-Telegram*, February 9, 1950.

Chapter 11

1. Wiggins, *Chief Bender*, 140–141.
2. Kashatus, *Money Pitcher*, 97.
3. Macht, *Connie Mack and the Early Years of Baseball*, 523.
4. *Ibid.*, 526.
5. Barry Sparks, *Frank "Home Run" Baker: Hall of Famer and World Series Hero* (Jefferson, NC: McFarland, 2006), 69.
6. *Ibid.*, 72.
7. *Ibid.*, 71.

8. *Ibid.*, 72–73.
9. *Ibid.*, 74.
10. Schoor, *The History of the World*.
11. Mack, "My Fifty Years in Baseball," Part 32.
12. Lieb, *Connie Mack*, 160.

Chapter 12

1. John Steadman, "A Visit with Home Run Baker," *Baseball Digest*, February 1962.
2. Frank Yeutter, "Baker Dreamed of Being a Baseball Hero, But 'Never, Never,' of Making Hall of Fame," *Philadelphia Bulletin*, February 13, 1955.
3. *Ibid.*
4. *Ibid.*
5. *Ibid.*
6. *Ibid.*
7. "I Could Hit 50 Now, Baker Says," United Press International/*New York World Telegram-Star*, July 25, 1955.
8. Mack, *My 66 Years in the Big Leagues*, 33.
9. *Ibid.*
10. Frank Baker and Bill Perry, "Frank Baker—The Original Home Run King ... as Star on Mack's Early Athletics," *The Sporting News*, February 9, 1955.
11. *Ibid.*

Chapter 13

1. Lieb, *Connie Mack*, 161–162.
2. Mack, "My Fifty Years in Baseball," Part 32.
3. Baseball Almanac Walter Johnson Quotes, www.baseballalmanac.com.
4. *Ibid.*
5. Lieb, 162.
6. *Ibid.*, 161.
7. Macht, *Connie Mack and the Early Years of Baseball*, 553.
8. Lieb, 162.
9. *Ibid.*
10. Mack, "My Fifty Years in Baseball," Part 32.

Chapter 14

1. Edward S. Plank and Joseph B. Bowles, "How I Got My Start," *Milwaukee Sentinel*, no date, 1910. Baseball Hall of Fame Library Archives.

2. *Ibid.*
3. *Ibid.*
4. "Plank May Be Pitching When 50 Years Old," unidentified newspaper clip, 1917. Baseball Hall of Fame Library Archives.
5. Jan Finkel, "Eddie Plank," Society for American Baseball Research Biography Project.
6. "Plank May Be Pitching When 50 Years Old."
7. Plank and Bowles, "How I Got My Start."
8. *Ibid.*
9. Ogden Nash, "Line-Up for Yesterday," *Sport Magazine*, January 1949.
10. Finkel, "Eddie Plank."
11. *Ibid.*
12. Harry Grayson, "Brilliant Southpaw Broke in at 26; Had Tough Luck in 5 Series," Newspaper Enterprise Association, no date. Baseball Hall of Fame Library Archives.
13. Mack, *My 66 Years in the Big Leagues*, 128.

Chapter 15

1. Macht, *Connie Mack and the Early Years of Baseball*, 580.
2. *Ibid.*
3. Tierney, *Jack Coombs*, 108.
4. Connie Mack, "My Fifty Years in Baseball," Part 33, *Philadelphia Inquirer*, October (no date), 1930. Baseball Hall of Fame Library Archives.
5. Macht, *Connie Mack and the Early Years of Baseball*, 581.
6. *Ibid.*, 584.
7. "Dream of Schang Causes Panic in East Aurora Hotel," no newspaper identification or date. Baseball Hall of Fame Library Archives.
8. The Old Scout (Herb Goren), "College Life Suits Big Jeff," *New York Sun*, June 9, 1944.

Chapter 16

1. William A. Young, *John Tortes "Chief" Meyers: A Baseball Biography* (Jefferson, NC: McFarland, 2012), 140.
2. Track and Field News website, www.trackandfieldnews.com.
3. Sparks, *Frank "Home Run" Baker*, 110.
4. *Ibid.*, 111.
5. Young, *John Tortes "Chief" Meyers*.
6. Macht, *Connie Mack and the Early Years of Baseball*, 593.
7. *Ibid.*
8. *Ibid.*, 595.

Chapter 17

1. John Montgomery Ward, "Were Star Infielders: Players of Older Generation Have Not Been Excelled," *Washington Post*, March 6, 1910.
2. Macht, *Connie Mack and the Early Years of Baseball*, 604.
3. *Ibid.*, 610.
4. *Ibid.*, 609.

Chapter 18

1. Tierney, *Jack Coombs*, 111.
2. Connie Mack, "My Fifty Years in Baseball," Part 34, *Philadelphia Inquirer*, October (no date), 1930. Baseball Hall of Fame Library Archives.
3. "Chief Bender Answers Call to Happy Hunting Grounds," *Necrology/The Sporting News*, June 2, 1954.
4. Kashatus, 111.
5. Leo Trachtenberg, "Bob Shawkey: A Yankee for Life," *Yankees Magazine*, October 13, 1988.
6. Pat Harmon, "Bressler Played Beside $100,000 Infield," *Cincinnati Post & Times-Star*, June 28, 1963.
7. Jim Baker, "'Bull' Still Kicking," *Durham News*, August 3, 1988.
8. Mack, "My Fifty Years in Baseball," Part 39, *Philadelphia Inquirer*, October (no date), 1930. Baseball Hall of Fame Library Archives.
9. Macht, *Connie Mack and the Early Years of Baseball*, 609.
10. Walter James "Rabbit" Maranville, *American Legion Monthly*, October 1935.
11. *Ibid.*
12. *Ibid.*
13. Grantland Rice, "Stallings, the Miracle Man," syndicated column, no date. Baseball Hall of Fame Library Archives.
14. George Stallings, "Stallings Tells How He Built Up the Boston Braves," *The Evening Sun*, August (no date), 1914.
15. Lee Greene, "The Miracle Braves," *Sport Magazine*, no date. Baseball Hall of Fame Library Archives.

Chapter 19

1. Greene, "The Miracle Braves."
2. *Ibid.*

3. Mack, "My Fifty Years in Baseball," Part 34.
4. Macht, *Connie Mack and the Early Years of Baseball*, 638–639.
5. Baker, "'Bull' Still Kicking."
6. Macht, *Connie Mack and the Early Years of Baseball*, 639.
7. Dick Leyden, "Dick Rudolph," Society for American Baseball Research Biography Project.
8. David Jones, "Bill James," Society for American Baseball Research Biography Project.
9. Lieb, *Connie Mack*, 176.
10. Wiggins, *Chief Bender*, 176.
11. Ibid., 178.
12. David Jones, ed., *Deadball Stars of the American League*, Society for American Baseball Research, 2006, 99.
13. Schoor, *The History of the World Series*.
14. Mack, *My 66 Years in the Big Leagues*, 35.
15. Macht, *Connie Mack and the Early Years of Baseball*, 643.
16. Ibid., 644.

Chapter 20

1. Mack, *My 66 Years in the Big Leagues*, 36.
2. Mack, "My Fifty Years in Baseball," Part 34.
3. Ibid.
4. Connie Mack, "My Fifty Years in Baseball," Part 35, *Philadelphia Inquirer*, October (no date), 1930. Baseball Hall of Fame Library Archives.
5. "Plank and Bender Put On Market," *New York Tribune*, November 1, 1914.
6. Ibid.
7. Sparks, *Frank "Home Run" Baker*, 125.
8. Macht, *Connie Mack and the Early Years of Baseball*, 654.
9. Ibid.
10. Ibid., 660.
11. Sparks, *Frank "Home Run" Baker*, 164.
12. Bill Fleischman, "Majors Paid Stiff Price to Kayo Outlaw Federal Loop," *The Sporting News*, April 5, 1969.
13. Joe Tinker, "Putting Across the Federal League," *Everybody's Magazine*, May 1914.
14. Wiggins, *Chief Bender*, 176.
15. "Feds Lost Only Half Million, Says Gilmore," no newspaper identification, December 28, 1916. Baseball Hall of Fame Library Archives.

16. United States Supreme Court Opinion, May 29, 1922.
17. Jon L. Wertheim, "Remembering the Athletics," *Sports Illustrated*, June 6, 2016.

Chapter 21

1. Harry Grayson, "Plank Had Longest Service; Offered Contract at 44," Newspaper Enterprise Association, April 14, 1943.
2. Stanley Woodward, "Views of College Sports," *New York Herald-Tribune*, January 31, 1937.
3. Edward V. Mitchell, "Jack Coombs Finds Fountain of Youth at Duke," *The Sporting News*, April 20, 1944.
4. Irving T. Marsh, "Coombs, Retiring, Now Seeks 'All the Catfish in Texas,'" *New York Herald-Tribune*, May 9, 1952.
5. Frederick G. Lieb, "Jack Coombs Dies at 73; Won 24-Inning Marathon," *The Sporting News*, no date. Baseball Hall of Fame Library Archives.
6. Wiggins, *Chief Bender*, 203.
7. Kashatus, *Money Pitcher*, 145.
8. "Chief Bender Answers Call to Happy Hunting Grounds," *The Sporting News*, June 2, 1954.
9. Stephen V. Rice, "Bob Shawkey," Society for American Baseball Research Biography Project.
10. Ibid.
11. Ron Anderson, "Joe Bush," Society for American Baseball Research Biography Project.
12. John McMurray, "Amos Strunk," Society for American Baseball Research Biography Project.
13. Roy Parsons, "Stuffy Is Gone, But His Legend Will Live Forever," *Gloucester Daily Times*, February 17, 1960.
14. Ibid.
15. Lou Mandarini, "Sports Insiders: Stuffy's Shot at Fame a Tough Sell," *Gloucester Daily Times*, February 17, 2000.
16. Paul Mittermeyer, "Eddie Collins," Society for American Baseball Research Biography Project.
17. Carl T. Felker, "Collins Left Shining Marks as Keystone King," *The Sporting News*, April 4, 1951.
18. Eddie Collins and Boyden Sparks, "From Player to Pilot," *Saturday Evening Post*, June 9, 1934.
19. "Jack Barry, Famed Member of $100,000 Infield, Dead," *The Sporting News*, May 3, 1961.

20. "Baker Was a Wrecker," Chicago Tribune Press Service, no date. Baseball Hall of Fame Library Archives.
21. Lieb, Frederick G., "Baker, Old-Time Slugging Champ, Dead At 77," *The Sporting News*, July 13, 1963.

Chapter 22

1. Connie Mack, "Our Number 1 Game," *American Legion Magazine*, May 1939.
2. *Ibid.*
3. Eddie Collins, "Connie Mack and His Mackmen," *American Magazine*, June 1914.
4. "Connie Mack—Psychologist of Baseball," *New York Herald*, March 10, 1912.
5. Ed Pollock, "Dykes and Mickey to 'Stay This Year,' For Mack," *The Sporting News*, March 29, 1950.
6. Art Morrow, "Pennant Cups to Crutches—A's Send K.C. Everything," *The Sporting News*, February 2, 1955.
7. Jimmy Cannon, "Ford Frick's Tribute: 'Always a Gentleman,'" *Philadelphia Daily News*, February 11, 1956.
8. Mel Singer, "Old Hometown to Pay Tribute to Mack Legend," no newspaper identified, June 27, 1970. Baseball Hall of Fame Library Archives.

Bibliography

Books

Hornbaker, Tim. *Fall from Grace: The Truth and Tragedy of Shoeless Joe Jackson*. New York: Sports Publishing, 2016.
Kashatus, William C. *Money Pitcher: Chief Bender and the Tragedy of Indian Assimilation*. University Park: Pennsylvania State University Press, 2006.
Levy, Alan H. *Rube Waddell: The Zany, Brilliant Life of a Strikeout Artist*. Jefferson, NC: McFarland, 2000.
Lieb, Frederick G. *Connie Mack: Grand Old Man of Baseball*. Kent, OH: Kent State University Press, 2012. First published 1945 by G.P. Putnam's Sons.
Macht, Norman L. *Connie Mack and the Early Years of Baseball*. Lincoln: University of Nebraska Press, 2007.
Mack, Connie. *My 66 Years in the Big Leagues*. Philadelphia: John C. Winston, 1950.
Schoor, Gene. *The History of the World Series*. New York: William Morrow, 1990.
Sparks, Barry. *Frank "Home Run" Baker*. Jefferson, NC: McFarland, 2006.
Tierney, John P. *Jack Coombs: A Life in Baseball*. Jefferson, NC: McFarland, 2008.
Wiggins, Robert Peyton. *Chief Bender: A Baseball Biography*. Jefferson, NC: McFarland, 2010.
Young, William A. *John Tortes "Chief" Meyers: A Baseball Biography*. Jefferson, NC: McFarland, 2012.

Magazines

American Legion Monthly
American Magazine
Baseball Digest
Everybody's Magazine
McClure's
Memories and Dreams
Saturday Evening Post
Sport Magazine
Sporting News
Sports Illustrated
Yankees Magazine

Newspapers

Baltimore Sun
Cincinnati Post & Times Star
Cleveland Plain-Dealer
Cleveland Press
Durham (NC) News
Freeman's Journal (NY)
Gloucester (MA) Daily Times
New York Herald-Tribune
New York Sun
New York Times
New York Tribune
New York World
New York World-Telegram
Philadelphia Bulletin
Philadelphia Daily News
Philadelphia Inquirer
Washington Post

Wire Services

Associated Press
Newspaper Enterprise Association
United Press International

Websites

www.baseballalmanac.com
www.baseballreference.com (statistical reference)
www.trackandfieldnews.com

Other

Society for American Baseball Research Biography Project, http:www.sabr.org/bioproject
World Series Program 1910

Index

Alexander, Grover Cleveland 69, 152
All-Star Game 62
Altoona (Pennsylvania) Mountain Citys 138
American Association 6, 138, 139
American Baseball Coaches Hall of Fame 192
American League 1, 2, 3, 8, 10, 15, 20, 22, 25, 27, 31, 33, 34, 38, 39, 42, 52, 53, 62, 63, 64, 67, 72, 78, 79, 83, 85, 91, 96, 97, 98, 101, 102, 103, 105, 119, 121, 122, 137, 139, 141, 142, 145, 147, 150, 151, 152, 153, 163, 170, 172, 173, 175, 177, 182, 188, 190, 193, 199
American League Championship Series (2004) 166
American Legion 197
Ames, Leon "Red" 72, 87, 88, 122
Anderson, South Carolina 18
Archduke Franz Ferdinand 152
Archer, Jimmy 44, 50
Atlanta Braves 138, 166
Atlantic City, New Jersey 117
Atlantic Ocean 100
Austria 152

Bagby, Jim 69
Baker, Frank "Home Run" 1, 17, 24, 29, 45, 47, 48, 49, 56, 57, 67, 68, 78, 79, 81, 82, 83, 84, 85, 86, 87, 88, 89, 90, 91, 92, 93, 94, 95, 96, 101, 102, 119, 127, 128, 131, 132, 135, 148, 151, 163, 165, 167, 170, 175, 188, 192, 193, 199
Ball, Phil 140, 177
Baltimore Orioles 1, 90, 132, 178
Baltimore Terrapins 152, 174, 178, 179, 184
Barnard, Ernest 20
Barry, Jack 1, 17, 29, 43, 47, 49, 56, 57, 67, 88, 90, 96, 101, 102, 119, 127, 130, 134, 148, 152, 163, 167, 170, 176, 192
Base Ball Players' Fraternity 142
Baseball Hall of Fame 1, 8, 10, 14, 25, 26, 34, 36, 40, 44, 47, 52, 58, 82, 92, 95, 98, 101, 104, 108, 110, 119, 137, 139, 140, 148, 149, 154, 171, 181, 182, 185, 186, 189, 190, 191, 192, 193, 197
Baseball Reference 149

Baylor University 65
Beaumont, Ginger 44, 49
Becker, Beals 77, 85, 87
Beckley, Jake 52
Bedient, Hugh 100
Bellevue-Stratford Hotel 51
Belmont Stakes 140
Bender, Albert "Chief" 1, 3, 10, 16, 22, 23, 31, 34, 36, 37, 38, 39, 40, 41, 45, 48, 50, 65, 77, 79, 81, 82, 86, 87, 89, 96, 101, 102, 104, 109, 110, 114, 115, 116, 119, 124, 126, 127, 128, 131, 132, 133, 134, 146, 147, 158, 160, 161, 162, 166, 167, 170, 173, 174, 178, 182, 184, 185, 186
Bentley, Jack 125
Birmingham, Joe 162
Black Sox Scandal 19, 98, 141, 191
Bloomer Girls 100
Blue Ridge Blue Sox 194
Boardman, Charlie 115, 121
Bohen, Pat 115, 121
Boston 164
Boston Beaneaters 138
Boston Braves (Rustlers) 54, 120, 126, 138, 153, 154, 155, 156, 157, 158, 159, 160, 161, 162, 163, 164, 165, 166, 167, 168, 169, 173
Boston Celtics 181
Boston Globe 190
Boston Red Sox 3, 10, 21, 25, 28, 33, 34, 54, 57, 93, 97, 99, 100, 101, 103, 104, 105, 112, 116, 120, 121, 122, 124, 125, 129, 147, 150, 153, 166, 167, 176, 186, 187, 189, 190, 192, 197
Bowdoin College 54
Braddock Hotel 76
Bradford, Pennsylvania 14
Brainerd, Minnesota 104
Bressler, Raymond "Rube" 109, 110, 146, 147, 148, 152, 176
Bridgeton, New Jersey 25, 194
Brockton, Massachusetts 100
Brooklyn Dodgers 11, 132, 142, 153, 174, 178, 183, 189
Brooklyn Tiptops 151, 171, 195

Index

Brown, Carroll "Boardwalk" 96, 102, 114, 116, 117, 118, 131, 144
Brown, Mordecai "Three Finger" 2, 44, 45, 47, 48, 50, 171
Browning, Pete 139
Brush, John T. 79
Bucknell University 73
Buffalo 7
Buffalo Blues 100
Buffalo Pullmans 120
Burns, George 122, 127, 134
Bush, (Leslie Ambrose) Joe "Bullet" 97, 104, 114, 115, 117, 120, 131, 132, 133, 146, 147, 160, 164, 165, 166, 170, 176, 187

Cabrera Miguel 57
Cahuilla Indians 77
California 86
Candlestick Park 34
Cano, Robinson 57
Cantillon, Joe 21
Canton Bulldogs 126
Capitol Park (Swampdoodle Grounds) 7
Carlisle Indian School 38, 126
Carlton, Steve 107
Caseyville, Illinois 76
Chalmers Motor Cars (and MVP) 42, 49, 76, 190
Chamberlain, Joba 128
Chance, Frank 2, 44, 48, 49, 50, 142, 154, 168
Chesbro, Jack 68
Chicago 20, 48, 51, 141, 198
Chicago Bears 181
Chicago Cubs (Chicago White Stockings) 2, 12, 14, 34, 42, 43, 44, 45, 46, 47, 48, 49, 50, 65, 68, 69, 75, 122, 138, 141, 142, 152, 153, 154, 162, 166, 171, 177, 197
Chicago Whales 140, 142, 152, 176, 177
Chicago White Sox 19, 34, 39, 43, 66, 68, 126, 166, 175, 176, 185, 191
China 141
Chippewa Indians 38
Cicotte, Ed 21, 66
Cincinnati Red Stockings (Reds) 6, 19, 29, 34, 137, 138, 142, 147, 148, 152, 171, 191
Civil War 5, 106
Clarke, Fred 168
Clarke, William "Boileryard" 91
Clarkson, John 68
Cleveland 28, 74
Cleveland Green Sox 140
Cleveland Naps (Bronchos, Indians) 8, 17, 19, 20, 25, 26, 29, 38, 39, 40, 104, 114, 121, 122, 141, 162, 189
Cobb, Ty 9, 24, 27, 28, 29, 47, 62, 63, 65, 66, 67, 68, 99, 108, 120, 151, 152, 191
Cochrane, Mickey 197
Cocreham, Gene 159
Coder, Pennsylvania 147
Colby College 31, 33
Cole, Leonard "King" 44, 45, 49, 50
College Baseball Hall of Fame 192
College World Series 192
Collins, Eddie 1, 17, 24, 25, 41, 47, 49, 50, 56, 57, 59, 60, 61, 62, 63, 65, 67, 68, 81, 83, 85, 87, 90, 93, 96, 101, 102, 110, 114, 119, 127, 128, 131, 132, 133, 135, 143, 148, 151, 163, 164, 165, 167, 170, 175, 183, 190, 191, 192, 194, 197
Collins, Eddie, Jr. 186
Collins, Jimmy 25, 93
Columbia Park 8
Columbia University 59, 60, 61, 139, 191
Columbian League 140
Comiskey, Charles 19, 141, 175
Conlon, Jocko 152
Connecticut State League 6
Connie Mack Day 199
Connie Mack League 12
Connie Mack Sportsmen's Club 12
Connie Mack Stadium 2, 198
Connolly, Joe 155, 161, 165
Connor, Roger 139
Coombs, Jack 2, 16, 22, 23, 31, 32, 33, 34, 35, 36, 37, 45, 47, 48, 49, 50, 65, 67, 68, 69, 79, 84, 85, 87, 88, 96, 102, 104, 109, 112, 113, 114, 115, 116, 118, 144, 145, 146, 173, 174, 178, 183, 184
Cooperstown, New York 26
Cooperstown Dreams Park 26
Cottrell, Ensign 115
Coveleski, Harry 104
Coveleski, Stan 97, 104
Covington (Kentucky) Blue Sox 140
Coyne, Marvin "Toots" 149
Crandall, James Otis "Doc" 72, 74, 87, 122, 127, 132, 152
Crane, Sam 150
Crawford, Sam 65
Crow Wing County, Minnesota 36
Crutcher, Dick 159
Cruthers, Press 149
Custer, George Armstrong 138
Cuyler, Kiki 152

Dandridge Ray 56
Danforth, Dave 65, 66, 96
Dartmouth College 123, 187
Davies, Lloyd Garrison "Chick" 149
Davis, Harry 8, 9, 17, 24, 41, 42, 47, 49, 52, 53, 54, 56, 58, 63, 64, 67, 71, 81, 86, 89, 96, 114, 135, 149
Deal, Charlie 155, 163, 164
Dean, Dizzy 41, 68
Delahanty Jim 65
Delaware River 165
Demaree, Al 122, 132, 133, 134
Derrick, Claud 54
Detroit Tigers 22, 24, 65, 68, 83, 117, 120, 121, 122, 152, 153, 183

Devore, Josh 77, 81, 84, 86, 87
DiMaggio, Joe 93
Donahue, Pat 28
Doubleday, Abner 197
Doyle, Larry 2, 76, 77, 81, 86, 88, 89, 122, 127, 128, 130, 132
Duke University 183
Dunlap, Fred 138
Durocher, Leo 11
Dygert, Jimmy 17

East Brookfield, Mass. 5, 6, 12, 199
Easterly, Ted 151
Eastern League 7
Easton, Maryland 94
Egypt 141
Ellsbury, Jacoby 128
Evans, Steve 151
Evers, Johnny 2, 44, 75, 142, 154, 155, 161, 162, 163, 167, 168

Faber, Urban "Red" 152
Factoryville, Pennsylvania 72
Falconer, New York 100
Falkenberg, Cy 171
Faust, Charles "Victory" 74, 75
Federal League 3, 100, 107, 137, 138, 139, 140, 141, 142, 143, 150, 151, 153, 154, 157, 161, 168, 170, 171, 172, 173, 174, 175, 176, 177, 178, 179, 182, 184, 185
Fenway Park 100, 103, 105, 120, 164, 166, 173
Fletcher, Art 77, 78, 87, 122, 127, 130, 131, 132, 134
Flick, Elmer 40
Ford, Russ 155
Fordham University 159
Foxx, Jimmie 94, 197
Frackville, Pennsylvania 54
France 141, 152, 154
Frazer, Pennsylvania 28
Frick, Ford 199
Fultz, David 142

Gandil, Charles "Chick" 98, 191
Gardner, Larry 101
Gehrig, Lou 59, 196
Gettysburg, Pennsylvania 8, 102, 106, 136
Gettysburg Academy 106
Gettysburg, Battle of 106
Gettysburg College 8, 38, 108, 183
Gilbert, Larry 165
Gilmore, James 141, 142, 178
Girard College 52
Gloucester, Massachusetts 54, 56, 190
Gloucester Times 190
Gowdy, Hank 154, 161, 163, 164, 165, 167
Granger, Texas 65
Grant, Eddie 130, 152
Greenville, South Carolina 18
Griffith, Clark 26, 98

Griffith Stadium 98
Grimes, Burleigh 152
Grimshaw, Moose 33
Grove, Lefty 69, 197

Hanlon, Ned 90
Harris, Joe 33
Hartford, Connecticut 7
Hartsel, Tully (Topsy) 26, 27, 61
Harvard University 56, 100, 190
Haw River, North Carolina 148
Hendrix, Claude 152
Herrmann, Garry 141
Herzog, Buck 77, 81, 82, 85, 130, 134
Hess, Otto 158
Hickman, Kentucky 21
Hillerich & Bradsby Company 139
Hilltop Park 70
H.O. Wilber & Sons Chocolate and Cocoa Manufacturing Company 64
Hofman, Solly 44, 49, 50
Holmes, Oliver Wendell Jr. 179
Holtzman, Jerome 116
Holy Cross College 56, 57, 192
Home Run Baker Park 193
Hooper, Harry 101
Hotel Majestic 42, 51
Houck, Bryan 97, 114, 116, 117, 121, 124
Houser, Ben 43, 54
Hoy, William "Dummy" 39
Hubbell, Carl 41
Hudson River 177
Huggins, Miller 187
Humpty Dumpty 179

Illinois 179
Indiana University 163
Indianapolis Hoosiers 140, 151, 152, 176
Iowa 31
Ireland 5
Ivy League 191

Jackson, Joe "Shoeless Joe" 17, 18, 19, 20, 22, 104, 195
Jackson, Katie 18
James, Bill "Seattle Bill" 154, 159, 160, 162, 163, 164, 165
James, Bill (statistician) 57
Jennings, Hugh 83, 91
Jersey City, New Jersey 195
Johnson, Arnold 198
Johnson, Ban 1, 2, 8, 85, 141, 173, 174
Johnson, Jing 180
Johnson, Walter 41, 69, 98, 99, 101, 110, 121, 125, 149, 151, 190
Jones, Sam 109
Joss, Addie 34

Kansas 74
Kansas City 99

Index

Kansas City Athletics 4, 199
Kansas City Cowboys 138
Kansas City Packers 140, 151
Kauff, Benny 151
Keller, Wee Willie 90
Kennedy, William "Brickyard" 125
Kennett Square, Pennsylvania 103
Kentucky Derby 140
King of Sweden 126
Kinney, Walt 180
Kivat, Abel 126
Klem, Bill 88, 89
Kling, Johnny 44
Knight, John 33
Kopf, Larry 148, 176
Krause, Harry 25, 65, 96
Kremer, Ray 125

Lajoie, Larry 9, 14, 40, 175, 179
Landis, Kenesaw Mountain 19, 141, 176, 178
Lapp, Jack 17, 27, 34, 67, 84, 85, 87, 88, 96, 102, 119, 130, 175
Lardner, Ring 35
Lee, Robert E. 91
Lehigh Valley Railroad 53
Lewis, Duffy 101
Link, Fred 40
Livingston, Paddy 17, 28, 29
Llanerch, Pennsylvania 189
Loma Prieta Earthquake 86
Lord, Bris (Bristol R.) 17, 19, 22, 26, 47, 50, 67, 81, 82, 84, 88, 96, 102, 195
Louisville (minor league) 66
Louisville, Kentucky 139
Louisville Colonels 14, 52
Louisville Slugger 139
Lucas, V. Henry 138
Lynch, Thomas 141

Mack, Connie 1, 2, 3, 4, 5, 6, 7, 8, 9, 10, 11, 12, 13, 14, 15, 16, 17, 18, 19, 20, 21, 22, 23, 24, 26, 27, 29, 30, 31, 34, 36, 38, 40, 41, 42, 43, 45, 48, 49, 50, 51, 52, 53, 54, 56, 57, 59, 60, 61, 62, 63, 64, 65, 69, 71, 72, 73, 75, 78, 82, 86, 89, 90, 94, 95, 96, 97, 98, 101, 102, 103, 104, 105, 106, 111, 112, 113, 114, 115, 116, 117, 118, 119, 120, 121, 122, 123, 124, 126, 128, 130, 131, 132, 133, 134, 135, 142, 143, 144, 145, 146, 148, 149, 150, 151, 156, 157, 158, 160, 161, 166, 167, 168, 170, 171, 172, 173, 174, 175, 176, 179, 180, 181, 184, 185, 186, 188, 189, 191, 192, 193, 196, 197, 198, 199
Mack, Earle 1, 28, 29, 30, 103, 147, 149, 193, 194, 198
Mack, Roy 194, 199
Maine 31, 33, 54
Mann, Lester 163, 165
Maranville, Walter "Rabbit" 154, 155, 161, 162, 163, 164, 167
Marichal, Juan 34

Marquard, Rube 2, 72, 73, 74, 82, 83, 84, 85, 87, 88, 122, 126, 127, 128, 133, 134
Martinsburg, West Virginia 194
Maryland 90, 94
Mathewson, Christy 2, 39, 41, 50, 69, 70, 72, 76, 79, 81, 82, 84, 85, 86, 87, 88, 105, 109, 122, 125, 126, 128, 129, 130, 135, 151, 152
Mays, Willie 27
McAvoy, Wickey 150
McClure's Magazine 11
McCormick, Harry "Moose" 127
McGinnity, Joe "Iron Man" 69, 76
McGraw, John 1, 2, 10, 51, 69, 70, 71, 72, 74, 75, 76, 77, 78, 81, 83, 84, 86, 87, 88, 91, 97, 122, 123, 124, 126, 131, 132, 134, 135, 141, 168, 192
McInnis, John "Stuffy" 1, 17, 41, 52, 54, 55, 56, 57, 64, 67, 71, 90, 96, 102, 119, 127, 131, 133, 148, 152, 164, 176, 179, 189, 190
McIntire, Harry 44, 45, 48, 49, 170
McKechnie, Bill 140
McLain, Denny 68
McLean, Larry 130, 132, 135
Meadows, Lee 125
Mercer, Sid 74
Merkle, Fred 75, 76, 87, 88, 122, 127, 134
Meriden, Connecticut 6
Meyers, John "Chief" 2, 77, 81, 83, 84, 87, 122, 126, 128
Milan, Clyde 98
Miller, Marvin 142
Millerton, New York 59
Mitchell, Fred 159
Milwaukee Braves 34, 138, 166
Milwaukee Brewers (minors) 7, 15
Minneapolis Millers 21
Minnesota 21
Minnesota Twins 98
Mobile, Alabama 122
Moline, Illinois 194
Montana 138
Montevallo, Alabama 179
Montgomery, Alabama 25
Montreal Canadiens 181
Moore, Ferdinand De Paige 150
Moran, Herbie 165, 167
Morey, Dave 115
Morgan, Cy 17, 22, 23, 43, 65, 96, 102, 115
Mullin, George 65, 152
Murphy, Charles 20
Murphy, Danny 17, 24, 25, 43, 47, 50, 61, 67, 86, 88, 92, 96, 102, 114, 117, 118, 174, 194, 195
Murphy, Eddie 118, 131, 132, 135, 148, 163, 164, 165, 176
Murray, John "Red" 77, 82, 132, 134
Mutt and Jeff 42
Myers, Elmer 179

Nabors, Jack 179
Nash, Ogden 109

Index

National Commission 141
National Football League 73, 126
National League 1, 2, 3, 6, 9, 10, 11, 14, 42, 43, 49, 68, 70, 71, 73, 75, 76, 79, 105, 110, 122, 123, 124, 137, 138, 139, 141, 151, 152, 153, 156, 160, 163, 166, 171, 173, 177, 178, 185
Nefh, Art 125
Negro Leagues 56
New Haven, Connecticut 194
New Orleans 19, 63
New York (state) 100, 120
New York City 25, 26, 82, 158, 159
New York Giants (New York Gothams) 1, 2, 3, 7, 12, 25, 39, 40, 41, 43, 50, 51, 52, 69, 70, 71, 72, 73, 74, 75, 76, 77, 79, 81, 82, 83, 84, 85, 86, 87, 88, 90, 94, 105, 122, 123, 124, 125, 126, 127, 128, 129, 130, 131, 132, 133, 134, 135, 137, 138, 141, 149, 151, 152, 153, 155, 159, 166, 187, 192
New York Highlanders (Yankees) 1, 3, 23, 26, 68, 70, 77, 78, 90, 93, 100, 104, 120, 121, 153, 166, 167, 175, 176, 186, 187, 192, 193, 194, 196, 199
Newark Domestics 7
Newark Eagles 56
Newark Peppers 140, 176, 177
North Carolina 183
Northern California Little League 149
Northern League 21
Norwich, Connecticut 25

Oakland Athletics 4, 86
O'Brien, Thomas "Buck" 100
O'Brien, Tom 25
O'Day, Hank 7
Ohio 8
Ojibwe (Indian tribe) 36, 185
Oklahoma 125
Oldring, Rube 17, 24, 25, 40, 48, 67, 81, 82, 87, 96, 102, 118, 131, 132, 134, 135, 148, 161, 163, 164, 165, 167, 176, 194
$100,000 Infield 1, 2, 27, 52, 56, 57, 58, 61, 90, 96, 148, 170, 189
Oorang Indians 126
Orr, Billy 149
Overall, Orval 44, 45, 46

Pacific Coast League 149
Paige, Satchel 108
Palestine, Texas 112, 184
Peabody, Massachusetts 149
Penn State University 139
Pennock, Herb 3, 97, 103, 104, 114, 124, 146, 147, 167, 170, 176, 186
Pennsylvania 38, 100, 117
Pennsylvania Supreme Court 9
Perdue, Hub 159
Pfiester, Jack 44, 49
Philadelphia 2, 15, 18, 19, 20, 25, 43, 51, 52, 82, 117, 120, 175, 199

Philadelphia Athletic Club 8
Philadelphia Athletics 1, 2, 3, 4, 7, 8, 9, 10, 11, 12, 13, 1, 15, 16, 17, 18, 20, 22, 23, 24, 25, 26, 27, 28, 29, 30, 31, 33, 37, 38, 39, 40, 42, 43, 44, 45, 46, 47, 48, 49, 50, 51, 52, 58, 59, 61, 63, 64, 65, 66, 69, 70, 71, 73, 76, 77, 78, 80, 81, 82, 83, 84, 85, 86, 87, 88, 89, 90, 92, 93, 96, 97, 99, 101, 102, 104, 105, 106, 108, 109, 110, 111, 112, 114, 115, 116, 117, 118, 119, 121, 122, 124, 125, 126, 127, 128, 129, 130, 131, 132, 133, 134, 135, 137, 141, 142, 143, 144, 145, 146, 147, 148, 149, 150, 151, 153, 156, 157, 158, 160, 161, 162, 163, 164, 165, 166, 167, 168, 169, 170, 172, 173, 174, 175, 176, 179, 180, 181, 182, 184, 185, 186, 187, 188, 189, 190, 191, 192, 193, 194, 195, 196, 197, 198, 199
Philadelphia Evening Telegraph 42
Philadelphia Historical Society 51
Philadelphia Phillies 1, 2, 9, 14, 122, 138, 153, 166, 185, 189
Philippines 141
Phillippe, Deacon 125
Pipgrass, George 187
Pittsburgh Alleghenys 138
Pittsburgh Pirates 5, 7, 10, 14, 52, 53, 115, 125, 187, 190
Pittsburgh Rebels 140, 176, 178
Plank, Eddie 1, 3, 8, 9, 10, 16, 22, 23, 31, 34, 38, 48, 65, 79, 82, 84, 88, 96, 102, 104, 106, 107, 108, 109, 110, 111, 112, 114, 115, 116, 119, 120, 121, 124, 125, 126, 128, 129, 130, 131, 135, 146, 147, 149, 160, 161, 162, 163, 164, 166, 170, 173, 174, 178, 182, 183
Plattsburgh, New York 59
Players' Association 142
Players' League 138, 139
Polo Grounds 7, 70, 77, 79, 82, 84, 87, 89, 126, 131, 134
Powers, Doc 33
Powers, John T. 140, 141
Prince Frederick, Maryland 195
Pro Football Hall of Fame 125
Providence Grays 68, 139
Purock 42

Quincy, Illinois 122
Quinn, Jack 151

Radbourn, Charles "Hoss" 68
Rainbow Division 154
Reading Pretzels 90, 94
Reese, John D. "Bonesetter" 45, 46
Reulbach, Ed 44, 48, 49, 171
Reynolds, Allie 128
Rice, Grantland 41, 190
Richie, Lew 44, 48
Richmond Colts 108
Rickey, Branch 11
Ripley's Believe It or Not 100
Robinson, Wilbert 91, 132

Index

Rochefort, Ben 149
"Rocky" (movie) 39
Roush, Edd 140, 148, 171
Rudolph, Dick 154, 159, 160, 161, 164, 166, 167, 169
Ruth, Babe 3, 83, 93, 139, 147, 188, 193, 196
Ryan, Bob 190

Sain, Johnny 154
St. Louis 21, 188
St. Louis Browns 20, 21, 66, 120, 121, 122, 138, 177, 187
St. Louis Cardinals 68, 74, 115, 138, 151
St. Louis Maroons 138
St. Louis Terriers 140, 152, 174, 176, 177, 178, 182
St. Paul (Minnesota) Apostles 138
San Antonio 112
San Francisco 16
San Francisco Giants 34, 86, 138
Schang, Bob 120
Schang, Wally 119, 120, 127, 132, 134, 135, 148, 163, 165, 170, 175, 188
Schmidt, Butch 155, 161, 163, 164
Schulte, Frank "Wildfire" 44, 49, 50
Seattle 194
Seay, Dick 56
Seeley, Blossom 74
Shafer, Tillie 122, 132, 134, 135
Shamokin, Pennsylvania 104
Shawkey, Bob 3, 114, 117, 121, 124, 146, 147, 160, 166, 167, 170, 176, 186, 187
Sheckard, Jimmy 47, 48, 49, 50
Sheehan, Tom 179
Sherman Anti-Trust Act 179
Shibe, Ben (Shibe Family) 2, 8, 11, 20, 42, 198
Shibe, Tom 198
Shibe Park 2, 23, 42, 43, 45, 61, 64, 67, 82, 85, 88, 93, 114, 128, 136, 160, 162, 170, 173, 176, 198
Shotton, Burt 11
Simmons, Al 197
Sinclair, Harry F. 140, 177
Sinclair Oil 140
Slaughter, Enos 27
Slippery Rock State (Pennsylvania) 187
Smith, Frank "Piano Mover" 39
Smith, James "Red" 155
Smith, Walter "Red" (journalist) 12
Snodgrass, Fred 77, 81, 84, 85, 122, 130
Sockalexis, Louis 38, 128
Somers, Charles 20, 141
South End Grounds 164
South Wales, New York 119
Southern Association 25, 122
Spahn, Warren 34, 107, 154
Speaker, Tris 92, 101, 152
Sports Illustrated 179, 180
Springfield, Ohio 28

Springfield Senators 76
Stahl, Jake 93, 101, 121, 124
Stallings, George 120, 153, 154, 155, 156, 157, 158, 160, 162, 163, 164, 165, 167, 168
Stengel, Casey 199
Strand, Paul 159
Stanford University 149
Strunk, Amos 27, 47, 48, 49, 61, 87, 96, 102, 118, 119, 130, 131, 134, 148, 170, 176, 179, 189
Sturgis, Dean 150
Summer Olympics, 1912 125
Summer Olympics, 1936 163
Suttles, Mule 56
Sweden 125

Taff, John 115
Taylor, Luther "Dummy" 39
Tener, John 141
Tesreau, Charles "Big Jeff" 122, 123, 127, 131, 132, 152
Texas 21, 184
Thomas, Ira 12, 17, 28, 40, 47, 55, 67, 86, 96, 114, 119, 149, 174, 175, 199
Thompson, James "Shag" 148, 149, 158, 161
Thorpe, Jim 38, 125, 126, 128
Three I League 76
Tinker, Joe 2, 44, 49, 142, 154, 177
Titanic 100
Tolowitzki, Troy 58
Toney, Fred 34
Trappe, Maryland 90, 91, 193
Triple Crown (horse racing) 140
Turner, Terry 40
Tyler, Lefty 159, 160, 164, 165

Union Association 138
United States Baseball League 140
United States Court of Appeal 178
United States Supreme Court 178
University of California (Berkeley) 46
University of Kansas 99
University of Maryland 66
University of Missouri 142
University of North Carolina 194
Upland (County), Pennsylvania 26, 175

Vaughan, Hippo 34
Villanova University 118
Vincent, Fay 86
Virginia 91, 108, 194
Virginia Hot Springs 23
Virginia League 185

Waco, Texas 65
Waddell, George Edward "Rube" 1, 10, 14, 15, 16, 17, 20, 21, 31, 38, 61, 74, 110, 115
Wagner, Honus 92, 110
Walsh, Ed "Big" 34, 35, 41, 68, 69
Walsh, Jimmy 119, 163, 167, 176
Ward, John Montgomery 138, 139

Index

Washington, D.C. 98
Washington Nationals (old) 52, 97
Washington Nationals (Statesmen) 7
Washington Senators 22, 33, 97, 98, 99, 101, 103, 104, 105, 121, 122, 125, 187, 190
Weeghman, Charles 177
Wells, Willie 56
West Side Grounds 48, 50
Western League 1
Western Washington State Hospital for the Insane 75
Wheat, Zach 128
Whitted, George 155, 161
Williamsport, Pennsylvania 147
Wilmington (Delaware) Quicksteps 138
Wiltse, George "Hooks" 72, 87, 88, 122, 130, 171
Wood, Joe "Smoky" 3, 69, 99, 100, 101, 104, 105, 121, 124
Woodbury, New Jersey 116
Worcester, Massachusetts 56, 192
World Series 1, 2, 3, 9, 10, 12, 19, 26, 39, 40, 42, 43, 44, 45, 46, 50, 52, 53, 56, 59, 64, 66, 68, 69, 70, 71, 72, 73, 75, 77, 78, 79, 81, 83, 84, 85, 86, 87, 89, 90, 92, 94, 96, 97, 104, 105, 109, 112, 119, 124, 125, 126, 127, 128, 129, 131, 135, 137, 142, 144, 151, 152, 153, 154, 157, 160, 161, 163, 164, 165, 166, 167, 168, 169, 170, 171, 172, 173, 176, 186, 188, 192, 195, 196
World War I 73, 137, 142, 152, 154, 177, 181, 182
World War II 181
Wright, David 58
Wright, George 137
Wright, Harry 137
Wrigley Field 48, 177
Wyckoff, Weldon 115, 121, 146, 147, 161

Yawkey, Tom 191
Yde, Emil 125
York, Rudy 128
Young, Cy 25, 34, 69, 98, 125
Youngstown, Ohio 45

Zev (racehorse) 110
Zimmerman, Heinie 44

www.ingramcontent.com/pod-product-compliance
Ingram Content Group UK Ltd.
Pitfield, Milton Keynes, MK11 3LW, UK
UKHW041958140426
5217IPUK00015B/860